Cast Out of the Covenant

Cast Out of the Covenant

Jews and Anti-Judaism in the Gospel of John

Adele Reinhartz

LEXINGTON BOOKS/FORTRESS ACADEMIC
Lanham • Boulder • New York • London

Published by Lexington Books/Fortress Academic
An imprint of The Rowman & Littlefield Publishing Group, Inc.
4501 Forbes Boulevard, Suite 200, Lanham, Maryland 20706
www.rowman.com

Unit A, Whitacre Mews, 26-34 Stannary Street, London SE11 4AB

British Library Cataloguing in Publication Information Available

Library of Congress Cataloging-in-Publication Data

Names: Reinhartz, Adele, 1953- author.
Title: Cast out of the covenant : Jews and anti-Judaism in the Gospel of John
    / Adele Reinhartz.
Description: Lanham : Lexington Books-Fortress Academic, 2018. | Includes
    bibliographical references and index.
Identifiers: LCCN 2018016848 (print) | LCCN 2018020694 (ebook) | ISBN
    9781978701182 (Electronic) | ISBN 9781978701175 (cloth : alk. paper)
Subjects: LCSH: Bible. John—Criticism, interpretation, etc. | Judaism
    (Christian theology)—Biblical teaching. | Christianity and other
    religions—Judaism—Biblical teaching. |
    Judaism—Relations—Christianity—Biblical teaching. | Christianity and
    antisemitism—Biblical teaching.
Classification: LCC BS2615.6.J44 (ebook) | LCC BS2615.6.J44 R45 2018 (print)
    | DDC 226.5/06—dc23
LC record available at https://lccn.loc.gov/2018016848

Dedicated to the blessed memory of
J. Louis Martyn (October 11, 1925–June 4, 2015)
Gregory A. Baum (June 20, 1923–October 18, 2017)

Contents

Contents

Preface and Acknowledgments

Writing a book over the course of many years on a much-studied topic inevitably calls to mind the sentiment expressed in Ecclesiastes 12:12: "Of making many books there is no end, and much study is a weariness of the flesh." And yet, John's tantalizing elusiveness ensures that when it comes to Johannine studies, there is always room for one more: "There are also many other things that Jesus did; if every one of them were written down, I suppose that the world itself could not contain the books that would be written" (Jn. 21:25).

The sheer volume of secondary literature on John's Gospel makes it impossible for any single person to have read everything in every relevant language; the practicalities of book publishing make it impossible to refer to all of the studies that would be relevant to every aspect of my topic. I thank the "Johannine community" of scholars, to which I am proud to belong, for the years of stimulating conversation, in person and in print, and request the understanding of those whose work I was unable to cite due to space limitations.

I am grateful to the many students and colleagues who have heard me out on the various aspects of this project during the last several years, at Boston College, Boston University, Brown University, Harvard Divinity School, the Institute of Advanced Studies in Princeton, McMaster University, Princeton University, the University of Toronto, Yale Divinity School, and at meetings of the Society of Biblical Literature, the Studiorum Novi Testamenti Societas, and the Colloquium Iohanneum. For their support of this project, I thank the Social Sciences and Humanities Research Council, the Hetty Goldman Fund at the Institute for Advanced Studies (2011–2012), and the Center for Christian-Jewish Learning, where I spent two wonderful years as the Corcoran Visiting Chair (2015–2017). I also wish to thank the University of Ottawa and my colleagues in the Department of Classics and Religious Studies, which continues to be a most congenial and collegial academic home, as well as the University of the Free State, Bloemfontein, South Africa, where I am a research fellow. On a less formal level, my thanks go out to the Princeton Public Library, where I finished the final draft of this book in October 2017, to Robert Goldenberg and Nina Wacholder for their warm hospitality during this self-imposed writing retreat, and to Sandy Sussman for showing up daily at just the right time.

The list of colleagues whom I would wish to thank is long. Two in particular—Alan Culpepper and Paula Fredriksen—have been frequent conversation partners over the course of many years. For his encouragement and patience, I thank Neil Elliott. At Lexington, my thanks to Judith Lakamper, Naomi Minkoff, and the production team. I am grateful to Dr. Tyler Smith, who read and commented on the entire manuscript, to Shoshana Walfish for the beautiful cover, to Ryan Mikalson for his able assistance with permissions and proofreading, and to Sergey Lobachev for the indexes. As always, I thank Simcha Walfish, Shoshana Walfish, Mordecai Walfish, Miriam-Simma Walfish, and Michael Rosenberg for support and encouragement, and Nehemia David, Adira Hana, and Shia Nochem for bringing such joy into my life. Most of all, I am grateful to Barry Walfish, not only for "being there for me" every day, and not only for being a sounding board and cheerleader, but also for going through every chapter, sometimes in several versions. Barry, I cannot thank you enough.

This book is dedicated to two scholars whose work has influenced my thinking, and this book, in numerous ways. J. L. Martyn was one of the sages and guiding lights of the scholarly Johannine community. Any attempt to understand the interrelationship between the Gospel and its intended, implied, or historical audience(s) must take account of Lou's work. I would hardly have engaged with this Gospel had my imagination not been captured by Lou's own compelling narrative of the Johannine community and its conflict with the synagogue. If in the end what I hear and see is different from what Martyn did, well, that is no different from everyday life in which, it is safe to say, no two members of the same community experience that community in quite the same way. The differences do not diminish my appreciation of his work and of J. L. Martyn himself, a man of grace and integrity.

Gregory Baum was a German Jew, a contemporary of my parents, and equally affected by the events of World War II. Gregory converted to Catholicism and became a theologian and priest. During the Second Vatican Council, he was a theological advisor at the Ecumenical Secretariat, and in that capacity he composed the first draft of the conciliar document Nostra Aetate, The Declaration on the Relation of the Church with Non-Christian Religions. Gregory was one of my professors at the University of Toronto, and when

I joined the Department of Religious Studies as a faculty member, I was privileged to have the office next to his at St. Michael's College. It was during this time—after Gregory had left the priesthood—that I got to know him well and came to understand his connections to my parents' Bundist circle of friends. I also learned that despite or perhaps even because of his conversion, he remained committed to fostering a positive relationship between Jews and Christians. And it is from Gregory that I realized that it is not only Jews who were concerned with the potential of the Christian scriptures to foster anti-Jewish sentiments.

May the memory of J. L. Martyn and Gregory Baum be for a blessing.

I am grateful for permission to reuse materials from the following previously-published works:

"The Johannine Community and its Jewish Neighbors: A Reappraisal." In *What is John? Vol. 2 Literary and Social Readings of the Fourth Gospel*, edited by Fernando F. Segovia. Pages 111–38. Atlanta: Scholars Press, 1998.

"To Love the Lord: An Intertextual Reading of John 20." In *The Labour of Reading: Essays in Honour of Robert C. Culley*, edited by Fiona Black, Roland Boer, Christian Kelm, Erin Runions. Pages 56–69. Semeia Studies. Atlanta: Scholars Press, 1999.

"John 8:31–59 from a Jewish Perspective." In *Remembering for the Future 2000: The Holocaust in an Age of Genocides*, vol. 2, edited by John K. Roth and Elisabeth Maxwell-Meynard. Pages 787–97. London: Palgrave, 2001.

"The Grammar of Hate in the Gospel of Love: Reading the Fourth Gospel in the Twenty-First Century." In *Israel und seine Heilstraditionen im Johannesevangelium*. Festschrift in honour of Johannes Beutler, S.J., edited by Dr. Michael Labahn et al. Pages 416–27. Paderborn: Verlag Schöningh, 2004.

"Reading History in the Fourth Gospel: A Response to J. L. Martyn." *"What You Have Heard From the Beginning": The Past, Present, and Future of Johannine Studies*, edited by Tom Thatcher. Pages 191–94. Waco: Baylor University Press, 2007.

"Building Skyscrapers on Toothpicks: The Literary-Critical Challenge to Historical Criticism." *Anatomies of Narrative Criticism*, edited by Tom Thatcher. Pages 55–76. Atlanta: Society of Biblical Literature, 2008.

"A Marginal Jew: Rethinking the Historical Jesus v 4 Law and Love," *The Catholic Biblical Quarterly* 72, no. 3 (July 2010): 602–4.

"Forging a New Identity: Johannine Rhetoric and the Audience of the Fourth Gospel." In *Paul, John, and apocalyptic eschatology: studies in honour of Martinus C. de Boer*, ed. Jan. Krans et al. Pages 123–134. Leiden: Brill, 2013.

"'Children of God' and Aristotelian Epigenesis in the Gospel of John," *Creation Stories in Dialogue: The Bible, Science, and Folk Traditions*, edited by R. Alan Culpepper and Jan G. van der Watt. Pages 243–252. Brill: Leiden, 2015.

"Story and History: John, Judaism, and the Historical Imagination." *John and Judaism: A Contested Relationship in Context*, edited by R. Alan Culpepper and Paul N. Anderson. Pages 113–26. Leiden: Brill, 2017.

"The Jews of the Fourth Gospel." *The Oxford Handbook of Johannine Studies*, edited by Judith M. Lieu and Martinus C. de Boer. Oxford: Oxford University Press, 2018. Pages 121–37.

A Note on Terminology

Virtually any historical study of the Gospels, first-century Judaism, or early Christianity quickly runs into a problem: the contested nature of our vocabulary. Terms that were foundational to the scholarly discussion in previous academic generations are now critiqued, deconstructed, and often discarded. This process of rethinking is important. As scholars strive towards new perspectives on the groups and events that shaped the early centuries of the common era, the limitations and assumptions behind familiar terminology urge us towards change. Questioning our language also helps us to think differently from the ways in which we were trained. On the other hand, no consensus has yet emerged on what our new vocabulary should be. Here I outline just a few of these terms, and explain the usage I will adopt in this book.[1]

"CHRISTIANS" AND "CHRISTIANITY"

For all that New Testament scholarship, including historical Jesus research, has embraced the Jewishness of Jesus and the movement that was created by his followers, the term "Christianity" remains in widespread use when speaking about that movement in the first century. This is particularly the case in Johannine studies, where many, myself included, have used the term "Johannine Christianity" to refer to what we find distinctive about the Fourth Gospel presentation of Jesus as Christ and Son of God, in comparison with other New Testament documents.

This nomenclature is problematic for two reasons. First, it is a relic of an earlier period of scholarship in which the tendency of scholars to retroject the modern distinctions between Judaism and Christianity (synagogues and churches) back into the first century went unchallenged, and perhaps even unnoticed. Second, it implies a level of unity and institutionalization among "Christians" that, all the evidence suggests, did not exist in the first century nor for some time thereafter (if, indeed, it ever existed).[2]

If Christians were not yet a well-defined and distinct group at the time the Gospel was written,[3] how should we refer to believers in Christ? Alternatives such as "Christ-confessors," "Christ-believers,"[4] or "Christ-followers"[5] are perhaps the best we can do, even as the cumbersome nature of such terms must be acknowledged.[6]

And if Christianity did not yet exist, how do we talk about that nebulous but nevertheless palpable sense of affiliation that Christ-believers had, not only with the other believers in their vicinity, but with the broader collectivity with which they shared some practices, beliefs, and institutions? One option is to resort to the generic term "community."

As Stanley Stowers has noted, "community," as used in New Testament studies, is a slippery term. It sometimes has a territorial or linguistic meaning; it may also denote less tangible concepts such as a "social and mental coherence, a commonality in mind and practice."[7] Stowers argues that in Gospel scholarship, these meanings are often built on "romantic ideas of communal creativity and communal authorship" that cannot be substantiated from the ancient evidence. Such claims may mean that the theology of an author or document originated within a particular group, and served to differentiate that group—that community—from others. Or they may mean that the Gospel author is addressing the circumstances of a particular community.[8] These perspectives are not mutually exclusive. They do, however, involve numerous undemonstrable assumptions about the relationships between the Gospels and their intended readers or hearers.

The idea of a Johannine community has been central to historical-critical analysis of the Gospel for at least fifty years. I have long been a critic of the expulsion hypothesis according to which the Gospel was written for a Johannine community that had experienced a traumatic expulsion from the synagogue.[9] Nevertheless, until recently, I counted myself among the vast majority of Johannine scholars who assume that a Johannine community already existed at the time that the Fourth Gospel reached its present form. In working on the present book, however, I have become convinced that while a community of sorts may have formed around the book itself, there is no evidence for its existence prior to the Gospel.

I will continue to use the term "community" without, I hope, any of the more complex nuances that Stowers criticizes. In the context of the present study, "community" refers primarily to the contemporaries of the Gospel writer(s) who encountered and responded positively to the Fourth Gospel. I will use the term interchangeably with other terms such as "group," "audience," and "hearers."

"JEWS," "JUDAISM," AND *IOUDAIOI*

Perhaps even more than "Christians" and "Christianity," "Jews" and "Judaism" are highly contested terms in the study of antiquity. I agree in principle with the view that "Judaism" seems inappropriate on the grounds that it refers to an essentializing abstraction that could not have existed in the first century. Nevertheless, I will at times (sparingly) use this term to refer to a "big tent" comprised of ideas, practices, groups, and individuals that are associated with those whom the Gospel, the writings of Josephus, inscriptions, and other texts and objects call *hoi Ioudaioi*.

Even more difficult is the term "Jews" in reference to those whom our sources refer to as *Ioudaioi*. Many argue that "Judeans" is a more accurate translation, on the assumption that "Jews" is a religious term and therefore should not be applied to a first-century group.[10] Others—including myself—argue that the term "Jews" could not in the past, and still cannot in the present, be limited to its religious sense, and that its connotations in English include a complex mix of practices, affiliations, identifications, and beliefs for which we find evidence in ancient sources. Mindful of the controversy, however, I use the transliterated forms extensively throughout the book. In keeping with my conviction that, in scholarship, the term "Jew" is the best translation, however, I also use the terms "Jew" and "Jews."[11]

"PAGANS" AND "GENTILES"

"Jews" and "Christians" are not the only labels that have been challenged in recent discussions about groups in antiquity. Some scholars now avoid all references to "pagans" and speak about "polytheists" instead. The argument for this position rests on what some argue are the pejorative connotations of the term "pagans." Although the term "polytheism" also implies a contrast with "monotheism," it is to be preferred as "a less nakedly offensive formulation than 'paganism.'"[12]

Others, however, continue to use the terms "pagan" and "paganism," while explicitly dissociating themselves from the negative connotations noted above. Christopher Jones acknowledges that the term "pagan" is inappropriate as a term for those who were neither Christian nor Jew. "Polytheist" may therefore seem like a plausible alternative but it blurs "the wide range of conceptions that 'pagans' had about the divine,"[13] given that some pagans were in effect monotheists while others had "a conception of a supreme being to whom all others are subservient or inferior." He concludes that while "paganism" is "potentially misleading" it is less so than the alternatives.[14] Raffaella

Cribiore adds that while the term "has been compromised by its Christian usage and moreover is far from precise" it is still the most serviceable.[15] It will be my choice in this book as well.[16]

NOTES

1. One might argue that the most contested term of all is "religion." The field of religious studies continues to be roiled by the question of whether there is such a thing as "religion," either in the past or in the present. The critique of "religion" as a constructed category shaped by Christian presuppositions is compelling. See, for example, Russell T. McCutcheon, *Critics Not Caretakers: Redescribing the Public Study of Religion* (Albany: State University of New York Press, 2001); Tomoko Masuzawa, *The Invention of World Religions or, How European Universalism Was Preserved in the Language of Pluralism* (Chicago: University of Chicago Press, 2007). For an application of this approach to the ancient world, see Carlin A. Barton and Daniel Boyarin, *Imagine No Religion: How Modern Abstractions Hide Ancient Realities* (New York: Fordham University Press, 2016).

On the other hand, "religion" remains a meaningful category for many scholars in "religion" or "religious studies" departments, and for many outside the academy, who use the term to refer to a complex set of ideas that include beliefs about how human beings situate ourselves in the cosmos, history, and community. I am of two minds about this issue when it comes to my teaching and my research in writing, for example, on "religion and film." In this book, however, and in my work on early Judaism and New Testament, I do not use the term, as I do not find it a helpful category for grappling with ancient texts, beliefs, practices, and societies.

2. Many others have come to the same conclusion. See the helpful discussion by Donald H. Juel, "The Future of the Religious Past: Qumran and the Palestinian Jesus Movement," in *The Bible and the Dead Sea Scrolls: The Second Princeton Symposium on Judaism and Christian Origins. 1, 1,* ed. James H. Charlesworth (Waco: Baylor University Press, 2006), 61–74.

3. This point is made by many. For one example, see Juel. See also Judith Lieu, *Christian Identity in the Jewish and Graeco-Roman World* (Oxford: Oxford University Press, 2004), 23.

4. Mikael Tellbe, *Christ-believers in Ephesus: A Textual Analysis of Early Christian Identity Formation in a Local Perspective* (Tübingen: Mohr Siebeck, 2009).

5. Paula Fredriksen, "How Later Contexts Affect Pauline Content, or: Retrospect Is the Mother of Anachronism," in *Jews and Christians in the First and Second Centuries: How to Write Their History*, ed. Peter J. Tomson and Joshua Schwartz, (Leiden: Brill, 2014), 17–51.

6. Paula Fredriksen, "Mandatory Retirement: Ideas in the Study of Christian Origins Whose Time Has Come to Go," *Studies in Religion* 35, no. 2 (2006): 231–46; Anders Runesson, "Inventing Christian Identity: Paul, Ignatius, and Theodosius I," in *Exploring Early Christian Identity* (Tübingen: Mohr Siebeck, 2008), 59–92; William

Arnal, "The Collection and Synthesis of 'Tradition' and the Second-Century Invention of Christianity*," *Method & Theory in the Study of Religion* 23, no. 3 (2011): 193–215, https://doi.org/10.1163/157006811X608359.

7. Stanley K. Stowers, "The Concept of 'Community' and the History of Early Christianity," *Method & Theory in the Study of Religion* 23, no. 3–4 (2011): 238.

8. Stowers, "The Concept of 'Community' and the History of Early Christianity," 240–41.

9. See Adele Reinhartz, "The Johannine Community and Its Jewish Neighbors: A Reappraisal," in *What Is John?* (Atlanta: Scholars Press, 1998), 111–38.

10. The most frequently cited article in support of this view is Steve Mason, "Jews, Judaeans, Judaizing, Judaism: Problems of Categorization in Ancient History," *Journal for the Study of Judaism in the Persian, Hellenistic and Roman Period* 38 (2007): 457–512.

11. Some scholars prefer to use "the Jews" in quotation marks. For my detailed argument against this usage, see Adele Reinhartz, "'Jews' and Jews in the Fourth Gospel," in *Anti-Judaism and the Fourth Gospel: Papers of the Leuven Colloquium, 2000,* ed. R. Bieringer, Didier Pollefeyt, and F. Vandecasteele-Vanneuville (Assen: Royal Van Gorcum, 2001), 341–56.

12. Garth Fowden, "Late Polytheism," in *The Cambridge Ancient History Volume 12. Volume 12.,* ed. Alan Bowman, Averil Cameron, and Peter Garnsey (Cambridge: Cambridge University Press, 2005), 522, http://dx.doi.org/10.1017/CHOL9780521301992.

13. Christopher P. Jones, *Between Pagan and Christian* (Cambridge, MA: Harvard University Press, 2014), 6.

14. Jones, *Between Pagan and Christian,* 6.

15. Raffaella Cribiore, *Libanius the Sophist: Rhetoric, Reality, and Religion in the Fourth Century* (Ithaca: Cornell University Press, 2013), 7.

16. See also Juel, "The Future of the Religious Past: Qumran and the Palestinian Jesus Movement," 62–63.

Introduction

"Will you walk into my parlour?" said the Spider to the Fly,
"'Tis the prettiest little parlour that ever you did spy;
The way into my parlour is up a winding stair,
And I have many curious things to show you when you are there."
"Oh no, no," said the little fly, "to ask me is in vain;
For who goes up your winding stair can ne'er come down again."

—The Spider and the Fly, Mary Howitt (1829)[1]

Some forty years ago, the Gospel of John beckoned me to enter its (deceptively) pretty little parlor. Although I manage from time to time to descend its winding stair, it calls me back again and again. My first forays focused on its mysterious signs. Like the messages spun into Charlotte's web, the Gospel's signs point to "no ordinary" subject (Jesus) and "no ordinary" creator (God).[2] Later, I followed one silken thread—Jesus as the Good Shepherd—to search its meanings in the Gospel and its subtexts in ancient views about death and resurrection.[3]

Over time, however, I became entangled in the sticky heart of the Gospel's web: the Jews, or, to be more specific, the Gospel's understanding and portrayal of "the Jews" (in Greek: οἱ Ἰουδαῖοι; *hoi Ioudaioi*).[4] I struggled to free myself by imagining the different perspectives from which I, as a Jewish reader, might respond to John's Gospel, and, more recently, by pondering matters of translation.[5] The present book is my final attempt to unravel this most difficult element—and this most troubling Gospel—from a rhetorical, historical, and ethical perspective.

Here is the problem. The Gospel's narrative, language, and worldview situate it squarely within the same orbit as other first-century Jewish texts written in Greek. With the exception of Pontius Pilate, the main characters are Jewish;

xix

with the exception of the Samaritan episode (John 4:1–42), the action takes place in Galilee and Judea, areas populated primarily by Jews.[6] The Gospel's theology is not at all unique within the "common Judaism" of the first century.[7] Jesus—the Gospel's Jewish protagonist—behaves in Jewish ways: he goes on pilgrimage to the Jerusalem Temple for the festivals; he quotes liberally from the Torah and Prophets; he argues from and with scripture in ways that resemble the midrashic arguments that later appear in rabbinic literature;[8] and he debates the same issues that concern other Jews in the Second Temple period.[9]

Nevertheless, with the exception of John 4:9, the Gospel does not refer to Jesus or his close disciples as *Ioudaioi*. The Gospel's implied author traces the escalation of the Jews' opposition to and enmity towards Jesus, from antagonistic interrogation (John 2:18–21), to persecution (5:16), attempts to stone (8:59; 10:31–33) and even kill him (5:18; 7:1), culminating in their successful plot to have him crucified by Pilate (11:49–52; 18:1–19:16). Although the Gospel of John's Jesus declares that "salvation is from the Jews" (4:22), he also states that the Jews have the devil as their father (8:44).

JEWISH AND ANTI-JEWISH?

Many have asked: How can a Gospel that is so Jewish also be so anti-Jewish?[10] Ancient commentators, such as Cyril of Alexandria, had a ready explanation. For Cyril, it is "altogether plain that the synagogue of the Jews rejected the Bridegroom from Heaven, and that the church of the Gentiles received Him, and that very gladly."[11] Because of this rejection, Christ, on God's behalf, "put the race of the Jews forth from the kingdom of heaven."[12] The Gospel's Jewishness reflects Jesus's own origins within "the synagogue of the Jews"; its anti-Jewishness reflects the divine judgement against the Jews on account of their refusal to recognize Jesus as God's son.

What was plain to Cyril, however, is neither obvious nor acceptable to modern scholars. Few today would say, with Cyril, that God truly has rejected the Jews, and few would entertain the possibility that the Gospel's implied author might have thought so. Although most scholars are highly motivated to smooth out the apparent contradiction between the Gospel's Jewish and anti-Jewish elements, our historical-critical sensibilities steer us away from cosmic explanations and towards the concrete circumstances and audiences for which the Gospel was written. Perhaps the *Ioudaioi* against whom John's Jesus railed were not the entire Jewish people but rather a subgroup.[13] Perhaps the Gospel's vituperative language does not reflect John's deep-seated views but is merely a convention of ancient polemics.[14] Maybe the hostility is simply a natural response to a traumatic experience—expulsion from the synagogue—that the intended audience suffered at Jewish hands.[15] Or maybe the anti-Jewish language is simply evidence of the differentiation that necessarily and inevitably accompanies the development of a new social identity.[16]

There is no single answer to the conundrum posed by the presence of both Jewish and anti-Jewish elements in the Fourth Gospel. As a Jew, I am glad that my colleagues reject Cyril's belief that God has abandoned the "synagogue of the Jews." As a scholar, however, I believe Cyril was onto something, not theologically but as a reader of John's Gospel.

To be sure, Cyril (378–444 CE) wrote long after the Fourth Gospel reached its final form, and he read the Gospel of John through the lenses of his own aims, ideas, and audiences. It seems to me, however, that the Gospel's implied author, like Cyril, was convinced that God's favor had turned away from the Jews to the Gentiles; that there is a deep rift between the synagogue and those who confess Christ as Messiah; and that this rift was initiated in Jesus's own lifetime. At the same time as the Fourth Gospel tells its version of Jesus's life story, it also narrates the story of God's repudiation of the Jews and the adoption of the Christ-confessors as God's covenant people. Although Jesus came to his own people—the Jews—they did not accept him (1:11).

Others did accept him, however (1:12), and, in doing so, replaced the Jews as God's own people. As God's people, they now had exclusive access to the valued tokens of Jewishness: the Jews' calendar (Sabbath and festivals), their scriptures, their Temple, and, most important, their God, or, more precisely, the special relationship with God through which all blessings flow. In this latter story, the Gospel's Jewish elements do not reflect an *approbation* of Jewishness that would in turn disarm its anti-Jewish statements. Rather, the Gospel argues that Jewish concepts and symbols no longer belong to the Jews, but solely to those who believe Jesus to be the Messiah.

For this reason, I disagree with those who describe the Fourth Gospel as both Jewish and anti-Jewish. On the contrary, I have come to see the Gospel as thoroughly anti-Jewish. This anti-Jewishness is evident not only in the Gospel's hostile comments about the Jews as children of the devil and in its portrayal of the Jews and their leaders as hounding Jesus unto death, but also in the very elements that were constitutive of first-century Jewish identity. The Fourth Gospel appropriates Jewishness at the same time as it repudiates Jews. In doing so, it also promotes a parting of the ways between those who believe that Jesus is the Messiah, the Son of God, and those who do not, that is, the *Ioudaioi*.[17]

"WRITTEN IN ORDER THAT . . ."

Like the myth of Arachne, the Gospel is an ancient tale spun in a web.[18] The motifs of appropriation and repudiation are woven deeply into its narration, its worldview, and the messages it conveys to its audience. Just as the spider uses its web to attract its prey, so did the implied author use his Gospel to attract his audience. Unlike the spider, the Gospel writer's aim was not predatory but rhetorical. He did not seek to consume his audience, or to overwhelm them with abstract ideas, but to persuade them by means of stories, metaphors, and exhortations to view history and the cosmos, Jesus and the Jews, as he did.

That the aim of the Gospel is indeed rhetorical, that is, persuasive, is stated explicitly in its own conclusion and statement of purpose. In John 20:30–31, the narrator declares that while "Jesus did many other signs in the presence of his disciples, which are not written in this book . . . these are written so that *you* [may come to] believe that Jesus is the Messiah, the Son of God, and that through believing *you* may have life in his name" (emphasis added).[19] In using the second person plural ("you") the Gospel addresses its audience directly and proclaims its intention to shape their very lives, present and future, in life and beyond death.[20]

My aims, too, are rhetorical. First, I seek to persuade you, my reader, that the Gospel does more than simply exhort its audience to believe its claims about Jesus. I will argue that, in exhorting them to believe, the Gospel offers its audience rebirth into a new family, the family of God, using a range of strategies that together constitute a *rhetoric of affiliation*.

Second, I will argue that participation in the family of God required not only affiliation with others who did the same, but also separation from the *Ioudaioi*. Through a *rhetoric of disaffiliation*, the Gospel insists that members of God's family enjoy exclusive access to the Father's scriptures and God's house, the very same assets that the Jews had claimed for themselves. By rejecting the claim that Jesus is the Messiah, God's Son, the Jews have removed themselves from God's care—God's flock, God's vine, God's elect people. For this Gospel, therefore, the *Ioudaioi* are those, who, by rejecting God's son, have forfeited their status as God's children. Just as one cannot simultaneously be a child of God (1:12) and a child of the devil (8:44), so also one cannot be a believer in Christ and a *Ioudaios*. In this sense, the Gospel rhetorically transfers the benefits of Jewishness—covenantal relationship with God—from the *Ioudaioi* to the "children of God."

Third, I will consider the rhetorical situation implied by the Gospel's rhetorical program, including its offer of rebirth, its appropriation of Jewishness, and its repudiation of the Jews. How might we situate the Gospel in the development of the Jesus movement of the late first century? For whom was it written, and what did it hope to achieve? Whereas the consensus position has been that the Gospel was written to comfort a Jewish-Christian group after its traumatic expulsion from the synagogue, I will propose that the Gospel's rhetoric can be explained just as well—or even better—by situating the Gospel in the context of the late first-century Gentile mission in Asia Minor.

THE FOURTH GOSPEL AS RHETORIC

To say that the Gospel of John has rhetorical—persuasive—intentions is hardly revolutionary. Although "rhetoric" is now often used derogatorily to refer to insincere, meaningless, or bombastic speech, it is fundamentally a neutral term that pertains to the persuasive function of speech.[21] Because all known societies, in all eras, used speech for persuasive purposes, rhetoric is a universal phenomenon, built into the very fabric of society and communication,[22] and the very nature of language itself.[23] For this reason, George Kennedy argues, "It is perfectly possible to utilize the categories of Aristotelian rhetoric to study speech in China, India, Africa, and elsewhere in the world, cultures much more different from the Greek than was that of Palestine in the time of the Roman empire."[24]

In approaching the Fourth Gospel as rhetoric, however, we need not look far from its own historical and geographical location. Rhetoric was deeply embedded in the Hellenistic and Greco-Roman cultures within which the New Testament texts were written.[25] As participants in these cultures, audiences were not only trained to absorb and learn from rhetorical discourse, but were also delighted by—and susceptible to—rhetorical strategies.[26] This capacity required neither literacy nor formal education in rhetoric; it was acquired through experience simply by participating in everyday life,[27] in the same way that twenty-first century movie goers, trained by many years of movie viewing, are skilled at interpreting and responding to Hollywood film. For these reasons, argues Kennedy, attention to rhetoric helps us "to hear the biblical texts as an ancient audience would hear them, and that means an audience familiar with classical rhetorical practice whether from study in school or from experience of the secular world."[28]

If the Gospel's audience would have been experienced in listening and responding to rhetorical compositions, the author(s) of the Gospel themselves must also have been adept at shaping the Gospel in ways that "sounded, resonated, and impressed . . . [itself] upon the mind and memory through the ear rather than the eye."[29] This does not mean that they had a rigorous classical education; we lack the evidence to know one way or another.[30] Because the New Testament was written in a cultural context infused with persuasive speech,[31] it is necessary to assume only that the Gospel's real author(s) were reasonably active participant(s) in this culture. Indeed, they could hardly have escaped it.[32] In seeking to persuade their audience that "life in his name" belongs to those who believe that Jesus is the Messiah, Son of God, they made use of the rhetorical toolkit common to both themselves and their audience.[33]

THE PRINCIPLES OF RHETORICAL ANALYSIS

Assumptions

The basic assumption underlying a rhetorical approach is that "texts are designed by authors in order to affect readers in particular ways, that those designs are conveyed through the words, techniques, structures, forms, and dialogic relations of texts as well as the genres and conventions readers use to understand them."[34] To view the Gospel as a rhetorical text we must attend both to the goals and to the techniques of its persuasive discourse. According to Kennedy, "Rhetorical criticism takes the text as we have it, whether the work of a single author or the product of editing, and looks at it from the point of view of the author's or editor's intent, the unified results, and how it would be perceived by an audience of near contemporaries."[35]

Like reader-response criticism, therefore, rhetorical criticism is concerned with the complex interrelationships among author, text, and reader.[36] But, as in reader-response criticism, the author and reader available to our analysis of ancient texts are not real or historical people but the authors and readers implied by the text itself, and imagined or constructed by ourselves. From this perspective, it is necessary to modify Kennedy's statement; in dealing with ancient texts (or perhaps any texts), I—or any reader—cannot know the intent of the *real* author or editor, but I can discern an intent of the *implied* author whom we have unavoidably constructed from our own reading of the text. Similarly, I cannot know how real audiences perceived John's Gospel, but I can imagine how the implied author might have hoped they would respond. In imagining this desired response, I also construct the Gospel's implied audience as a compliant one, composed of individuals who sincerely, enthusiastically, and uncritically accept the Gospel's claims. In practice, few real readers, even those who claim to engage in literalist interpretations of scripture, are fully compliant. Nevertheless, for the purpose of discerning the potential impact of the Gospel's rhetorical intent and strategies, it is the unreservedly compliant audience that I will construct.[37]

Types of Rhetoric

Ancient authors, following Aristotle (*Rhet.* 3.1.1358a), distinguish among three types of rhetoric: deliberative, judicial, and epideictic. Judicial rhetoric is used to persuade an audience that needs to make a judgment about a past event.[38] Deliberative rhetoric is used to persuade an audience to take a specific action.[39] Epideictic rhetoric is used to persuade an audience to accept a particular belief, position, or stance.[40]

For my purposes it is not important to determine which type of rhetoric, if any, is dominant in the Fourth Gospel; the Gospel used all three types in order to convey its message, urgently and passionately, to its audience.[41] Nevertheless, the Gospel does draw on the three principal elements of classical rhetoric—invention, arrangement, and style[42]—in its attempt to persuade its audience that faith in Jesus as the Christ and Son of God is the foundation for eternal life.

The Elements of Rhetoric: The Rule of Three

All three types of rhetoric depend on three elements: invention, arrangement, and style.[43]

Invention can be based on either external or internal ("artistic") proofs. In New Testament rhetoric, states Kennedy, there are three common forms of external proof: scriptural quotations, evidence of miracles, and the naming of witnesses.[44] Internal, or artistic proofs, also fall into three categories: *Ethos*, *Pathos*, *Logos*. These categories, according to Aristotle, inhere in the speaker, the audience, and the discourse respectively. *Ethos* depends upon the credibility of the author or speaker; *Pathos* refers to the ability of the orator or writer to play upon the emotions of the audience; *Logos* refers to the argumentation used to demonstrate one point or another.[45]

Arrangement refers to the most effective ordering of the discourse's elements. Judicial oratory is the most elaborate, consisting of a proem, narration, proposition, refutation, and epilogue. Deliberative oratory typically is arranged as proem, proposition, proof, and epilogue. Epideictic oratory typically opens with a proem, and then presents an orderly sequence of topics relevant to the life of the individual or the topic under consideration before concluding with an epilogue.[46] With regard to arrangement, the Fourth Gospel resembles epideictic oratory, as it opens with the Prologue (1:1–18), closes with an epilogue (21:1–25), and in between presents a series of *semeia* (signs) and discourses that develop particular topics.

Style can be plain, grand, or various subcategories in-between; it entails *lexis* (appropriate word choice) and *synthesis* (the appropriate arrangement of those words into phrases, clauses, and sentences, including figures of speech and figures of thought).[47]

The Gospel uses these elements of classical rhetoric to persuade the audience that belief in Jesus as the Messiah, Son of God, is essential for eternal life. The goal of rhetoric, however, is not only to move an audience to be-lief, knowledge, and understanding. Rhetoric is also meant to move them to action.[48] Augustine quotes a "great orator"—Cicero—as saying that "an eloquent man must speak so as to teach, to delight, and to persuade. Then he adds: To teach is a necessity, to delight is a beauty, to persuade is a tri-umph."[49] The goal of persuasion is not mere intellectual assent, but action: "And as the hearer must be pleased in order to secure his attention, so he must be persuaded in order to move him to action."[50] We cannot know pre-cisely what actions the Gospel's, historical first audience took in response to John's Gospel. By attending to its rhetoric, however, we can discern the actions towards which the Gospel guided its audience. These actions can be categorized broadly as affiliation with other believers and disaffiliation, or separation from, those who do not believe. To convey the need for these ac-tions, the Gospel draws not only on the elements of classical rhetoric but also on a range of other, specifically crafted, rhetorical strategies.

These customized rhetorical strategies can be perceived not only in the lan-guage, patterns, and ideas expressed in Jesus's discourses, but also through the characters and plot that constitute the narrative. The idea that rhetoric can be found in narrative as well as in expository discourse has been explored at length by James Phelan. Phelan argues that "narrative is not just story but also action, *the telling of a story by someone to someone on some occasion for some purpose"* (italics in original).[51] To approach narrative as rhetoric re-quires that we take seriously "the complex, multilayered processes of writing and reading, processes that call upon our cognition, emotions, desires, hopes, values, and beliefs."[52] For this reason we will seek the Gospel's rhetoric not only in the discourses attributed to Jesus but also in the ways in which the Gospel tells the story and depicts its characters.

ON METHOD

According to Kennedy, "Rhetorical criticism takes the text as we have it, whether the work of a single author or the product of editing, and looks at it from the point of view of the author's or editor's intent, the unified results, and how it would be perceived by an audience of near contemporaries."[53] Kennedy describes an orderly procedure for analyzing the rhetoric of a given New Testament document: first, determine the rhetorical unit to be analyzed; then, construct the rhetorical situation that prompts the rhetorical document—the other side of the conversation, so to speak—by considering the arrange-ment of material and stylistic devices; finally, evaluate the piece's success, or failure, in addressing the rhetorical situation.[54]

Kennedy and others have amply demonstrated that the Fourth Gospel is amenable to rhetorical analysis and that it made use of classical rhetorical techniques to tell its story and drive home its messages.[55] My book will add further evidence of the Gospel's rhetorical nature, but this is not its main goal. I will modify Kennedy's step-by-step approach in order to address my own three principal aims. Because the rhetorical unit—the Gospel of John in its final form[56]—is already known, I begin by examining the Gospel's rhetorical aims and the rhetorical strategies deployed to potentially achieve those aims. On the basis of this rhetorical analysis, I will extrapolate—imaginatively construct—a rhetorical situation for which those aims, arguments and strategies might plausibly have a persuasive impact.

CONSTRUCTING THE
RHETORICAL SITUATION: IMAGINING HISTORY

Rhetorical analysis will allow us to get at the Gospel's persuasive purposes, which, I will argue, are twofold: to construct a new and idealized identity for its audience, and to urge their estrangement from the *Ioudaioi*. From a rhetorical-critical perspective, the Gospel is one side of an engaged conversation between the Gospel writer and a particular audience. Moving from rhetoric to history requires us to imagine the other partners to the conversation. What were their issues, questions, concerns? What might they have wanted from the Gospel, and why?[57]

This is a circular approach: first, I analyze the text and then I extrapolate an audience and historical situation from that analysis. Circular reasoning is problematic, to be sure. Yet, unless we forego historical questions altogether, it is inevitable in cases where we have only a single source and no reliable external evidence, and acceptable, in my view, as long as one refrains from reifying one's own constructions.

Constructing the rhetorical situation builds on the rhetorical analysis but it also depends upon our assumptions regarding the Gospel's provenance, the concrete situations in which it would have been encountered by auditors or readers, and the Gospel's relationship to a history external to itself, that is, to events prior to or contemporaneous with the time of writing. The fact that the identity and concrete situation of the audience can be imagined in different, often mutually exclusive ways, points to the constructed nature of any hypothesis, including my own. If, in the words of Clifford Geertz, we human beings are animals "suspended in webs of significance" of our own construction,[58] the same is true of the significance that we weave from the strands of this Gospel.

TRUE CONFESSIONS AND GUIDING PRINCIPLES

Finally, I wish to acknowledge three points: 1) the situatedness of interpretation; 2) the need for humility; and 3) the fundamental role of the imagination.

1) *Situatedness*. I come to the Gospel of John as a Jewish scholar for whom the New Testament is fascinating and important, but neither canonical, nor divinely inspired. Even more important, I come to this study as the daughter of Holocaust survivors who lived their post-war lives with zest, optimism, and gratitude to Canada as a land of opportunity, social responsibility, and freedom from overt anti-Semitism. My interest in the New Testament did not begin with a concern about its role in the history of Jewish-Christian relations, but over time, it has settled there. That concern will be evident throughout this book

2) *Humility*. Humility is a desideratum in all scholarship, and, indeed, in all of one's endeavors. Humility is not the same as false modesty. Humility allows room for me to believe sincerely that I have something to say about the Gospel of John that would be interesting and even important for other scholars to hear or to read, and yet to acknowledge that others can legitimately arrive at different conclusions based on the same evidence. In Johannine studies, humility is required by the simple fact that there is little to no external evidence to support any historical hypothesis whatsoever—whether that pertains to authorship, audience, purpose, or historical context. Furthermore, when it comes to evidence from the Gospel itself, there is no theory that accounts for all aspects of the Gospel or that cannot be refuted by starting from a different set of principles. We must make room for alternative interpretations and acknowledge the limitations of our own efforts, even as we argue vigorously for our own hypotheses.

3) *Imagination*. Like humility, imagination is essential to every scholarly study. The wide and numerous gaps in our knowledge about the historical context of the Gospel, its author, and the broader Greco-Roman world, allow considerable scope for historical imagination. Over many years of reading historiography as well as historical fiction, I have become convinced that both are highly dependent on the same strategies and express the same impulses: to fill in the gaps, to seek causal links among events, and to help ancient people and situations come alive for modern readers.[59]

HISTORY, FICTION, AND THE IMAGINATION

I have neither the desire nor the ability to write historical fiction. Where, I ask, would all the footnotes go? But I am not above a bit of fictionalizing to aid the historical imagination of myself and my readers. To that end, I will imagine the Gospel's implied author(s) as an individual named John (the name is hardly original but the figure is nevertheless a figment of my imagination). Every work prompts its readers to construct an implied author who may share all, some, or none of the characteristics of the real (historical) author. The implied author is also not the narrator. The narrator, as "the voice that tells the story and speaks to the reader" is a rhetorical device.[60] In the Fourth Gospel, however, with the possible exception of chapter 21, the implied author is indistinguishable from the narrator.[61] For that reason, (my construction of) John is the one whose voice, convictions, and rhetorical intentions, are heard in the Fourth Gospel.

I imagine John as man who is confident in—and passionate about—his belief that Jesus is the Messiah and Son of God, and utterly committed to persuading others to be the same. I do not know whether he knew Hebrew or had spent time in the Galilee, Judea, or Samaria, but I picture him as a Greek-speaking and -writing Jew from Asia Minor immersed both in Jewish scriptures and traditions as well as in Hellenistic modes of thought.[62] He has absorbed not only the knowledge that is common to Jews of his time and place, but also a Jewish way of seeing the world. He believes that the world is created and presided over by the God of Israel, and that God has chosen a people with whom to be in an exclusive covenantal relationship. He differs from at least some of the Jews of his time and place, however, because he understands Jesus as the divinely-given mediator in that relationship. Perhaps it is for that reason that John—as I imagine him—does not call himself a *Ioudaios*. John is a fine orator, and a well-known presence in his city or town.

Alongside John, the implied author, I imagine a second fictional figure. I call her Alexandra. Alexandra stands in for the compliant audience—a part I cannot play on my own. She is a person who responds wholeheartedly to John's message; in absorbing his story of Jesus, she is stirred to faith and called to action.[63] John's explanations of the festivals and other Jewish practices suggest that she does not know much about Jewish ritual life. Whether Alexandra is already a Christ-follower—or not yet one—I do not know for certain. Nor do I know her age, hair color, sexual orientation, or personal circumstances. I do know—as the one who created her—that she is open to persuasion and that she is attracted, by birth and/or by inclination, to the idea of covenantal relationship with the God of Israel.

ORALITY

How would Alexandra have encountered John's message? Given the relatively low rate of literacy, it is likely that she, and all other members of John's implied audience, would have heard the Gospel read or proclaimed aloud, ⊘

⊘ See Harrison, 5 (note 71 below) for the additional point that even private reading for oneself may have been aloud.

rather than reading it to themselves.[64] That at least some New Testament texts were meant to be experienced orally is supported by references in 1 Thessalonians and the book of Revelation. In 1 Thess 5:27, Paul "solemnly command[s]" his addressees that "this letter be read to all of them," that is, all the "brothers and sisters" (1 Thess 5:26).[65] Revelation declares that "blessed is the one who reads aloud the words of the prophecy, and blessed are those who hear and who keep what is written in it; for the time is near" (Rev. 1:3); and later, warns "everyone who hears the words of the prophecy of this book: if anyone adds to them, God will add to that person the plagues described in this book; if anyone takes away from the words of the book of this prophecy, God will take away that person's share in the tree of life and in the holy city, which are described in this book" (Rev. 22:18–19). Although the Gospel of John does not refer explicitly to the mode by which it is to be encountered— by hearing or by reading—these examples suggest that oral experience of written texts was not unusual in the circles attracted to and/or affiliated with this fledgling movement in the mid to late first century.

The oral transmission of written texts was widespread and crossed ethnic, cultural, and social boundaries within the broad Greco-Roman world, classical and Hellenistic. According to Carol Harrison,

> Classical culture was wholly directed towards the hearer, in that its educational system, its legal and political practice, its ceremonies, literature, and art, were all founded upon the art and practice of rhetoric; the art of speaking in such a way that the hearer's mind and emotions should be impressed and moved by what they heard, so that they assented to, and acted upon it.[66]

The assumption that the books were heard more often than read is consistent with research that suggests a relatively low level of full literacy (the ability to read and write) among Jews and pagans in Greco-Roman society. Harry Gamble stresses that the level of literacy in the ancient church was probably not any higher than in the surrounding Greco-Roman society. Indeed, full literacy may not have been widespread at all.[67] Gamble suggests that "this is true in spite of the importance the early church accorded to religious texts, for acquaintance with the scriptures did not require that all or even most Christians be individually capable of reading them and does not imply that they were."[68]

The emphasis on oral reception did not, however, diminish the value accorded to written texts. As Gamble points out,

> If most Christians were illiterate, it did not prevent them from participating in literacy or from becoming familiar with Christian texts. Those who had only a cursory contact with Christianity through missionary preaching or propaganda could hardly have failed to notice its reliance on texts and to hear them quoted. Those who were drawn to Christianity were intensively schooled in its literature, especially scripture.[69]

Furthermore, the Gospel's contemporaries would have been accustomed to hearing and responding to oral texts. Carol Harrison emphasizes that "classical and early Christian culture was very much a rhetorical culture; one based on the practice and power of the spoken word." For this reason, "the unlettered were able to 'read' and understand reality through the shared, often tacit, markers of complicit understanding, customary practice, and habitual ways of thinking created by speaking and hearing."[70] Even if we imagine Alexandra as a "lettered" woman who was able to read for herself, the strongly rhetorical nature of the Gospel suggests that she still may well have become familiar with the Gospel by hearing rather than, or in addition to, reading.[71] *(See note 71)*

Imagine, then, Alexandra's encounter with John's rhetorical Gospel, taking place somewhere, perhaps in Asia Minor, and perhaps in Ephesus.[72] If your imagination needs some stimulation, just look again at the front cover of this book, and the way in which artist Shoshana Walfish visualized this encounter, inspired by the work of Raphael and Pontormo.[73] Alexandra and John may or may not have known each other personally. For John, Alexandra was probably just another face in the crowd; for Alexandra, John may just have been an orator whose words resonated with her.[74] But if the Gospel had any power at all, it was to foster an encounter not so much between an author and a reader or listener, but between Jesus—some of whose signs are written in "this book" (20:30)—and those who are moved to be reborn, "not of blood or of the will of the flesh or of the will of man, but of God" (1:13).

OUTLINE OF CHAPTERS

The book is divided into three main sections, corresponding to each of the three aims discussed above.

Part I: The Rhetoric of Affiliation

Chapter 1, "'Ask and you will receive': The Rhetoric of Desire and Fulfillment," examines the varied rhetorical strategies that the Gospel uses to develop two core propositions: that human beings desire eternal life—or, at the very least, freedom from death—and that faith in Jesus as the Christ and Son of God is the only way to fulfill this desire. To persuade its audience that faith is indeed the answer to their deepest desires, the Gospel draws on standard categories of Greek rhetoric such as external proof, artistic evidence, and style.

Chapter 2, "'Love one another': The Rhetoric of Transformation," focuses on the actions that the Gospel calls on individuals to take once they are persuaded that belief in Jesus leads to eternal life. The next step is to discern the cosmological context and meaning of Jesus's sojourn in the world, and to situate oneself within that cosmological realm. This discernment requires a transformation of personal identity but the transformation is incomplete without corporate affiliation, that is, a joining together with others who are undergoing or have undergone the same transformation. Eternal life cannot be achieved outside this collective framework.

Part II: The Rhetoric of Disaffiliation

Chapter 3, "'Casting off the withered branch': The Rhetoric of Expropriation," documents the rhetoric of appropriation and expropriation that marks the new cosmological reality in which believers reside. The Gospel's narrative is structured around the Jewish Sabbath, the Jewish festivals, and Jewish institutions of synagogue and Temple. These features, however, function rhetorically not to include John's audience within a broader Jewish corporate entity but, perhaps ironically, to exclude that broader entity from the divine covenant. In appropriating the scriptures, the Temple, and covenantal language for its audience, the Gospel rhetorically expropriates, casts out, expels the Jews from that covenant. The Jewishness of the Gospel is not an antidote to its anti-Jewishness, but part and parcel thereof.

Chapter 4, "'The world has hated you': The Rhetoric of Repudiation," looks closely at the negative rhetoric employed by the Gospel to encourage separation from the *Ioudaioi*. In this chapter I argue that the Gospel's use of the labels *Ioudaios/Ioudaioi*, while not uniform, in general expresses a rhetoric of vituperation that casts aspersions on the *Ioudaioi*. This rhetoric paints the *Ioudaioi* as unbelievers and "the children of Satan" who are unwilling and, indeed, incapable of hearing and responding to the promise of eternal life offered by Jesus through the Gospel.

Chapter 5, "Rhetorical *Ioudaioi* and Real Jews," surveys the theories concerning the historical referents of *Ioudaioi* as used in the Fourth Gospel, and considers briefly the fraught question of how best to translate this term into English. The difficulty in pinning down the referent suggests that for John, as for the church fathers, *Ioudaioi* was not primarily a historical designation but rather a hermeneutical, rhetorical, and theological category used for the purposes of self-identification, boundary-drawing, and polemics. Nevertheless, in identifying the enemies of Christ and his followers as *Ioudaioi*, the Gospel potentially creates distrust and separation from the flesh-and-blood *Ioudaioi*—Jews who did not believe in Christ—whom its audience may have known.

Part III: Imagining the Rhetorical Situation

The third section of the book moves outside the framework of the Gospel's rhetoric in order to imagine the "real" identities of both the historical audience and the *Ioudaioi* over against whom the Gospel defines the children of God.

Chapter 6, "'The Jews had already agreed': J. L. Martyn and the Expulsion Theory," considers Martyn's construction of the Gospel's audience, purpose, and historical situation. On the basis of three passages that refer to the *aposynagōgos*—the one who is distanced from the synagogue—Martyn argued that the Gospel reflects the traumatic expulsion of the "Johannine community" from the synagogue in the years immediately preceding the final version of Gospel itself. Martyn's work has shaped historical study of the Fourth Gospel for a half century, yet it is based on some problematic and unverifiable assumptions.

Chapter 7, "'We wish to see Jesus': John, Alexandra, and the Propulsion Theory," proposes an alternative to the expulsion hypothesis. The very practice of rhetoric presupposes a particular audience in a specific historical, geographical, and social location.[75] The challenge is to reconstruct that audience in the absence of any external evidence, that is, on the basis of the rhetoric alone. Although a majority of scholars have argued for a Jewish audience, I will suggest that the rhetoric of the Gospel may have appealed most directly to a Gentile audience interested in, but not yet fully committed to, the idea of becoming children of God by participating in a group dedicated to faith in Jesus as the Messiah and Son of God. If so, the Gospel can be viewed as a participant in the Gentile mission of the first century.

The Conclusion summarizes the argument and considers the ethical implications of the rhetorical analysis for the issue of Jews and anti-Judaism in the Gospel of John.

NOTES

1. This poem, including its minor variations, is in the public domain. For the full poem, see http://holyjoe.org/poetry/howitt.htm (accessed December 13, 2017).

2. "But we have received a sign, Edith—a mysterious sign. A miracle has happened on this farm . . . in the middle of the web there were the words 'Some Pig' . . . we have no ordinary pig." "Well," said Mrs. Zuckerman, "it seems to me you're a little off. It seems to me we have no ordinary spider." E. B. White, *Charlotte's Web* (New York: Harper & Brothers, 1952), 80–81. See Adele Reinhartz, "John 20:30–31 and the Purpose of the Fourth Gospel" (McMaster University, 1983).

3. Adele Reinhartz, *The Word in the World: The Cosmological Tale in the Fourth Gospel* (Atlanta: Scholars Press, 1992).

4. Unless otherwise specified, all translations of the Fourth Gospel and other biblical books are from the New Revised Standard Version (2006).

5. Adele Reinhartz, *Befriending the Beloved Disciple: A Jewish Reading of the Gospel of John* (New York: Continuum, 2001). Adele Reinhartz et al. "Jew and Judean: A Forum on Politics and Historiography in the Translation of Ancient Texts," *The Marginalia Review of Books*, accessed August 26, 2014, http://marginalia.lareviewofbooks.org/jew-judean-forum/.

6. On the ethnic makeup of the Galilee in the first century, see Mark A. Chancey, *The Myth of a Gentile Galilee* (Cambridge: Cambridge University Press, 2002); Bradley W. Root, *First Century Galilee: A Fresh Examination of the Sources* (Tübingen: Mohr Siebeck, 2014).

7. For discussion of "common Judaism," see E. P. Sanders, *Judaism: Practice and Belief, 63 BCE–66 CE* (London: SCM Press, 2016); Wayne O. McCready and Adele Reinhartz, *Common Judaism: Explorations in Second-Temple Judaism* (Minneapolis: Fortress Press, 2008).

8. Peder Borgen, *Bread from Heaven; an Exegetical Study of the Concept of Manna in the Gospel of John and the Writings of Philo.* (Leiden: E.J. Brill, 1965); Peder Borgen, *The Gospel of John: More Light from Philo, Paul and Archaeology: The Scriptures, Tradition, Exposition, Settings, Meaning* (Leiden: Brill, 2014).

9. In John 5:17, for example, Jesus claims that God the Father works on the Sabbath. This would seem to contradict Genesis 2:2, which states that God rested on the seventh day, but the question of whether God worked on the Sabbath was very much a live issue in the Second Temple and rabbinic periods. See Philo of Alexandria, *Cher.* 8 6–890; *Leg All.* 1. 5–6; Exod Rabbah 11:10; 30:9.

10. The formulation is often traced back either to C. K. Barrett, *The Gospel According to St. John: An Introduction with Commentary and Notes on the Greek Text* (London: SPCK, 1965), 71 or to Wayne A. Meeks, "'Am I a Jew?'—Johannine Christianity and Judaism," in *Christianity, Judaism and Other Greco-Roman Cults: Studies for Morton Smith at Sixty*, ed. Jacob Neusner (Leiden: Brill, 1975), 163.

11. Cyril of Alexandria, *Commentary on John*, Book 2. http://www.tertullian.org/fathers/cyril_on_john_02_book2.htm (accessed October 9, 2017).

12. Cyril of Alexandria, *Commentary on John,* Book 5. http://www.tertullian.org/fathers/cyril_on_john_05_book5.htm (accessed October 9, 2017).

13. Daniel Boyarin, "The IOUDAIOI of John and the Prehistory of Judaism," in *Pauline Conversations in Context: Essays in Honor of Calvin J. Roetzel*, ed. Janice Capel Anderson et al. (London: Sheffield Academic Press, 2002), 216–39. For detailed discussion and bibliography, see chapter 7.

14. Luke Timothy Johnson, "The New Testament's Anti-Jewish Slander and the Conventions of Ancient Polemic," *Journal of Biblical Literature* 108, no. 3 (September 1, 1989): 419–41.

15. J. Louis Martyn, *History and Theology in the Fourth Gospel* (Louisville: Westminster John Knox Press, 2003).

16. Raimo Hakola, *Identity Matters: John, the Jews, and Jewishness* (Leiden: Brill, 2005), http://public.eblib.com/choice/publicfullrecord.aspx?p=280605; Raimo Hakola, *Reconsidering Johannine Christianity: A Social Identity Approach* (New York: Routledge, 2015).

17. Please note: To declare the Gospel anti-Jewish is *not* to blame the text or its author for the history of Christian anti-Semitism, for the attitudes and events that paved the way for the Holocaust, or for the ongoing appropriation of the "Jews as devil" motif by contemporary neo-Nazi groups. Rather, I consider the Gospel to be anti-Jewish insofar as those who hear or read it in a compliant or uncritical way—accepting its worldview as their own—are likely to come away with negative views of Jews. Such compliant readings may well have reinforced anti-Jewish or anti-Semitic views and behaviors but it strains credulity to imagine that the Gospel's author(s) had such consequences in mind in portraying the Jews as they did.

Further, while I read the Gospel as anti-Jewish, and as fostering anti-Judaism in its compliant audience, I wish to emphasize that, in my experience, the vast majority of New Testament scholars active today—including those that will bristle at my claims about the Gospel of John's anti-Jewishness—are neither anti-Jewish nor anti-Semitic.

18. In classical mythology, Arachne was a well-known weaver who challenged the goddess Athena to a weaving competition. Out of jealousy, and irritation at her portrayal of the gods' scandalous behavior, Athena destroyed Arachne's tapestry and turned Arachne herself into a spider. Anthony Grafton et al., *The Classical Tradition* (Cambridge, MA: The Belknap Press of Harvard University Press, 2010), 57.

19. For a discussion of the text critical issues in 20:31, see chapter 7.

20. On the selectivity of signs in Greco-Roman literary context, see Craig S. Keener, *The Gospel of John: A Commentary* (Peabody: Hendrickson, 2003), 2.1214.

21. On the negative perception of rhetoric and its connection to Plato, see Richard Toye, *Rhetoric: A Very Short Introduction* (Oxford: Oxford University Press, 2013), 1–2, http://dx.doi.org/10.1093/actrade/9780199651368.001.0001.

22. George A. Kennedy, *New Testament Interpretation through Rhetorical Criticism* (Chapel Hill: University of North Carolina Press, 1984), 10.

23. Kenneth Burke, *A Rhetoric of Motives* (Berkeley: University of California Press, 1969), 43.

24. Kennedy, *New Testament Interpretation through Rhetorical Criticism*, 10.

25. C. Clifton Black, *The Rhetoric of the Gospel: Theological Artistry in the Gospels and Acts* (St. Louis: Chalice Press, 2001), 3.

26. Carol Harrison, *The Art of Listening in the Early Church* (Oxford: Oxford University Press, 2013), 40.

27. Harrison, 40.

28. George A. Kennedy, *Classical Rhetoric and Its Christian and Secular Tradition from Ancient to Modern Times* (Chapel Hill: University of North Carolina Press, 1980), 147.

29. Harrison, *The Art of Listening in the Early Church*, 1. This is not to suggest, however, that the Gospel of John was composed in performance or solely for the sake of performance. See the discussion in Larry W. Hurtado, "Oral Fixation and New Testament Studies?: 'Orality', 'Performance' and Reading Texts in Early Christianity," *New Testament Studies* 60, no. 3 (2014): 321–40, doi:10.1017/S0028688514000058. Kelly R. Iverson, "Oral Fixation or Oral Corrective?: A Response to Larry Hurtado," *New Testament Studies* 62, no. 2 (2016): 183–200, https://doi.org/10.1017/S0028688515000430.

30. Neyrey posits that the evangelist did have an education that included rhetoric. Jerome H. Neyrey, "Encomium versus Vituperation: Contrasting Portraits of Jesus in the Fourth Gospel," *Journal of Biblical Literature* 126, no. 3 (2007): 529.

31. Black, *The Rhetoric of the Gospel*, 84. See also Kennedy, *New Testament Interpretation through Rhetorical Criticism*, 9.

32. Kennedy, *New Testament Interpretation through Rhetorical Criticism*, 10. My enterprise intersects with Vernon Robbins's socio-rhetorical approach, though his is more elaborate in that it addresses "complex correlation between a text and the contexts in which a text has been read and reread, including various dynamic inter-relations between creator and contemplators, past and present." David B. Gowler, "Socio-Rhetorical Interpretation: Textures of a Text and Its Reception," *Journal for the Study of the New Testament* 33, no. 2 (2010): 191. For detailed information on the approach, see note 57 below and Robbins's website and the bibliography there. http://www.religion.emory.edu/faculty/robbins/SRI/index.cfm

33. Kennedy, *New Testament Interpretation through Rhetorical Criticism*, 3.

34. James Phelan, "Rhetorical Literary Ethics and Lyric Narrative: Robert Frost's 'Home Burial,'" *Poetics Today* 25, no. 4 (2004): 631.

35. Phelan, "Rhetorical Literary Ethics and Lyric Narrative," 4.

36. Although Kennedy distinguishes between rhetorical and literary criticism, his definition implies a close connection between these two approaches. Kennedy, *New Testament Interpretation through Rhetorical Criticism*, 4. On reader response criticism, see Seymour Benjamin Chatman, *Story and Discourse: Narrative Structure in Fiction and Film* (Ithaca: Cornell University Press, 1978), 267 and the helpful diagram and discussion in R. Alan Culpepper, *Anatomy of the Fourth Gospel: A Study in Literary Design*, Foundations and Facets: New Testament (Philadelphia: Fortress Press, 1983), 6–10.

37. For detailed discussion of compliant and other sorts of readers, and analysis of how these different readers might respond to the Gospel of John, see Reinhartz, *Befriending the Beloved Disciple*.

38. Kennedy, *New Testament Interpretation through Rhetorical Criticism*, 20. Judicial rhetoric is evident, for example, in John 5, in which Jesus calls several witnesses to testify on his behalf. On the lawsuit motif in John, see Andrew T. Lincoln, *Truth on Trial: The Lawsuit Motif in the Fourth Gospel* (Peabody: Hendrickson Publishers, 2000); George L. Parsenios, *Rhetoric and Drama in the Johannine Lawsuit Motif* (Tübingen: Mohr Siebeck, 2010).

39. Deliberative rhetoric is used in the exhortations to abide in faith, as in the farewell discourses (e.g., 15:9). For a detailed rhetorical analysis of the Farewell Discourse, following George Kennedy's approach, see John Carlson Stube, *A Graeco-Roman Rhetorical Reading of the Farewell Discourse* (London: T & T Clark, 2006).

40. Kennedy, *New Testament Interpretation through Rhetorical Criticism*, 19. Deliberative rhetoric can be discerned in the statements such as 16:24, in which Jesus instructs his disciples to "Ask and you will receive, so that your joy may be complete." On deliberative rhetoric in John, see, briefly, Jo-Ann A. Brant, *Dialogue*

and Drama: Elements of Greek Tragedy in the Fourth Gospel (Peabody: Hendrickson Publishers, 2004), 234.

41. The Fourth Gospel exhibits all three types of rhetoric. Scholars disagree as to which type predominates. Jo-Ann Brant, for example, places John firmly in the category of epideictic rhetoric. Jo-Ann A. Brant, *John* (Grand Rapids: Baker Academic, 2011), 12. This conclusion is consistent with the view of most scholars that the Gospel aims to strengthen the faithful rather than bring new believers to the movement. George Parsenios argues that the rhetorical categories are not nearly so straightforward; most ancient texts, John included, exhibit a hybrid form of rhetoric. George L. Parsenios, *Rhetoric and Drama in the Johannine Lawsuit Motif*, 12–14, 27. See also See also Alicia D. Myers, "'Jesus Said to Them . . .': The Adaptation of Juridical Rhetoric in John 5:1 9–47," *Journal of Biblical Literature* 132, no. 2 (2013): 415–430. Even in ancient rhetoric, however, these three categories are not always distinct. Thomas Conley comments on the artificial nature of Aristotle's three categories, and notes that the "pervasive infiltration of 'epideictic' *topoi* of praise and blame into forensic oratory . . . is not only permissible, but essential." Thomas M. Conley, "Topics of Vituperation: Some Commonplaces of 4th-Century Oratory," in *Influences on Peripatetic Rhetoric: Essays in Honor of William W. Fortenbaugh*, ed. David C. Mirhady (Leiden: Brill, 2007), 235.

42. Kennedy, *New Testament Interpretation through Rhetorical Criticism*, 14.

43. Kennedy, 14.

44. Kennedy, 14.

45. Kennedy, 15.

46. Kennedy, 23–24.

47. Kennedy, 25–27.

48. Jim A. Kuypers, *Rhetorical Criticism: Perspectives in Action* (Lanham: Lexington Books, 2009), 6.

49. St. Augustine, *On Christian Doctrine*, Book 4 Chapter 12. Augustine, *On Christian Doctrine*, ed. J. J Shaw (Mineola: Dover Publications, 2009), 141.http://www.ccel.org/ccel/schaff/npnf102.v.IV_1.12.html. The reference is to Cicero's treatise *De Oratore* 1.15.69. Marcus Tullius Cicero, *De Oratore*, ed. H. Rackham, trans. E. W. Sutton (Cambridge, MA: Harvard University Press, 1976), 51.

50. Augustine, *On Christian Doctrine*, 141. See also Burke, *A Rhetoric of Motives*, 50.

51. James Phelan, *Narrative as Rhetoric: Technique, Audiences, Ethics, Ideology*, (Columbus: Ohio State University Press, 1996), 8.

52. Phelan, 19. Carol Harrison (Harrison, *The Art of Listening in the Early Church*, 137) notes that "Scripture itself fell a long way short of classical eloquence, being a somewhat crudely written, rather vulgar text, belonging to an alien culture which did not recognize or value such rules or practices. Its translators had not helped matters either." Kennedy (Kennedy, *New Testament Interpretation through Rhetorical Criticism*, 128) notes that: "The Gospels are unique works which do not exactly fit any classical literary genre and which have a subtle internal rhetoric of their own."

53. Kennedy, 4.

54. Kennedy, *New Testament Interpretation through Rhetorical Criticism*, 33–38. Kennedy describes these steps in detail.

55. For example, Margaret Davies, *Rhetoric and Reference in the Fourth Gospel* (Sheffield: Sheffield Academic Press, 1992); Stube, *A Graeco-Roman Rhetorical Reading of the Farewell Discourse*; Douglas Estes, *The Questions of Jesus in John: Logic, Rhetoric and Persuasive Discourse* (Leiden: Brill, 2013).

56. I will omit the *pericope adulterae* (story of the adulterous woman in 7:5 2–8:11) from consideration on textual-critical grounds, but I will consider John 21 to be an epilogue that is nevertheless integral to the Gospel as such.

57. Vernon K. Robbins has developed an approached, socio-rhetorical criticism to address this type of question. See, for example, Vernon K. Robbins, *Exploring the Texture of Texts: A Guide to Socio-Rhetorical Interpretation* (Valley Forge: Trinity Press International, 1996); Vernon K. Robbins, *Jesus the Teacher: A Socio-Rhetorical Interpretation of Mark* (Minneapolis: Fortress Press, 2009); Vernon K. Robbins, Robert H. Von Thaden, and Bart B. Bruehler, *Foundations for Sociorhetorical Exploration: A Rhetoric of Religious Antiquity Reader*, 2016, http://lib.myilibrary. com?id=951528. Robbins defines socio-rhetorical criticism as: "An approach to literature that focuses on values, convictions, and beliefs both in the texts we read and in the world in which we live. It views texts as performances of language in particular historical and cultural situations. It presupposes that a text is a tapestry of interwoven textures, including *inner texture, intertexture, social and cultural texture, ideological texture*, and *sacred texture*. A major goal of socio-rhetorical interpretation is to nurture an environment of interpretation that encourages a genuine interest in people who live in contexts with values, norms, and goals different from our own." http:// www.religion.emory.edu/faculty/robbins/SRI/defns/s_defns.cfm [accessed October 9, 2017]. Although, in general terms, my approach can fall into this category, I prefer to use the categories of classical rhetoric rather than concepts such as "inner texture" or "intertexture."

58. Clifford Geertz, *The Interpretation of Cultures: Selected Essays* (New York: Basic Books, 1973), 5.

59. For further discussion, see Adele Reinhartz, *Caiaphas the High Priest* (Columbia: University of South Carolina Press, 2011), 4–6 and the references there.

60. Culpepper, *Anatomy of the Fourth Gospel: A Study in Literary Design*, 16.

61. On text critical grounds, 7:5 3–8:11 are also excluded.

62. The authorship of the Gospel is unknown. And while it seems clear that the Gospel underwent a process of composition that may have included prior sources and/ or multiple redactions, no hypothesis or reconstruction has yet created a stable consensus among scholars. For the sake of convenience, I shall use "John" and masculine singular pronouns to refer to the Gospel's implied author. Although arguments have been made for female authorship, on the basis of the Gospel's relatively positive and high profile given to female characters, the consensus is that the author or authors were likely male. For examples of source and redaction theory, see Robert Tomson Fortna, *The Gospel of Signs: A Reconstruction of the Narrative Source Underlying the Fourth Gospel* (London: Cambridge University Press, 1970); Raymond Edward Brown, *The Community of the Beloved Disciple* (New York: Paulist Press, 1979);

Urban C. von Wahlde, *The Gospel and Letters of John*, 3 vols. (Grand Rapids: Eerdmans, 2010). On the possibility of a female implied author, see Davies, *Rhetoric and Reference in the Fourth Gospel*, 254–56.

63. John 11, which features Mary and Martha, suggests that there were Jewish women who became Christ-followers. On pagan women converts or God-fearers see Shelly Matthews, *First Converts: Rich Pagan Women and the Rhetoric of Mission in Early Judaism and Christianity*, Contraversions (Stanford: Stanford University Press, 2001), https://login.proxy.bib.uottawa.ca/login?url=http://hdl.handle.net/2027/heb.04314. Culpepper uses the term "ideal narrative audience" to refer to the stance that I call compliant. Culpepper, *Anatomy of the Fourth Gospel: A Study in Literary Design*, 208.

64. Harrison, *The Art of Listening in the Early Church,* 2.

65. "Brothers and sisters" is the NRSV translation of the Greek masculine that literally means "brothers," ἀδελφός (masculine accusative plural).

66. Harrison, *The Art of Listening in the Early Church*, 37. For an example of modern dramatic performance, see https://www.youtube.com/watch?v=unL8m3PV58s. On the relationship between John and ancient drama, see Brant, *Dialogue and Drama: Elements of Greek Tragedy in the Fourth Gospel*; Parsenios, *Rhetoric and Drama in the Johannine Lawsuit Motif*. Orality was the norm not only in Greek-speaking societies but also in the Hebrew/Aramaic circles within which rabbinic literature arose; as Shemaryahu Talmon notes, "all reading was aloud, and most probably intoned, in a sing-song voice." Shemaryahu Talmon, "Oral Tradition and Written Transmission, or the Heard and the Seen Word in Judaism of the Second Temple Period," in *Jesus and the Oral Gospel Tradition*, ed. Henry Wansbrough (Sheffield: JSOT Press, 1991), 150. According to Talmon (Talmon, 137) there is an evident emphasis on aural reception in Hebrew Bible and apocrypha, e.g. Neh 8:2; Jer 36:6. See also Terence C. Mournet, *Oral Tradition and Literary Dependency: Variability and Stability in the Synoptic Tradition and Q* (Tübingen: Mohr Siebeck, 2005), 135–37.

67. Harry Y. Gamble, *Books and Readers in the Early Church: A History of Early Christian Texts* (New Haven: Yale University Press, 1995), 5.

68. Gamble, 5.

69. Gamble, 8.

70. Harrison, *The Art of Listening in the Early Church*, 4.

71. Even people who could and did read to themselves read aloud, thereby hearing the words as well as seeing them. See Harrison, *The Art of Listening in the Early Church*, 5. For general studies of orality and literacy, see the classic studies Walter J. Ong, *Orality and Literacy: The Technologizing of the Word* (London: Methuen, 1982); Werner H. Kelber, *The Oral and the Written Gospel: The Hermeneutics of Speaking and Writing in the Synoptic Tradition, Mark, Paul, and Q* (Bloomington: Indiana University Press, 1997), http://search.ebscohost.com/login.aspx?direct=true&scope=site&db=nlebk&db=nlabk&AN=11058.

72. The tradition that the Gospel of John was written in Ephesus is based on a number of ancient sources, including Polycrates (late second century) as quoted in Eusebius, HE 5.24. 2–7; Papias (c. 125) as quoted by Eusebius (HE 3.39. 3–4) and Irenaeus (ca. 13 0–200), who was the first to claim explicitly that the Gospel

was written in Ephesus (*Adv Haer* 3.1.1; 3.3.4). Recently first-century archaeo-logical remains have been discovered. See http://www.haaretz.com/jewish/archae ology/1.736389. (The article appeared on August 11 2016 and was accessed on De-cember 28, 2016.) Some scholars accept Ephesus as the Gospel's provenance. See Paul R. Trebilco, *The Early Christians in Ephesus from Paul to Ignatius* (Tübingen: Mohr Siebeck, 2004), 237. See the helpful discussion of provenance in Keener, *The Gospel of John*, 142–49.

73. For example, "Saint Paul delivering the Aeropagus Sermon in Athens," by Raphael (Raffaello Sanzio), 1515 (Victoria and Albert Museum, London) and "The Madonna with Child and Saints," by Jacopo Pontormo (1516) housed in the church of San Michele Visdomini in Florence.

74. On the basis of sociolinguistic analysis, David Lamb sees no evidence of a personal "interactiveness" or personal relationship between the implied author and audience. David A. Lamb, *Text, Context and the Johannine Community: A Sociolin-guistic Analysis of the Johannine Writings* (London: Bloomsbury T & T Clark, 2014), 200. This, of course, does not mean that "John" could not have known or known of "Alexandra" or other people who heard his words, but it does caution us against pre-suming a priori, for example, that he was preaching to a congregation or gathering of people familiar to him.

75. Jim A. Kuypers and Andrew King, "What Is Rhetoric?" in *Rhetorical Criticism: Perspectives in Action*, ed. Jim A Kuypers (Lanham: Lexington Books, 2009), 8.

○ recent discoveries in Ephesus: 1st century
○○ Trebilco; Keener on Ephesus & the Gospel of John
○○○ alternative to a "Johannine community" audience (rather, the community may have formed, in part, with repeated listenings to the Gospel) (xxxi—xxxiii)

Part I

THE RHETORIC OF AFFILIATION

Chapter One

"Ask and you will receive"

The Rhetoric of Desire and Fulfillment

The Gospel's stance towards Jewishness and Jews rests on an elaborate scaffold of claims and beliefs that are themselves based on a particular way of viewing God, Jesus, and the world. In presenting this worldview, John makes a fundamental claim: that belief in Jesus as the Messiah, Son of God, is the way to eternal life. This claim, however, is based on an unstated assumption: that the dread of death—and desire for eternal life—are universal human traits common to all cultures and all eras.[1]

John is not the only ancient author to make such an assumption. On the contrary, the dread of death is a theme in numerous Greek, Hellenistic, and Roman sources. The mystery cult of Isis, for example, promised life beyond death, or, at least, ongoing existence in the afterlife to its adherents.[2] Philosophers such as Epicurus (d. 270 BCE) offered psychological advice: people can and should change their attitudes towards death in order to avoid their distress at its inevitability.[3] Lucretius (99–55 BCE) acknowledged that "the love of life . . . is natural in all sentient creatures, and so all creatures go to death with reluctance."[4]

John's approach, however, draws more directly on the book of Genesis than on the traditions of Greek philosophy. In its focus on eternal life, the Fourth Gospel builds on the creation stories in Genesis. The opening words "In the beginning" echo those of Genesis 1:1: "In the beginning when God created the heavens and the earth," and the Prologue as a whole evokes the cosmic setting and scope of primordial creation: "In the beginning was the Word, and the Word was with God, and the Word was God. . . . All things came into being through him . . ." (1:1–4). Like Genesis 1, John's Prologue brings a narrative world into being, and sets that story world into the context of divine creation. The Prologue situates the Word in the process by which

3

God created all things, set light against darkness (Gen 1:3–4), and breathed life into humankind (Gen 2:7).

The narratives in Genesis 1–3 assert that unending life is the ideal, God-given state of humankind. Mortality is the consequence of Adam and Eve's consumption of the fruit of the tree of knowledge of good and evil, in contravention of God's explicit command: "You may freely eat of every tree of the garden; but of the tree of the knowledge of good and evil you shall not eat, for in the day that you eat of it you shall die" (Gen 2:16–17).

This command introduces an ominous note. All human beings know that death awaits them; all who heard or read God's warning in Genesis 2:16–17 knew that the primordial couple did eventually disobey. The transgression is described in Genesis 3, in which the sly serpent misleads the woman: "You will not die," the serpent tells her, "for God knows that when you eat of it your eyes will be opened, and you will be like God, knowing good and evil" (Gen 3:4–5). After they eat the fruit, God expels the man and woman from the garden lest the man "reach out his hand and take also from the tree of life, and eat, and live forever" (Gen 3:22). Although the man and woman did not die immediately, their act forfeited eternal life for them and all humankind. In promising "life in his name" to those who believe, the Gospel of John implicitly promised to reverse the death decree of Genesis and restore believers, if not humankind as a whole, to a primordial state of life without death.

Whether she is familiar with Genesis, with Hellenistic authors, both, or neither, Alexandra too—as a member of John's compliant audience—must have experienced the dread of death. But in case she and other members of John's compliant audience were not strongly motivated by such dread, John presents eternal life as both highly desirable, and universally desired.

THE RHETORIC OF DESIRE

The desire for eternal life is explicit or implicit at numerous points in John's account of Jesus's signs.[5] The anxiety of the gentile official, who approaches Jesus to heal his son in Capernaum (4:46–54), eloquently testifies to the desire to avoid death: "Sir, come down before my little boy dies" (4:49). The same is implied by Jesus's comment upon hearing that his friend Lazarus was ill: "This illness does not lead to death; rather it is for God's glory, so that the Son of God may be glorified through it" (11:4).

The desire for eternal life is also expressed directly by several characters within the Gospel narrative. When Jesus offers the Samaritan woman "a spring of water gushing up to eternal life" the woman eagerly responds: "Sir, give me this water, so that I may never be thirsty or have to keep coming here to draw water" (4:14–15). In 6:68 Simon Peter speaks on behalf of the disciples when he asserts that they, unlike many others, will not turn away from Jesus: "Lord, to whom can we go? You have the words of eternal life" (John 6:68).

Jesus's exchange with Nicodemus, a Jewish ruler, also presumes this desire. Nicodemus's nighttime approach suggests both secrecy and anxiety (3:2). Initially Nicodemus surmises only that Jesus is "a teacher who has come from God; for no one can do these signs that you do apart from the presence of God" (3:2). But John soon turns the conversation to eternal life, for which belief in Jesus, and the death of Jesus, are necessary prerequisites: "And just as Moses lifted up the serpent in the wilderness, so must the Son of Man be lifted up, that whoever believes in him may have eternal life" (3:15). He then pronounces the principle underlying the connection between belief and eternal life: "For God so loved the world that he gave his only Son, so that everyone who believes in him may not perish but may have eternal life" (3:14–16).

As the dialogue with Nicodemus implies, Jesus offers the gift of eternal life to all: "*Anyone* who hears my word [ὁ τὸν λόγον μου ἀκούων—the one who hears my word] and believes him who sent me has eternal life, and does not come under judgment, but has passed from death to life" (5:24, emphasis added; see also 7:37 and 9:51). This offer extends to the Jews, but in discussing it with Jewish audiences, Jesus presumes not only their desire but also their refusal to believe: "You search the scriptures because you think that in them you have eternal life; and it is they that testify on my behalf. Yet you refuse to come to me to have life" (5:39–40). Similarly, the Jews, who initially beg for the bread "which comes down from heaven and gives life to the world" (6:33), later depart (6:66) when Jesus demands that they drink his blood and eat his body (6:53–58).

The Fourth Gospel, Genesis, and other ancient texts may or may not be correct in presuming a universal desire for eternal life. Nevertheless, this assumption is central to the Gospel's rhetorical program. Indeed, from a rhetorical perspective, the Gospel not only presumes this desire but also, in some sense, creates it. The creation of desire is not a unique or unusual aspect of narrative, but rather is inherent in the narrative form as such. As Kenneth Burke notes, "Form in literature is an arousing and fulfillment of desires. A work has form in so far as one part of it leads a reader to anticipate another part, to be gratified by the sequence."[6]

At a minimum, the reader's desire pertains to the progress of the narrative itself, such as the desire for resolution, a happy ending, or catharsis. Often, however, the narrative work builds upon and, indeed, manipulates the prior desires of the reader: "The artist's manipulations of the reader's desires involve his use of what the reader considers desirable. If the reader believes in monogamist marriage, and in the code of fidelity surrounding it, the poet can exploit this belief in writing an *Othello*."[7] Burke takes his examples from the plays of Shakespeare and other classic works of Western literature. But the same is patently true in the Fourth Gospel, which presumes its audience's prior desire for eternal life, but also accentuates this desire by articulating it and, even more importantly, providing a path to fulfilling that desire.

Depending on her background and education, Alexandra may or may not catch the Prologue's allusions to Genesis or the resonances with Greek philosophy or the mystery cults. She probably shares the dread of death that John imputes to humankind, but she may not have given it much prior thought. Anticipating this possibility, John not only draws her attention to Jesus's capacity to offer life to those who believe, but also causes her to recognize her own latent desire.

THE RHETORIC OF FULFILLMENT

John insists that the desire for eternal life can be fulfilled only by believing that Jesus is the Messiah, Son of God. This message is conveyed not only in the Gospel's statement of purpose in 20:30–31 but throughout the Gospel. Of the three primary strategies of classical rhetoric—invention, arrangement, and style—the most important for our purposes are invention and style.[8] Arrangement, referring to the overall structure of a rhetorical discourse,[9] is not used strategically in this Gospel, given that the sequence of stories and discourses is constructed not topically, as in expository writing, but chronologically, as in much narrative writing. In what follows, I shall consider how the Gospel uses invention and style to convey that faith in Jesus as Messiah and Son of God is indeed the key to eternal life.

Invention

External Proofs

Invention can be based on either external or internal ("artistic") proofs. External proofs are derived from the "real world" outside the text in question. New Testament rhetoric relies on three principal forms of external proof: miracles, the scriptures, and witnesses. John includes the first two forms of external proof—miracles and scriptures—as subcategories of the third category, witnesses.

Throughout the Gospel, the Johannine Jesus testifies about himself: ". . . just as the Father raises the dead and gives them life, so also the Son gives life to whomever he wishes" (5:21). But in John 5, and throughout the narrative, a series of other witnesses are called upon to testify to Jesus's identity as the Messiah and Son of God, and, whether directly or indirectly, to his role as the one who fulfills the desire for eternal life.[10]

1) John the Baptist (5:31; cf. 1:7, 15, 32, 34; 3.26). In 5:32–33, Jesus calls John the Baptist to the witness stand: "There is another who testifies on my behalf, and I know that his testimony to me is true. You sent messengers to John, and he testified to the truth." John the Baptist witnesses to Jesus in 1:29: "Here is the Lamb of God who takes away the sin of the world!"

2) The works. Jesus next calls attention to the testimony that his works have provided with regard to his identity as God's Son: "The works that the Father has given me to complete, the very works that I am doing, testify on my behalf that the Father has sent me" (5:36; see also 10:25). The types of acts that Jesus refers to as works are called signs (*semeia*) by the narrator and other characters within the Gospel.[11] In the Gospel's rhetorical repertoire, the signs constitute evidence for the claims about Jesus's identity as God's son and, in the case of the raising of Lazarus (John 11), for Jesus's ability to restore life to the dead.

3) The Father. In John 5:37, Jesus calls upon the Father to testify on his behalf. God provides testimony in John 11 and 12. At the graveside of his friend Lazarus, Jesus thanks God for having heard him, and adds: "I knew that you always hear me, but I have said this for the sake of the crowd standing here, so that they may believe that you sent me" (11:41–42). Jesus then calls Lazarus forth from the grave, an act that presumably he does on God's behalf. This act demonstrates, as already noted, Jesus's power to grant eternal life to those who hear him, believe in him, and love him. In Jesus's last public appearance, he calls upon God to glorify his name. "Then a voice came from heaven, "I have glorified it, and I will glorify it again" (12:28).

4) The Scriptures and Moses. The final witnesses that Jesus calls in chapter 5 are the scriptures.[12] In 5:39 Jesus himself calls attention to the scriptures' role as confirming the Gospel's claims when he tells the Jews, "You search the scriptures because you think that in them you have eternal life; and it is they that testify on my behalf." At numerous points, the Gospel portrays Jesus as the fulfillment of scripture. At Jesus's crucifixion, for example, the casting of lots for Jesus's clothing (19:24), and Jesus's thirst (19:28) are both described as fulfillment of scripture.[13]

5) Disciples. In 15:27, Jesus refers to the disciples as witnesses: "You also are to testify because you have been with me from the beginning" (15:27). Whereas the other witnesses are described as testifying to others within the Gospel narrative, the disciples testify directly to the extradiegetic audience. The Gospel does not depict the disciples as speaking to an audience other than their fellow disciples. Their testimony is accessible, therefore, to those

hearing or reading the Gospel, but not to the other characters within it. The external addressees of the disciples' testimony are hinted at in 17:20–21, in which Jesus prays "not only on behalf of these [the disciples], but also on behalf of those who will believe in me through their word, that they may all be one. As you, Father, are in me and I am in you, may they also be in us, so that the world may believe that you have sent me." Among the disciples, the most important witness is the Beloved Disciple, whose testimony is said to underlie the book as a whole (19:35, 21:24).[14]

6) The Gospel as testimony. For the Gospel's audiences, the Gospel itself is the primary, indeed, the only, witness through which Jesus's words and deeds are available. The Gospel encompasses and conveys all of the other testimony. Only by hearing the Gospel can others hear the words and "see"—perceive, learn about—the works of Jesus for themselves.

7) The paraclete. In his final discourses to the disciples, Jesus also refers to the Paraclete (Advocate: NRSV) as a witness: "When the Advocate comes, whom I will send to you from the Father, the Spirit of truth who comes from the Father, he will testify on my behalf" (15:26).

It may seem odd to refer to these witnesses as "external proofs." The idea that God, the scriptures, John the Baptist, or any of the other proofs constitute witnesses to Jesus's identity is clearly John's own construct and therefore does not seem to be external. John, however, depicts them as external to Jesus—and therefore as evidence that Jesus's claims are not grounded soley in his self-testimony (5:31).

Artistic Evidence

Internal, or artistic proofs, also fall into three categories: *Ethos*, *Pathos*, and *Logos*. These categories, according to Aristotle, inhere in the speaker, the audience, and the discourse respectively. Ethos depends upon the credibility of the author or speaker; pathos refers to the ability of the orator or writer to play upon the emotions of the audience; logos refers to the argumentation used to demonstrate one point or another.[15]

Ethos

Ethos is defined as "the persuasive power of the speaker's authoritative character."[16] Aristotle views ethos as a key component of the art of persuasion: "Persuasion is achieved by the speaker's personal character when the speech is so spoken as to make us think him credible" (*Rhetoric* (1.2.1356a).[17] In Aristotelian rhetoric, ethos is entirely internal to the speech, but in the New Testament, the authoritativeness of the speaker as such is equally important.[18]

The narrator introduces Jesus at the very beginning of the Gospel as God's pre-existent Word through whom "all things" were created (1:1–4) and as God's only begotten son (1:14). This introduction is extradiegetic, accessible only to the book's external audience. In this way, John establishes Jesus's ethos, and his own, from the very beginning of the book, and provides that audience with the important key to understanding the story that will follow.

The disciples point to Jesus's authority by labeling him christologically with titles associated with Jewish messianic expectations (Lamb of God, Messiah), apocalyptic salvation (Son of Man), and Greco-Roman divinity (Son of God). In 1:49, Nathanael declares: "Rabbi, you are the Son of God! You are the King of Israel!" In 6:69 Peter proclaims on behalf of the disciples, "We have come to believe and know that you are the Holy One of God." In 20:28, Thomas confesses Jesus to be "My Lord and my God!"

Although the crowds are not privy to this testimony, the signs and discourses done in their presence throughout John 1–12 provide them with the opportunity to acknowledge Jesus's authority. Jesus's use of the phrase *ego eimi* ("I am") also emphasizes this point. This formula evokes God's self-declaration in Exodus 3:14, in which God answered Moses's request for his name with the pithy but enigmatic self-description: "I AM WHO I AM" and then added: "Thus you shall say to the Israelites, 'I AM has sent me to you.'" (Exod 3:14). When, for example, the Samaritan woman states, "I know that the Messiah is coming" (4:25), Jesus responds, "I am he [literally, "I am"], the one who is speaking to you" (4:26).[19] In addition, Jesus reveals his identity through numerous metaphors, such as the bread of life, the shepherd, the gate, and, most famously, "the way, and the truth, and the life" (14:6).

Jesus's authority is not immediately accepted by the crowds who hear his discourses after healing the disabled man (John 5) or on the festivals (Passover, John 6; Tabernacles, John 7). And the *Ioudaioi* reject it altogether, as is evident in John 8:31–59 and throughout the Gospel. But although *Jesus* addresses the diegetic audience, *John* is addressing those who live after the Easter event (20:29); even if they are not already believers, their access to the Prologue and other explanations provided by John gives them the background needed to view Jesus as an authoritative speaker and to interpret his words correctly, that is, as John wishes them to do.[20]

Pathos

In *Rhetoric* 1.2.1356a, Aristotle emphasizes that persuasion is a matter not only of reason but also emotion: "Persuasion may come through the hearers, when the speech stirs their emotions. . . . It is towards producing these effects, as we maintain, that present-day writers on rhetoric direct the whole of their efforts." Modern thinkers agree. As Bruce Lincoln has noted, "discourse is not only an instrument of persuasion, operating along rational (or pseudo-rational) and moral (or pseudo-moral) lines, but also an instrument of sentiment evocation. Moreover, it is through these paired instrumentalities—ideological persuasion and sentiment evocation—that discourse holds the capacity to shape and reshape society itself."[21]

The Gospel creates pathos through its use of emotive language throughout the narrative. The signs stories showcase Jesus's ability to resolve all problems. Audiences can share in the delight of the wine steward at the unexpected abundance of superb wine (2:10) and the surprise, joy, and awe experienced by the others who are helped: the nobleman whose son was healed (4:53); the lame and blind men (5:9; 9:15); and the risen Lazarus and his loving sisters (11:45).

The Gospel also evokes emotion when it associates Jesus with his flock's safety from deceit and danger (10:11–16); portrays the joyous celebration of those who witness the triumphal entry (12:13; cf. 12:19); provides hope of a future dwelling place with Jesus in God's house (14:2); and promises the disciples' future joy (15:11; 17:13). Particularly evocative is the imagery in 16:21–22: "When a woman is in labor, she has pain, because her hour has come. But when her child is born, she no longer remembers the anguish because of the joy of having brought a human being into the world. So you have pain now; but I will see you again, and your hearts will rejoice, and no one will take your joy from you."

Metaphors are also used emotively.[22] John 8:12 uses the light/darkness contrast that was established in the Prologue: "I am the light of the world. Whoever follows me will never walk in darkness but will have the light of life." John 4:14 uses the metaphor of water: "those who drink of the water that I will give them will never be thirsty. The water that I will give will become in them a spring of water gushing up to eternal life." John 6 uses bread, as in 6:35: "I am the bread of life. Whoever comes to me will never be hungry, and whoever believes in me will never be thirsty." The idea is repeated throughout the Bread of Life discourse, in language that to later readers, if not to the initial readers, evoked the language of the Eucharist: "Those who eat my flesh and drink my blood have eternal life, and I will raise them up on the last day" (6:54).[23] Emotive language and the stark contrast between positive and negative terms would stir a compliant listener like Alexandra to desire what Jesus has to offer and follow the path that John lays out.

Another everyday metaphor depicts Jesus as the gate. In 10:7–10, Jesus tells his listeners:[24] "Very truly, I tell you, I am the gate for the sheep. All who came before me are thieves and bandits; but the sheep did not listen to them. I am the gate. Whoever enters by me will be saved, and will come in and go out and find pasture. The thief comes only to steal and kill and destroy. I came that they may have life, and have it abundantly." This metaphor emphasizes Jesus's role as the access point to relationship with God. In the Prologue, the narrator declares: "No one has ever seen God. It is God's only Son, who is close to the Father's heart, who has made him known" (1:18). In the Farewell discourses, Jesus assures Thomas: "I am the way, and the truth, and the life. No one comes to the Father except through me. If you know me, you will know my Father also. From now on you do know him and have seen him" (14:6–7).

These metaphors are taken from everyday experience. Productive work is accomplished in the daytime, whereas dangers lurk at night; water and bread are fundamental to physical survival. In using these metaphors to express Jesus's essential role in fulfilling the human desire for eternal life, the Gospel is asserting that faith is connected to eternal life even more profoundly than light, darkness, water, and bread are connected to mundane existence. To fulfill the desire for eternal—in contrast to temporal—life, one must acknowledge the centrality of Jesus as the one who provides for humankind's most essential needs, not for the impermanence of this world, but for the eternal life with God.

Freedom is another metaphor that expresses Jesus's role as the one who fulfills the desire for eternal life. In 8:31–32 Jesus holds out a promise to "the Jews who had believed in him," that "If you continue in my word, you are truly my disciples; and you will know the truth, and the truth will make you free." The Jews fail to understand this promise and reject the idea that they are now enslaved. But Jesus continues: "[E]veryone who commits sin is a slave to sin. The slave does not have a permanent place in the household; the Son has a place there forever. So if the Son makes you free, you will be free indeed" (8:34–36). The discussion deteriorates from there, but in these initial statements, Jesus clearly contrasts the present life characterized by sin, and therefore slavery, with the future life of true freedom in God's household. This discussion alludes to the Baptist's identification of Jesus as the Lamb of God who takes away the sin of the world. It is not only the Jews who sin; every human being does so, and in that sense everyone is a slave to sin until or unless they continue in Jesus's word.

Logos

In *Rhetoric* 1.2.1356a, Aristotle discusses the value of speech, or *logos*, as evidence, stating that "persuasion is effected through the speech itself when we have proved a truth or an apparent truth by means of the persuasive arguments suitable to the case in question." And, as noted above, logoi were thought not merely to persuade but also to move the emotions.

The most important example of logos as persuasive argument is the enthymeme. An enthymeme is a deductive proof that commonly takes the form of a claim followed by a reason supporting that claim. For that reason, enthymemes are often signaled by the conjunction "for" (γὰρ) or "therefore" (οὖν).

The Gospel frequently uses enthymemes to express Jesus's life-giving capacity. The most famous example is 3:16, which declares that Jesus's death is evidence of God's love of the world: "For [γὰρ] God so loved the world that he gave his only Son, so that everyone who believes in him may not perish but may have eternal life." Specific characters also use enthymemes. For example, Nicodemus explains his reason for coming to Jesus as follows: "Rabbi, we know that you are a teacher who has come from God; for [γὰρ] no one can do these signs that you do apart from the presence of God" (3:2). John the Baptist explains why he is happy rather than displeased at the increase in Jesus's following compared to his own: "He who has the bride is the bridegroom. The friend of the bridegroom, who stands and hears him, rejoices greatly at the bridegroom's voice. For this reason [οὖν] my joy has been fulfilled" (3:29).

In some cases the statement's form may be more important rhetorically than the content of the statement per se. Examples of such enthymemes include: "He whom God has sent speaks the words of God, for [γὰρ] he gives the Spirit without measure" (3:34); "You worship what you do not know; we worship what we know, for [ὅτι] salvation is from the Jews" (4:22); "For [γὰρ] just as the Father has life in himself, so he has granted the Son also to have life in himself" (5:26); "Yet even if I do judge, my judgment is valid; for it is not I alone who judge, but I and the Father who sent me" (8:16). In and of themselves, these lines are self-referential and obscure.[25] Yet their logical structure (two clauses connected by the conjunctions "for," "because," "then") and their use of positively-coded language (spirit, truth, life, God, Son) gives them a persuasive force that is not dependent on the ability to discern their full meaning.

Using the rhetorical techniques pertaining to ethos, pathos, and logos, the Gospel continuously and persistently draws the reader or hearer back to the one essential point: Jesus is the Son of God and the one through whom the desire for eternal life can be fulfilled. The fulfillment is based on faith. The next step is to show that faith, while an individual matter, cannot achieve its full expression unless it is in unity with others who are of similar faith.

Style

As a rhetorical strategy, style entails *lexis* (appropriate word choice) and *synthesis* (the appropriate arrangement of those words into phrases, clauses, and sentences, including figures of speech and figures of thought).[26] Both work together to support the Gospel's contention that Jesus offers eternal life—the fulfillment of desire—to those who believe.

A key example is the pattern of seeking and finding that runs through the Gospel's narrative and discourses. The Gospel presents several examples of characters who seek Jesus as the conduit to eternal life and either find him, by accepting that he is the Messiah, or do not find him, by rejecting this message.

On a narrative level, this pattern—combining word choice with word arrangement—emerges much more clearly in Greek than in English transla- tion. The verb "to seek" (ζητέω) is used throughout the Gospel and forms the thread that allows one to discern this theme. English translations such as the NRSV, however, use several different verbs, including seeking (e.g., 7:18), looking for (e.g., 8:37), wanting (e.g., 4:27), and trying to (e.g., 7:20).

Most praiseworthy are those who seek and immediately find. The two most obvious instances of this pattern bookend the Gospel narrative, in the call of the first disciples (1:38) and the finding of the empty tomb (20:15). In the first example, two disciples of John the Baptist follow Jesus after the Baptist identifies him as the Lamb of God. He turns around and asks them: Whom are you seeking? (τί ζητεῖτε; "What are you looking for?" NRSV 1:38). He invites them to come with him and they remain with him (1:39). One of these is Peter, who, despite his later denial, abides with Jesus to the end of the book (John 21).

The other seeker is Mary Magdalene, whom Jesus finds weeping at his tomb. He poses the same question to her (in the singular form) as he did to the two disciples in chapter 1: What (or whom) are you seeking? (τίνα ζητεῖς; "Whom are you looking for?" NRSV 20:15). These seekers fall into the cat- egory of true worshippers, those who not only seek but also are sought by God, implying that humankind and God are bound in mutual desire. As Jesus comments to the Samaritan woman, "the hour is coming, and is now here, when the true worshippers will worship the Father in spirit and truth, for the Father seeks (ζητεῖ) such as these to worship him" (4:23).

As faithful seekers, these characters succeed in finding Jesus. The first disciples realize that they have found the Messiah, as Andrew tells his brother Simon (Peter) in 1:41 and Philip tells Nathanael in 1:45 (εὑρήκαμεν τὸν Μεσσίαν; 1:41; Ὃν ἔγραψεν Μωϋσῆς ἐν τῷ νόμῳ καὶ οἱ προφῆται εὑρήκαμεν, "We have found him about whom Moses in the law and also the prophets wrote," 1:45).

No seekers, however, not even true worshippers, will be able to find Jesus immediately after the crucifixion. Jesus tells the crowds at Tabernacles that "You will search for me (ζητήσετέ με), but you will not find me; and where I am, you cannot come" (7:34). He says the same to a group of Jews who had believed in him:[27] "I am going away, and you will search for me (ζητήσετέ με), but you will die in your sin. Where I am going, you cannot come" (8:21). This has a more ominous ring to it; these seekers, Jesus implies, will never see eternal life, no doubt because of their eventual refusal to believe (8:46). The disciples too will face a time when they will seek Jesus without success: "Little children, I am with you only a little longer. You will look for me (ζητήσετέ με); and as I said to the Jews so now I say to you, 'Where I am going, you cannot come'" (13:33).

None of these groups truly understands Jesus's meaning (7:35–36; 16:19). But by this point in the story, Alexandra and other members of John's audience know that it is not enough merely to seek Jesus; one must seek him for the right reasons. Hence Jesus's rebuke to those who sought him after eating the bread and fish: they seek him (ζητεῖτέ με—"you are looking for me"; 6:26) only because they ate their fill, not because they saw signs.

The language of seeking and finding, like darkness and light, death and life, describes everyday experience, and in itself does not require us to search for its source. Nevertheless, this language, especially in 20:19, may also evoke the Song of Songs, particularly 3:1–5, in which the female lover speaks about her beloved:

> Song 3:1 Upon my bed at night
>   I sought (ἐζήτησα) him whom my soul loves;
>   I sought (ἐζήτησα) him, but found him not;
>   I called him, but he gave no answer.
> 2 "I will rise now and go about the city,
>   in the streets and in the squares;
>   I will seek (ζητήσω) him whom my soul loves."
>   I sought (ἐζήτησα) him, but found him not.
> 3 The sentinels found (εὔροσάν) me,
>   as they went about in the city.
> "Have you seen him whom my soul loves?"
> 4 Scarcely had I passed them,
>   when I found (εὗρον) him whom my soul loves.
> I held him, and would not let him go
>   until I brought him into my mother's house,
>   and into the chamber of her that conceived me.

Because John never quotes the Song directly, it is hard to say whether he intended to compare the risen Jesus and Mary Magdalene to the Song's two lovers.[28] But the allusions remain suggestive nonetheless, particularly in light of the early tradition of allegorical interpretation of the Song as representing the relationship between God and Israel or Jesus and believers. Like John's Gospel, the Song of Songs plays on seeking and not finding and the consummation that occurs when the one who is sought is indeed found.[29]

Erotic subtexts can also be found in the Johannine stories of encounters between Jesus and women who followed him: the Samaritan woman and the Bethany sisters Mary and Martha. Jesus's encounter with the Samaritan woman recalls the stories in Genesis and Exodus in which biblical heroes meet the women they will marry at a well.[30] In anointing Jesus's feet with expensive nard (12:3), Mary of Bethany may be compared to the female lover in Song 1:12: "While the king was on his couch, my nard gave forth its fragrance."[31] The references to Jesus as the bridegroom—at the wedding at Cana and in the context of baptizing activity—also evoke this semantic field.[32]

The erotic allusions add depth to the rhetoric of searching and finding, and emotion to the desire for eternal life. They also attribute an all-consuming intensity to the relationship between Jesus and the believer, one whose dimensions extend far beyond the cognitive and even the emotive to include also the sensual.[33]

THE CONTENT OF BELIEF:
JESUS, GOD, AND THE COSMOS

John's rhetoric of desire and fulfillment promises eternal life to those who believe in Jesus as the Christ and Son of God. Throughout the Gospel, Jesus, the narrator, and some of the characters refer to him in a variety of ways. He is the lamb of God, the savior of the world, the Son of Man, a prophet, a king of Israel, and the Messiah, a Hebrew term that the narrator correctly translates as "anointed" (1:41). The Gospel also associates Jesus with a number of traits or activities: he takes away the sin of the world (1:29), provides food for the hungry, heals the sick, and raises the dead. And for John, Jesus is preeminently the Son of God, the pre-existent Word, who does God's works in the world.

What does it mean, exactly, to believe that Jesus is the Messiah, the Son of God? John encourages his audience to see this belief in relation to God's desire to save the world (3:16) and as a necessary condition for eternal life. The Gospels of Matthew and Luke begin with infancy narratives that describe a set of material circumstances under which Jesus was indeed conceived as the Son of God and a human mother, Mary.[34] The Gospel of John famously lacks such a narrative; indeed, it gives Jesus's mother a very small role in its drama and does not even mention her by name. This absence suggests a primarily metaphorical meaning for Jesus's identification as the Son of God.[35]

The varied nature of the relationship between a human father and son can certainly be viewed as a metaphor for the complex and intimate relationship between God and Jesus, which otherwise eludes human description and in which the believer is also invited to participate.[36] Yet, I would argue, the Gospel too describes Jesus concretely, materially, and genealogically, as God's son, on the basis of Aristotelian theories of procreation that were popular in the first century Mediterranean world.[37]

The Gospel's Prologue proclaims the pre-existence of Jesus as the Word of God, who "in the beginning" was both with God and was God (John 1:1–2). Through this prologue, the Gospel establishes that Jesus's true place is with God in the eternal time and space that is God's realm. But the Johannine Gospel must also bring Jesus into the human realm. Only this way can the good news be accessible to humankind and the narrative proceed. And so we learn, in John 1:14, that "the Word became flesh and lived among us" (1:14a).

At this point, the language shifts; no longer does the Prologue speak about the Word in relationship but of the only-begotten son (μονογενής) in relationship with the Father. John 1:1–18 implies that the incarnation—the becoming flesh—itself transformed the nature of the relationship between God and Jesus to that of father and son. In this sense, the Prologue, as the story of Jesus's conception and birth, is this Gospel's infancy narrative, analogous to, if radically different from, the infancy narratives of Matthew and Luke.

The language of the Prologue echoes that of the Aristotelian theory of epigenesis. Aristotle described the act of generation as being set in motion by the male sperm, which is the *logos*, or Word. The *logos* is the motive and final cause of the reproductive process, and the vehicle for the male *pneuma*, or spirit, that determines the form and characteristics of the offspring. Aristotle likens it to the principle [ἡ ἀρχή] in fig-juice or rennet that causes milk to coagulate. (GA 729a10–12). The role of the female is to provide the medium of growth for the offspring. The generative process (ἡ γένεσις) as such has its source and analogue in the upper cosmos (ἄνωθεν; GA 731b24).[38] In this way, Aristotle's theory of epigenesis does not limit itself to the mechanical and physical aspects of reproduction but also places reproduction in a broader, even cosmic, context.

Aristotle's theory, and particularly the role it ascribes to the male seed, dominated Greco-Roman embryology,[39] including Second Temple Jewish wisdom texts.[40] Reading the Prologue's use of phrases and terms, such as Ἐν ἀρχῆ, ὁ λόγος, and various forms of the verb γίνομαι as allusions to epigenesis identifies God as the first principle of generation, whose *logos*, or rational principle, was given human life and form and sent into the human world as Jesus, the divine father's only-begotten son.

To believe that Jesus is the Messiah, the Son of God, Alexandra must therefore comprehend, fully and deeply, not only that Jesus is God's anointed one, but that he is actually, physically and spiritually, the offspring of God, God's only begotten son. Believing this crucial fact will also open her eyes to the true significance of the Gospel narrative. The Gospel, like its Synoptic counterparts, is a story of Jesus, set in a particular time and place. But from the very first words of this Gospel, including its insistence on Jesus's identity as God's Son, the Gospel sets this particular story within the eternal and cosmic relationship between God and humankind. On this cosmological level, the Gospel story, from Jesus's arrival in the world until his return to the Father, is an important turning point in the long history of God's engagement with humankind that (from John's point of view) began with Genesis. This turning point, as we shall see, changed the terms of the agreement—the covenant—between God and humankind.

THE MEANING OF LIFE

Believing that Jesus is the Messiah, the Son of God, allows human beings to participate in the cosmic relationship between God and humankind. Although not stated explicitly, this participation may well be the "life in his name" that is promised to those who believe. Although the Gospel does not directly define "life," "life in his name," or "eternal life," some attributes of this desirable state can be teased out of Jesus's discourses.[41] Eternal life is something granted by God who has in turn handed authority to his Son "over all people, to give eternal life to all whom you have given him" (17:2). Like the statements placed in the mouths of various characters within the narrative, this verse suggests that the desire for eternal life is not limited to those who hear or read the Gospel, but to all humankind. John has no "two covenant" theology.[42] There is only one path to eternal life.

Second, eternal life is connected in some way to knowledge of God: "And this is eternal life, that they may know you, the only true God, and Jesus Christ whom you have sent" (17:3). It is not clear whether knowledge precedes eternal life or whether, perhaps, knowledge of God—true and profound knowledge—is itself eternal life. Another related concept is hearing the word: "Very truly, I tell you, anyone who hears my word and believes him who sent me has eternal life" (5:24).

Third, faith and eternal life overturn the accepted world order and our assumptions about everyday life: "Those who love their life lose it, and those who hate their life in this world will keep it for eternal life" (12:25).

Fourth, eternal life is freedom from death. In John 10, Jesus contrasts himself, "the good shepherd," with a thief who "comes only to steal and kill and destroy. I came that they may have life, and have it abundantly" (10:10). To his sheep, the shepherd gives "eternal life, and they will never perish. No one will snatch them out of my hand" (10:28). After her brother Lazarus's death, Jesus reassures Martha that: "I am the resurrection and the life. Those who believe in me, even though they die, will live, and everyone who lives and believes in me will never die" (11:25–26).

Those who believe and therefore have eternal life are freed not only from death but also from other aspects of the mortal condition: thirst, hunger, and darkness, all of the conditions that create fear and can lead to death. In 4:14, Jesus promises the Samaritan woman that "those who drink of the water that I will give them will never be thirsty. The water that I will give will become in them a spring of water gushing up to eternal life." In 6:27, John urges his audience to work not "for the food that perishes, but for the food that endures for eternal life, which the Son of Man will give you." And in 8:12, Jesus tells a group of Jews that "Whoever follows me will never walk in darkness but will have the light of life."

From this perspective, the deceptively simple exhortation and promise of John 20:31—to believe in Jesus thereby to enjoy life in his name—calls on Alexandra, as a member of John's compliant audience, not only to assent to certain ideas about Jesus as savior, but, more profoundly, to reorient her understanding about the radical transformation in God's relationship to the world that began with Jesus's incarnation. To find a place for herself within that relationship, Alexandra, along with the rest of John's audience, too must undergo change. Such change, as we shall soon see, has both an individual and a collective dimension. But while it is portrayed as the means to fulfill the desire for eternal life, the reorientation that is required will also transform Alexandra's stance towards, and, potentially, her relationship with, those who reject the claim that Jesus is the Messiah and the Son of God.

NOTES

1. This desire is implicit in our own lives, for example, in the modern expectation that medicine can prolong life and postpone the inevitable. This claim about universal human desires is not meant to ignore the fact that individual human beings may for various reasons and under various circumstances have no fear of death or even desire it.

2. Bruce W. Longenecker, "The Empress, the Goddess, and the Earthquake: Atmospheric Conditions Pertaining to Jesus-Devotion in Pompeii," in *Early Christianity in Pompeiian Light: People, Texts, Situations*, ed. Bruce W. Longenecker (Minneapolis: Fortress Press, 2016), 83.

3. http://www.epicurus.net/en/menoeceus.html. This passage is quoted, in slightly different translation, in Martha Craven Nussbaum, *The Therapy of Desire: Theory and Practice in Hellenistic Ethics* (Princeton: Princeton University Press, 1994), 192.

4. Nussbaum, 200. http://www.perseus.tufts.edu/hopper/text?doc=Perseus%3Atext%3A1999.02.0131%3Abook%3D5%3Acard%3D146: "Whosoever/Hath been begotten wills perforce to stay/In life, so long as fond delight detains; But whoso ne'er hath tasted love of life,/ And ne'er was in the count of living things,/What hurts it him that he was never born? (accessed October 9, 2017).

5. For a discussion of *semeia* in the Gospel, see, for example, Fortna, *The Gospel of Signs*; Marinus de Jonge, "Signs and Works in the Fourth Gospel," in *Miscellanea Neotestamentica 2*, ed. T. Baarda, A. F. J. Klijn, and W. C. van Unnik, NovTSup 48 (Leiden: Brill, 1978), 107–25;; Urban C. von Wahlde, *The Earliest Version of John's Gospel: Recovering the Gospel of Signs* (Wilmington: Michael Glazier, 1989).

6. Kenneth Burke, *Counter-Statement.* (Los Altos: Hermes Publications, 1953), 124.

7. Burke, 146.

8. Kennedy, *New Testament Interpretation through Rhetorical Criticism*, 14. The handbooks also include memory and delivery, which are less pertinent to the rhetorical analysis of texts.

9. Kennedy, 23–24.

10. On forensic language in the Gospel, see Lincoln, *Truth on Trial*; Parsenios, *Rhetoric and Drama in the Johannine Lawsuit Motif.*

11. John generally refers to Jesus's healing and other miraculous acts as signs, pointing towards their significance for the believer and the Gospel's audience, whereas Jesus sometimes refers to them in general terms as works, pointing to the evidentiary role they play as witnesses to his filial relationship with God. For discussion, see Raymond Edward Brown, *The Gospel According to John* (Garden City: Doubleday, 1966), 2.526. See also de Jonge, "Signs and Works in the Fourth Gospel."

12. Although the Fourth Gospel was written before the Jewish scriptures were formally canonized, the New Testament's use of quotations of and allusions to the Torah (Pentateuch) and the prophetic writings indicates that these books already had authoritative and even sacred status for Jews. On the Gospel's use of the Tanakh, see Bruce G. Schuchard, *Scripture within Scripture: The Interrelationship of Form and Function in the Explicit Old Testament Citations in the Gospel of John* (Atlanta: Scholars Press, 1992); Jaime Clark-Soles, *Scripture Cannot Be Broken: The Social Function of the Use of Scripture in the Fourth Gospel* (Boston: Brill Academic Publishers, 2003), http://site.ebrary.com/id/10090611; Ruth Sheridan, *Retelling Scripture "the Jews" and the Scriptural Citations in John 1:19–12:50* (Leiden: Brill, 2012). See also Eva Mroczek, *The Literary Imagination in Jewish Antiquity* (New York: Oxford University Press, 2016).

13. Clark-Soles, *Scripture Cannot Be Broken*; Schuchard, *Scripture within Scripture*.

14. On the Beloved Disciple as a witness, see the standard commentaries as well as Andrew T. Lincoln, "The Beloved Disciple as Eyewitness and the Fourth Gospel as Witness," *Journal for the Study of the New Testament* 85 (March 2002): 3–26. Lincoln argues that the Beloved Disciple's testimony is a "literary device with a

legitimating function" which speaks to the authenticity of the Gospels confessional perspective rather than facticity per se (Lincoln, 3).

15. Lincoln, 15.

16. C. Clifton Black and Duane Frederick Watson, *Words Well Spoken: George Kennedy's Rhetoric of the New Testament*, vol. 8, Studies in Rhetoric and Religion; 8 (Waco: Baylor University Press, 2008), 7.

17. Aristotle, *The Works of Aristotle.*, ed. W. D. Ross, vol. 9 (Franklin Center. PA: Franklin Library, 1978), 7, http://books.google.com/books?id=8OskAQAAMAAJ.

18. George A. Kennedy, *New Testament Interpretation through Rhetorical Criticism*, 15.

19. Among the many treatments of the *ego eimi* formulation, see, for example, David Mark Ball, *"I Am" in John's Gospel Literary Function, Background, and Theological Implications* (Sheffield: Sheffield Academic Press, 1996), http://public .eblib.com/EBLPublic/PublicView.do?ptiID=742500.

20. Alicia D. Myers, "Prosopopoetics and Conflict: Speech and Expectations in John 8," *Biblica* 92, no. 4 (2011): 588.

21. Bruce Lincoln, *Discourse and the Construction of Society: Comparative Studies of Myth, Ritual, and Classification* (Oxford: Oxford University Press, 2014), 7. See also Chad Kile, "Feeling Persuaded: Christianization and Social Formation," in *Rhetoric and Reality in Early Christianities*, ed. Willi Braun (Waterloo: Published for the Canadian Corporation for Studies in Religion/Corporation canadienne des sciences religieuses by Wilfrid Laurier University Press, 2005), 219–48.

22. On metaphors in John, see, for example, Beth M. Stovell, *Mapping Metaphorical Discourse in the Fourth Gospel: John's Eternal King.* (Leiden: Brill, 2012), http:// dx.doi.org/10.1163/9789004230460; Jörg Frey et al., eds., *Imagery in the Gospel of John: Terms, Forms, Themes, and Theology of Johannine Figurative Language* (Tübingen: Mohr Siebeck, 2006); J. G. van der Watt, *Family of the King: Dynamics of Metaphor in the Gospel According to John* (Leiden: Brill, 2000).

23. On the debate with regard to Eucharistic language in John 6, see, for example, Esther Kobel, *Dining with John: Communal Meals and Identity Formation in the Fourth Gospel and Its Historical and Cultural Context* (Leiden: Brill, 2011), http://search.ebscohost.com/login.aspx?direct=true&scope=site&db=nlebk&db=nlab k&AN=408440 and Meredith J. C. Warren, *My Flesh Is Meat Indeed: A Nonsacramental Reading of John 6:51–58* (Minneapolis: Fortress, 2015).

24. The context is unclear as to who the audience is. There is no obvious change of scene from chapter 9. In that case, Jesus would be speaking to the Pharisees. But according to 10:19 it is a more general Jewish crowd that is divided in its response to Jesus's words.

25. Wayne A. Meeks, "Man from Heaven in Johannine Sectarianism," *Journal of Biblical Literature* 91, no. 1 (March 1, 1972): 44–72. For Meeks, the Gospel's self-referentiality and esoteric language suggests that it is written within and for a sectarian group.

26. Kennedy, *New Testament Interpretation through Rhetorical Criticism*, 25–27.

27. The narrative does not signal a change of audience (leaving aside 7:53–8:11, which is not Johannine). On the latter, see Brown, *The Gospel According to John*, 1.335–36.

28. Adele Reinhartz, "To Love the Lord: An Intertextual Reading of John 20," in *The Labour of Reading: Essays in Honour of Robert C. Culley*, ed. Fiona Bladk et al., Semeia Studies (Atlanta: Scholars Press, 1999), 56–69.

29. For a detailed analysis of the possible contacts between John and Song, see Ann Roberts Winsor, *A King Is Bound in the Tresses: Allusions to the Song of Songs in the Fourth Gospel* (New York: P. Lang, 1999).

30. This point was made persuasively by Lyle Eslinger, "The Wooing of the Woman at the Well: Jesus, the Reader and Reader-Response Criticism," *Literature and Theology* 1, no. 2 (1987): 167–83.

31. Adeline Fehribach, *The Women in the Life of the Bridegroom: A Feminist Historical-Literary Analysis of the Female Characters in the Fourth Gospel* (Collegeville: Liturgical Press, 1998), 93.

32. See Jocelyn McWhirter, *The Bridegroom Messiah and the People of God: Marriage in the Fourth Gospel* (Cambridge: Cambridge University Press, 2006).

33. For detailed discussion of the connection between the erotic and the spiritual, see David McLain Carr, *The Erotic Word: Sexuality, Spirituality, and the Bible* (New York: Oxford University Press, 2003), http://www.dawsonera.com/depp/reader/protected/external/AbstractView/S9780195343557.

34. See Raymond E. Brown, *The Birth of the Messiah: A Commentary on the Infancy Narratives in the Gospels of Matthew and Luke* (New York: Doubleday, 2008).

35. Van der Watt, *Family of the King*, 196 and passim.

36. The idea that there is a literal foundation to this language does not of course rule out the possibility that it is also used metaphorically in this Gospel.

37. For detailed discussion of this point, see Adele Reinhartz, "'And the Word Was Begotten': Divine Epigenesis in the Gospel of John," *Semeia*, no. 85 (1999): 83–103. So also Turid Karlsen Seim, who built upon my argument to discuss in detail the role of motherhood in the Gospel and more broadly in Greco-Roman antiquity. Turid Karlsen Seim, "Descent and Divine Paternity in the Gospel of John: Does the Mother Matter?" *New Testament Studies* 51, no. 3 (2005): 361–75; Turid Karlsen Seim, "Motherhood and the Making of Fathers in Antiquity. Contextualizing Genetics in the Gospel of John," in *Women and Gender in Ancient Religions: Interdisciplinary Approaches*, ed. Stephen P. Ahearne-Kroll, Paul A. Holloway, and James A. Kelhoffer (Tübingen: Mohr Siebeck, 2010), 99–123. Alternatives have been suggested, however. In her discussion of ancient physiology as a branch of philosophy, Yii-Jan Singh concedes that John 1:14 "might *possibly* allude to the enlivening of female matter by the male pneumatic *sperma* but it does not *necessitate* an Aristotelian framework." Singh does not, however, provide an argument against the idea that the Prologue uses language that might resonate with an audience familiar even indirectly with Aristotelian thought. Yii-Jan Singh, "Semen, Philosophy, and Paul," *Journal of Philosophy & Scripture* 4, no. 2 (2007): 40. A more detailed critique is offered by Clare Rothschild, who argues that the Gospel's idea of divine generation is based on the theory of *parthenogenesis* (a theory of plant generation according to which "a female gamete is activated spontaneously on its own with fusion with a male reproductive element or sperm") rather than that of *epigenesis*. Clare Rothschild, "Embryology, Plant Biology, and Divine Generation in the Fourth Gospel," in *Women and Gender in Ancient*

Religions: Interdisciplinary Approaches, ed. Stephen P. Ahearne-Kroll, Paul A. Holloway, and James A. Kelhoffer (Tübingen: Mohr Siebeck, 2010), 125–51. Rothschild bases this argument primarily on a detailed analysis of John 3:3–10. The appeal of the theory, in my view, is the interpretation of 3:8 as referring to the wind blowing the seed far and wide "to a natural landing place in which it can be generate and grow." Rothschild, 139. The essay does not, however, directly address the language of the Prologue or the nature of the Father-Son relationship in John, which are the principle arguments in favor of the idea that epigenesis directly or indirectly lies in the background of the John's generative language as applied to Jesus.

38. Cf. Daryl McGowan Tress, "The Metaphysical Science of Aristotle's Generation of Animals and Its Feminist Critics," in *Feminism and Ancient Philosophy*, ed. Julie K. Ward (New York: Routledge, 1996), 44.

39. Joseph Needham and Arthur F. W. Hughes, *A History of Embryology.* (New York: Abelard-Schuman, 1959), 60.

40. Needham and Hughes, 64.

41. On life in his name as divine love and eternal life, see Rudolf Schnackenburg, *The Gospel According to St. John* (New York: Seabury Press, 1980), 2.339.

42. This is contrary to what some have claimed for Paul in Romans 9–11. For this view on Paul, see Krister Stendahl, *Paul among Jews and Gentiles, and Other Essays* (Philadelphia: Fortress Press, 1976), 1–77; John G. Gager, *The Origins of Anti-Semitism: Attitudes toward Judaism in Pagan and Christian Antiquity* (New York: Oxford University Press, 1983); Lloyd Gaston, *Paul and the Torah* (Vancouver: University of British Columbia Press, 1987). For a counter argument, see A. Andrew Das, *Paul and the Jews* (Peabody: Hendrickson, 2003).

Chapter Two

"Love one another"

The Rhetoric of Transformation

As Augustine, and Cicero before him, recognized, rhetoric's persuasive strategies not only reorient thought but also propel action. It is not surprising, then, that John wants Alexandra, his compliant audience member, not only to understand his claims but to transform her life as a consequence of that understanding. What this means concretely will depend on her circumstances, but at the very least it involves a dramatic shift in her way of looking and being in the world. This shift may also lead to a break with family and friends. This private, individual set of changes, however, is only the first step. The process will be incomplete until Alexandra affiliates with others engaged in the same process. What John wants from Alexandra, in other words, is a profound transformation of personal and communal identity. John's success will be measured by the ability of his Gospel to create a new community of those who see themselves in a radically new way as a consequence of their encounter with his story of Jesus.[1]

In explicitly stating his rhetorical goals, John promotes his Gospel as a vehicle through which its audience can achieve this transformation. The signs that he records are written *in order that* (ἵνα) the Gospel's audience will believe its claims about Jesus, and, in so believing, have life in his name. In other words, hearing or reading the Gospel provides an avenue through which the audience can come to believe the claims made by this Gospel and in so doing achieve life in his name. This assertion is supported by the appeal to the Beloved Disciple as the authority behind the Gospel's narrative. In 19:35, the narrator emphasizes that "he who saw this [the blood and the water coming out from the wound in Jesus's side] has testified so that you also may believe. His testimony is true, and he knows that he tells the truth." And in the final verses of the Gospel, the narrator proclaims that "This is the disciple who is testifying to these things and has written them, and we know that his testimony is true" (21:24).[2]

THE NEED FOR MEDIATION

That transformation requires human mediation is conveyed throughout John's narrative. In chapter 1, the call of the disciples exhibits a pattern of invitation and response in which human mediation plays a central role. The first two disciples are pointed in Jesus's direction by John the Baptist (1:35–36); they follow Jesus (1:37), and stay with him (1:39). One of them, Andrew, brings his brother Simon to Jesus, just as John the Baptist had brought him (1:40–41). Jesus changes this brother's name to Cephas (Peter), after which Peter becomes a stalwart follower. Jesus himself recruits Philip, who follows him (1:43) and also brings Nathanael (1:45). Andrew tells Simon that "we have found the Messiah" (1:41); Philip tells Nathanael that "We have found him about whom Moses in the law and also the prophets wrote" (1:45), and Nathanael proclaims, "Rabbi, you are the Son of God! You are the King of Israel!" (1:49). In each case, the new recruit's openness to Jesus is followed by a direct encounter, mediated by someone who already believes.

This two-step process occurs also in the story of the Samaritan woman. After Jesus offers her living water and reveals his messianic identity (4:26), she runs off to tell her fellow Samaritans, leaving her water jug behind (4:28). On the basis of the woman's testimony, the Samaritans come to meet Jesus, and he stays with them for two days (4:39–40). This personal encounter convinces them that he is the Messiah: "It is no longer because of what you said that we believe, for we have heard for ourselves, and we know that this is truly the Savior of the world" (4:42).

And then there is Mary Magdalene. On the Sunday after Jesus's death, Mary goes to the tomb alone. She finds the tomb empty and presumes that the body has been taken away. She confronts a man whom she believes to be the gardener, but when he calls her by name, she recognizes him as her teacher Jesus. (20:16). In one of the Gospel's most enigmatic verses, Jesus then tells her: "Do not hold on to me, because I have not yet ascended to the Father" (20:17).[3] This is not a rejection, however. Jesus goes on to bid Mary to "go to my brothers and say to them, 'I am ascending to my Father and your Father, to my God and your God'" (20:17). Mary goes to the disciples and announces that she has seen the Lord, and tells them "that he had said these things to her" (20:18).

John does not divulge how, or whether, the disciples responded to Mary's proclamation.[4] But like the Samaritan woman, Mary exercised an apostolic function by mediating Jesus's words to others. In this case, it is not the word about Jesus's identity as the Messiah, but the word that she has seen him, that is, he has risen from the dead, as he had prophesied. This news marks the beginning of the disciples' deeper knowledge, fulfilling John's comments about matters that they did not or could not understand until Jesus was raised from the dead (e.g., 2:22).[5]

Finally, Doubting Thomas provides a negative example that reinforces the need for human mediation. On the evening after Mary Magdalene discovers the empty tomb, Jesus appeared among the disciples (20:19–23). Thomas the Twin was absent, but when the others told him "We have seen the Lord" he was skeptical: "Unless I see the mark of the nails in his hands, and put my finger in the mark of the nails and my hand in his side, I will not believe" (20:24–25). A week later, Jesus appeared and offered him the proof he sought (20:27). Although Thomas then confessed "My Lord and my God" (20:28), Jesus downplays his confession. Jesus's parting words to Thomas—"Have you believed because you have seen me? Blessed are those who have not seen and yet have come to believe" (20:29)—imply that Thomas should have believed the disciples' testimony without needing his own visual and tactile proof. Jesus's rebuke bolsters the extradiegetic audience, none of whom had the option of first-hand proof and therefore needed to rely on the testimony of others. It also sets up the Gospel's self-proclaimed status as a foundation for the faith of its audience, which immediately follows in 20:30–31.

These stories illustrate a point that is essential to the Gospel's rhetorical program: encounters with Jesus must be mediated by another's witness to Jesus's identity. While the disciples play this role for each other in the call narrative, Mary herself mediates Jesus's resurrection and ascension to the disciples. The disciples in turn will do so for others who, unlike Thomas, will have the faith to believe their testimony (cf. John 17:20).

John promotes his Gospel—the record of the disciples' testimony—as the mediator that brings those living after the Easter event into a direct encounter with Jesus. This encounter takes place in the very process of hearing or reading John's account of Jesus's deeds, and, even more perhaps, John's report of Jesus's discourses.

NARRATIVE AS RHETORIC: CHARACTER IDENTIFICATION

Social psychologists Melanie Green and Timothy Brock acknowledge what many of us experience: the power of narrative to change our lives.[6]

Green and Brock argue that attachment to characters, as sources of information or models of specific beliefs or attitudes, can play a critical role in what they term "narrative-based belief change."[7] The power of character identification is experienced by anyone who can, on occasion, become lost in—"transported" by—a short story, novel, play, or movie. This power was already noted by Plato, who expressed concern that the spectacle of actors shuddering with fear at the prospect of death would provoke such fear in the viewers as well.[8]

The literary theorist Suzanne Keen notes that character identification can result from a broad range and combination of elements, including "naming, description, indirect implication of traits, reliance on types, relative flatness or roundness, depicted actions, roles in plot trajectories, quality of attributed speech, and mode of representation of consciousness."[9] Following Wayne Booth, however, she cautions that character identification cannot be attributed to a single factor; all narratives, from the classical to the post-modern, are complex and polyvocal.[10]

Some theorists suggest that readers identify most strongly with characters whose goals, plans, or experiences resonate with their own.[11] This theory accounts, for example, for the fact that children may identify with fictional children who engage in the sorts of adventures that fill their own fantasy lives or that correspond to their own experiences (welcoming a new baby, having two moms or dads, living through the divorce of their parents, or the death of a grandparent). The corollary is that authors shape their stories in ways that they believe will appeal to audiences who have undergone the experiences that they narrate.[12]

Narrative identification, however, can also be aspirational. As many have noted, the diverse characters within the Gospel model possible responses to Jesus.[13] This modeling has rhetorical implications. Through its modes of characterization, the Gospel steers its audience towards identification with characters who move towards faith in Jesus as the Messiah and Son of God.[14]

The Disciples

As the ones who set aside their previous lives to follow Jesus, the disciples, with the significant exception of Judas, provide the Gospel's hearers with the most direct—if nevertheless imperfect—models of profound transformation. For that reason they constitute the Gospel's most powerful models for identification.[15] Although their understanding is only partial during Jesus's lifetime, they dedicate themselves to following him and do their best to understand his message and his identity. Their imperfections are important as they convey the point that perfect discipleship, and complete faith, are aspirations. Even Peter's denial, shocking as it is, does not affect his status as a disciple; indeed, the epilogue identifies him as the one who will tend Jesus's flock after his return to the Father (21:15–17).[16]

As we have seen, most of the disciples become followers through the word of others. This word brings them to a face-to-face contact with Jesus, upon which they leave their former lives behind and follow him. Their role as witnesses to, or mediators of, Jesus's identity does not end, however, with their call to discipleship. The Gospel does not portray them as preaching to others; there is no Johannine equivalent to the sending out of the disciples in Matthew 10. Nevertheless, John 4:31–38 implies that they were meant to engage in such activities.

While Jesus converses with the Samaritan woman, the disciples are in the city buying food (4:8). When they return, they urge Jesus to eat. Just as Jesus did not apparently drink the water that he asked of the Samaritan woman (4:7), so too does Jesus apparently refrain from consuming the food brought by his disciples. Instead he insists, "I have food to eat that you do not know about" (4:32). Like Nicodemus, they initially misunderstand; perhaps, they say to one another, someone else has brought him food to eat while they were gone (4:33). But no. Jesus's food, he says, is to do the Father's will and complete his work (4:34). Jesus then describes the disciples' role in the divine economy: "Look around you, and see how the fields are ripe for harvesting. The reaper is already receiving wages and is gathering fruit for eternal life, so that sower and reaper may rejoice together. . . . I sent you to reap that for which you did not labor. Others have labored, and you have entered into their labor" (4:35–38). While this passage defies easy explanation, it implies that the harvesting ("gathering fruit for eternal life") consists of spreading the word so that more and more people will fulfill the desire for eternal life.

The theme of testimony recurs in chapter 17. Here Jesus prays that God sanctify the disciples, whom Jesus has sent into the world just as God has sent his Word into the world (17:17–18). He then continues, "I ask not only on behalf of these, but also on behalf of those who will believe in me through their word, that they may all be one. As you, Father, are in me and I am in you, may they also be in us, so that the world may believe that you have sent me" (17:20–21). Here Jesus describes testimony—bringing others to faith through their word—as the essential task of the disciples, and the task that will accomplish the goals that Jesus shares with the Father: "that they may all be one."

Dialogue Partners

The disciples are the only major recurring characters in the Gospel, aside from Jesus himself. Nevertheless, the encounters of individual characters with Jesus model a range of possible responses to Jesus and therefore illustrate the different ways (good and bad) that Alexandra might situate herself within John's narrative.

Nicodemus. Nicodemus is introduced as a Pharisee and a leader of the Jews (3:1). Given the heavily symbolic association between night (darkness), secrecy, and death, however, his approach is ambiguous from the outset. A listener may be excused for wondering whether he is a model to be emulated because he initiates contact with Jesus, or to be avoided, like Judas, who was with "the light" and yet betrayed him in darkness (13:30).

Nicodemus begins on the right foot, however, by acknowledging that "we" (the Pharisees? A faction among the Pharisees?) have been convinced that he is a "teacher who has come from God" (3:2). Jesus does not respond directly to Nicodemus's assertion but makes a generalized declaration: "Very truly, I tell *you*, no one can see the kingdom of God without being born from above" (3:3; emphasis added). Although these words are directed to Nicodemus (using the second person singular), they enunciate a general principle. We may speculate that hearers attuned to the Gospel's rhetoric would have understood the principle of rebirth as applying to them as well.[17]

The next section of the conversation revolves around what it means to be born from above or born again; the Greek ἄνωθεν can mean either, and perhaps John's Jesus has both in mind.[18] In typical Johannine fashion, Nicodemus takes Jesus's words literally as an absurd statement: "How can anyone be born after having grown old? Can one enter a second time into the mother's womb and be born?" (3:4). The question provides Jesus with the opportunity to explain, to Nicodemus and to the audience outside the Gospel, that this is no physical rebirth but a rebirth born of water and spirit (3:5). Nicodemus does not understand ("How can these things be?" [3:9]) but those who have heard or read the Prologue and the first two chapters will know that Jesus is talking not about ordinary existence but eternal life.

Whether Nicodemus takes these words to heart is unclear; John does not describe a dramatic transformation. Nevertheless, he retains a positive stance towards Jesus. In the aftermath of Jesus's appearance at the feast of Tabernacles, he defends Jesus to the authorities who dismiss the possibility that Jesus could be the Messiah. When the Temple police, who had been charged to arrest Jesus (7:32), return without him, the chief priests and Pharisees accuse the police of having been deceived like so many others. Nicodemus, "who had gone to Jesus before, and who was one of them [the Pharisees]," (7:50) intervened: "Our law does not judge people without first giving them a hearing to find out what they are doing, does it?" (7:51). After Jesus's death, Nicodemus, along with Joseph of Arimathea, prepares Jesus's body for burial, bringing "a mixture of myrrh and aloes, weighing about a hundred pounds" (19:39).

Nicodemus's defense of Jesus and his providing of (an excessive amount of) spices for the burial cast him in a positive light.[19] At the very least, John 3 showcases his initial curiosity in Jesus, and the later references demonstrate his ongoing interest. Nevertheless, Nicodemus does not commit himself to following the way that leads to eternal life. Rather, he represents the "many authorities" who believed in him but "because of the Pharisees they did not confess it, for fear that they would be put out of the synagogue" (12:42). Still, the Gospel narrative holds out hope for him, given the risk he took in defending Jesus (7:51) and in anointing Jesus's body for burial (19:38–40). Nicodemus is attracted to Jesus but refrains from entering into the full faith that would lead to transformation and eternal life. In this regard, he does not model the transformation towards which John urges his audience.

The Samaritan woman. In sharp contrast to Nicodemus is Jesus's conversation partner in John 4:7–29. Like Nicodemus, the Samaritan woman represents a broader group in which she may have some authority. And like Nicodemus, she is interested in what Jesus has to say. Now it is Jesus who makes the first move when they meet at a well in Samaria where he has stopped to rest. The scene is reminiscent of those biblical scenes in which boy meets girl at a well—Abraham's servant meets Isaac's future wife Rebekah (Genesis 24:15–24), Jacob meets his future wife Rachel (Genesis 29:9–12), and Moses meets his future wife Zipporah (Exodus 2:16–22). In this story, Jesus is not meeting his future wife; he knows that the Samaritan woman has had five husbands and is currently living with a man to whom she is not married (John 4:18).[20] Yet Jesus makes the Samaritan woman a life-changing offer: What if she could have living water, instead of the ordinary water that she must draw daily from the well? (4:13–14). The woman responds: "Sir, give me this water, so that I may never be thirsty or have to keep coming here to draw water" (4:15). Whether she is fully convinced by the end of the exchange is unclear. Nevertheless, it is significant that she leaves her water jug behind when she goes to testify to her fellow Samaritans. This gesture suggests that, having accepted the living water that Jesus offered, she has no more need to draw water from the well on a daily basis.

The introduction of the disciples, Nicodemus, and the Samaritan, acquaint the audience with the concepts of faith and rebirth that will help them understand the rest of the story. The stories would prod Alexandra to identify with the Samaritan woman rather than Nicodemus, while still leaving the door open to those who cannot yet fully take the step of believing and testifying to others.

The Healed

Some of the Gospel's minor characters also present some of the traits that John encourages in his audience.

The nobleman's son. The nobleman who begs Jesus to heal his son (4:46–54) acquires the faith that Jesus can and will heal from a distance. Although Jesus does not do what the nobleman begs him to do—come down to Capernaum and heal his son (4:47)—he assures the distraught father that his son will live (4:50).[21] The man believes, even before he receives confirmation that his son's fever had broken (4:52), at the very moment Jesus said, "Your son will live" (4:53a). Anyone can identify with the father's dread and anguish, and empathize with his relief and gratitude. Although the father is not promised that his son will live forever, Jesus's actions prevent the death of his son, thereby fulfilling the father's immediate desire. The story supports the Gospel's rhetorical claim concerning the close connection between faith and life, and conveys the message that, like the nobleman, hearers who turn to Jesus will have their desires fulfilled, though not necessarily in the ways that they might expect. It also illustrates two points that can be important to the post-Easter audience: Jesus can fulfill human desires even if not physically present in the world; and it is not necessary to see with one's own eyes in order to believe.

The disabled man. John 5 focuses on the plight of a disabled man who has been ill for 38 years and has been waiting beside the Sheep Gate pool for someone to help him (5:6). The man unquestioningly obeys Jesus's command to "Stand up, take your mat and walk" (5:8). Like the nobleman, the disabled man has his longstanding desire fulfilled. The chronic nature of his plight, as well as his frustration, may contribute to Alexandra's empathy, though perhaps less poignantly than the desperate father of 4:46–53.

These episodes provide graphic illustration of Jesus's statement to the disciples that "I will do whatever you ask in my name, so that the Father may be glorified in the Son. If in my name you ask me for anything, I will do it" (14:13–14). We may imagine that these stories could provide Alexandra with the hope that she too will find her deepest desires fulfilled through faith, despite Jesus's absence from the physical world.

The man born blind. John 9, in which Jesus heals a man who has been blind from birth, provides a more detailed illustration of the connection between faith and transformation. As Jesus told his disciples, the man's impairment was not due to his or his parents' sins, but "that God's works might be revealed in him" (9:3). Not only the account of the miracle but also the man's response is more developed than the nobleman or disabled man encountered in chapters 4 and 5. When the Jewish authorities question him, he challenges them: "I have told you already, and you would not listen. Why do you want to hear it again? Do you also want to become his disciples?" (9:27). When they revile him, he retorts: "Here is an astonishing thing! You do not know where he comes from, and yet he opened my eyes. . . . If this man were not from God, he could do nothing" (9:30–33). This exchange shows that in acquiring physical sight, the man born blind has also acquired spiritual insight: an understanding that Jesus is the source of his own transformation. In the aftermath of the man's confrontation with the Jewish authorities, Jesus reveals his identity and receives his confession of faith (9:36–38).

More than either the nobleman or disabled man, the man born blind provides a model for identification. The man has a condition which Jesus remedies; he credits Jesus with the remedy; and most importantly, he understands the broader implications of what he has just experienced. The same might be said of Alexandra and other members of the Gospel's implied audience: they have a condition—mortality—which needs a remedy. Jesus provides that remedy and, with the help of the Gospel, they understand its true meaning and divine source. Whereas the man born blind first experienced the remedy and then believed and worshipped, Alexandra and company must first believe in order to experience the remedy. But the point is the same: the need to understand and experience Jesus for who he really is—the Messiah, the Son of God sent by the Father to save the world (3:16).

Lazarus. The Gospel's most spectacular healing story comes at the climax of Jesus's public ministry. From a narrative perspective, this episode is the catalyst for the Jewish authorities' plot against Jesus's life (11:49–52). This story is also the most important from a rhetorical perspective as it models a stance of profound and fully developed faith.

In contrast to the other healing stories, the victim, Lazarus, is someone whom Jesus not only knew but also loved prior to this event (11:3). But when Jesus hears of Lazarus's grave illness, he does not rush to his friend's bedside, as one might expect. As a result, he arrives in Bethany after Lazarus has already been dead and buried for four days.[22] After Jesus arrives at the graveside, he orders the stone taken away. He then prays audibly to God ("Father, I thank you for having heard me" [11:41]). He does so for the sake of the onlookers, and, we might speculate, for the Gospel's audience itself: "I knew that you always hear me, but I have said this for the sake of the crowd standing here, so that they may believe that you sent me" (11:42). He then calls Lazarus out of the grave, and orders his shroud to be removed (11:44). This event illustrates a point made in the discourse in John 5: "Very truly, I tell you, the hour is coming, and is now here, when the dead will hear the voice of the Son of God, and those who hear will live" (5:25).

The raising of Lazarus enacts the promise of John's rhetoric: that those who have faith in Jesus as Messiah and Son of God will overcome death. Whether Lazarus lived forever is not stated. Certainly those who aimed to kill him (12:10) assumed that he remained subject to the laws of mortality. But in emerging from the tomb, he demonstrated that love of Jesus loosens the bonds of death.

Lazarus himself does not utter a word in this Gospel. His sisters, Mary and Martha, act as his surrogates. Mary's faith is emphasized in the narrator's aside that identifies her as the "one who anointed the Lord with perfume and wiped his feet with her hair" (11:2); Martha's faith is expressed more directly in her highly-charged conversation with Jesus prior to Lazarus's raising. In 11:21, Martha accuses Jesus of delaying his arrival unnecessarily: "Lord, if you had been here, my brother would not have died." But she follows up immediately with a statement of her faith: "But even now I know that God will give you whatever you ask of him" (11:22). Jesus then promises that Lazarus will rise again (11:23). Martha understands this promise eschatologically (11:24). Jesus persists by asking for a confession of faith: "I am the resurrection and the life. Those who believe in me, even though they die, will live, and everyone who lives and believes in me will never die. Do you believe this?" (11:25–26). Martha obliges: "Yes, Lord, I believe that you are the Messiah, the Son of God, the one coming into the world" (11:27).

The lives of all three siblings are transformed by their brother's resurrection. Those who witnessed the resurrection—the Jews who had come to mourn with Mary and Martha—must also reckon with this extraordinary event. Some become believers; others betray Jesus to the Jewish authorities and thereby set in motion the leaders' plan to do away with him (11:46–53). But the focus is on the sisters. The story traces their emotional journey from concern (their brother's illness), grief (their brother's death), and disappointment (Jesus's delay) to unexpected joy. This emotional journey foreshadows the metaphor by which Jesus foretells the disciples' emotional journey from pain to joy in the aftermath of the crucifixion: "When a woman is in labor, she has pain, because her hour has come. But when her child is born, she no longer remembers the anguish because of the joy of having brought a human being into the world. So you have pain now; but I will see you again, and your hearts will rejoice, and no one will take your joy from you" (16:21–22).

Like the Jews who mourned with the Bethany family, Alexandra bears witness to Lazarus's resurrection as she listens to this story. She faces the same choice put before the Jewish crowd: to believe or to turn their backs. She also vicariously rides Mary and Martha's emotional roller coaster, an experience that might well have increased her desire to imitate Martha's confession of faith.

Narrative Flow

The order in which characters are presented promotes an ever-deepening sense of engagement and character identification. The early chapters of the Gospel introduce the disciples as ongoing characters connecting the entire narrative, and Nicodemus, whose nighttime visit prompts Jesus to proclaim the need for rebirth from above. Later, starting in John 9 (the story of the man born blind) and continuing in John 11 (the raising of Lazarus), however, the stories linger on the description of the miracle (restoration of sight; resurrection from death) and its impact on the audience within the narrative (the Pharisees; the Jewish mourners).[23] After a lengthy narrative pause—the three chapters of Jesus's farewell discourses (John 14–16) and his final prayer (John 17) John's story resumes with the betrayal, trials, and crucifixion, before wending to its startling conclusion.

COMMUNITY OF BELIEVERS

Stories can create empathy not only for individual characters but also for in-groups, that is, those who display the positive traits encouraged by the narrative.

Suzanne Keen describes three varieties of collective empathizing. The first is what she terms bounded strategic empathy, which *"occurs within an in-group, stemming from experiences of mutuality, and leading to feeling familiar with others."* Second is *"ambassadorial strategic empathy* [which] *addresses chosen others with the aim of cultivating their empathy for the in-group, often to a specific end."* And the third is *"broadcast strategic empathy* [which] *calls upon every reader to feel with members of a group, by emphasizing our common vulnerabilities and hopes"*[24] (italics in the original). To these I would add a fourth variety, less relevant perhaps to contemporary fictional literature (Keen's main focus) but pertinent to the Gospels: an evangelizing empathy that aims to persuade the audience to join the disciples, the Bethany family, and other positive characters in following Jesus.

The idea that individual belief must be combined with communal identification is supported by social identity theory, according to which individual identity derives from or is dependent upon group identity.[25] But the integral relationship between the individual and the group was recognized long before such theories were developed. Jewish law and practice acknowledged this relationship in its focus on communal prayer.[26] Greek philosophers also acknowledged it. According to Martha Nussbaum, Aristotle had stressed that "a life in community with others is the only life that will be accepted as complete by a being who identifies itself as human."[27] Furthermore, notes Nussbaum, Hellenistic philosophers were concerned not only with the individual as such but also with the individual's participation in a "therapeutic community," which was often set over against mainstream society and based on a different set of norms and priorities.[28]

Whatever their background, it seems likely that John's intended audience would have understood and accepted the close tie between individual and communal identity.

The Individual in Community

Whereas John's narrative encourages identification with certain characters and groups, the discourse sections more explicitly convey the importance of community. To be sure, the discourses are framed by narrative material, and, with some exceptions, have identifiable addressees within the Gospel's story world. Nevertheless, some of the longer discourses beckon the extradiegetic audience to imagine that Jesus is addressing the discourse to them directly. This type of response is unlikely in the case of discourses addressed to the skeptical crowds at the Feast of Tabernacles (7:15–31) or to the unbelieving *Ioudaioi* (8:31–58). It can easily be imagined, however, in response to the shepherd and sheep discourse in John 10 and the farewell discourses in John 14–16.

Each of these two sections includes an extended metaphor: the sheepfold (John 10) and the vine (John 15). The *paroimia* (figure) of the shepherd and the sheep (10:1–6) and its accompanying explanation (10:7–18) use a collective image—the flock of sheep—well-known from biblical literature, to describe the collectivity of believers.[29] The *paroimia* identifies Jesus as the "good shepherd" who stands out in contrast to a number of villains: the thief and bandit (10:1), the hired hand and the wolf (10:12). As the good shepherd, Jesus lays down his life for the sheep (10:11), including the sheep from other sheepfolds: "I have other sheep that do not belong to this fold. I must bring them also, and they will listen to my voice. So there will be one flock, one shepherd" (10:16). Jesus's sacrifice is carried out not for the sake of discrete individuals but for the sake of a group—a community—defined by their participation in one flock.[30]

The collective dimension is also emphasized in the metaphor of the vine and the vinegrower in 15:1–6. This metaphor identifies Jesus as the true vine and God as the vinegrower (15:1). Only by connecting to Jesus, the Father, and one another, can the disciples and, with them, the audience, bear fruit for eternal life. Implicit in the metaphor is the fact that the branches are connected to one another by virtue of their organic connection to the vine. The branches together make up a single plant, and collectively constitute the vine that is tended by the vinegrower.

Pronouns

More subtly, the Gospel conveys the importance of groupness through the use of pronouns, in both the discourse sections and, on occasion, in Jesus's conversations with his diegetic conversation partners. Through the strategic use of first person plural pronouns, John invites Alexandra and company to join the "we" to which he belongs. And the second person plural pronouns ("you") in Jesus's discourses, especially when not required by the context, reach out beyond the diegetic audience to address the post-Easter audience. Through these plural pronouns, John both asserts the importance of community and also mediates an encounter with Jesus for his audience. These plural forms are an example of classical rhetorical style; they present affiliation—"groupness"—as a positive and desirable goal.[31]

In most passages, John uses "we" in the usual ways: to designate plural speakers within the narrative context, as in John 12:34, in which a crowd tells Jesus: "We have heard from the law that the Messiah remains forever." The Prologue, however, contains two exceptions. In John 1:14 and 1:16, it is the narrator who uses the first person plural. John 1:14 reads: "And the Word became flesh and lived among us, and *we* have seen his glory, the glory as of a father's only son, full of grace and truth" (emphasis added). The thought is continued in 1:16: "From his fullness *we* have all received, grace upon grace" (emphasis added).

Any narrator (who, we must remember, is a literary construct like the other figures in the story he or she narrates) may use "we" to differentiate between her- or himself and the audience, that is, to stress her or his membership in a group to which the hearers do not belong. So, for example, a teenager may tell her mother that "we are going out to the movies" referring to herself and her friends, a group from which her mother is excluded. In other cases, however, a narrator may use "we" to indicate, or rhetorically to create, fellowship between the narrator and the audience. This is the case in 1:14 and 1:16.

Exactly what is promised to "us" is difficult to pinpoint. Nevertheless, it is obvious that seeing the glory of the Word and receiving grace upon grace are highly positive experiences. These "we" statements create the desire in the audience to do what is necessary in order to receive these gifts. The Prologue includes its readers alongside the narrator as members of that plurality—that group or community—that will be blessed as Jesus promises in 20:29, and that will have life in his name, as promised in 20:31.

Second Person Plural

The use of pronouns is an example of the rhetorical strategy of *lexis*, or word choice. As we have seen, John 20:31 reaches out to its late first-century audience by using the second person plural form: "these are written so that *you may come to believe* that Jesus is the Messiah, the Son of God, and that through believing *you may have life* in his name" (emphasis added). Second person plural forms, however, are found throughout the Gospel.

In many cases, of course, John's use of the second person singular or plural is governed by the narrative situation. It is unsurprising, for example, that Jesus addresses Simon Peter using the singular (1:42) and the disciples using the plural (e.g., 13:13–20). In some cases, however, a plural pronoun is used when a singular might have been expected, suggesting that Jesus or the narrator is looking beyond the story world to include the audience outside the narrative. In 4:48, for example, Jesus chastises the centurion who has asked him to heal his son, as follows: "Unless you [plural] see signs and wonders you [plural] will not believe (Ἐὰν μὴ σημεῖα καὶ τέρατα ἴδητε, οὐ μὴ πιστεύσητε)."

In John 14:9–10, Jesus's discourse, prompted by a question posed by Philip, moves between the plural and the singular: "Have I been with *you* [plural] all this time, Philip, and *you* [singular] still do not know me? Whoever has seen me has seen the Father. How can *you* say [singular], 'Show us the Father'? *Do you not believe* [singular] that I am in the Father and the Father is in me?" (14:9–10a; emphasis added). In the middle of 14:10, however, the tense shifts exclusively to second person plural:

> The words that I say *to you* [plural] I do not speak on my own; but the Father who dwells in me does his works. *Believe me* [plural] that I am in the Father and the Father is in me; but if you do not, then *believe me* [plural] because of the works themselves. Very truly, I tell *you* [plural], the one who believes in me will also do the works that I do and, in fact, will do greater works than these, because I am going to the Father. I will do whatever *you ask* [plural] in my name, so that the Father may be glorified in the Son. If in my name *you ask* [plural] me for anything, I will do it. (14:10b–14; emphasis added)

In this passage, Jesus's direct criticisms of Philip use the second person singular. But in his references to what he has taught, or how believers will benefit, he uses the second person plural. Alexandra may well have perceived Jesus as addressing herself as well.

Through the use of the second person plural throughout the farewell discourses, Alexandra and the rest of John's compliant audience would also have learned:

1) That they will receive whatever they ask for (14:14).
2) That they will receive another advocate ("paraclete") who will be with them always, the Spirit of Truth that will abide with them (14:15–17, 26; 15:26; 16:13).
3) That they will see Jesus even when the world no longer can (14:19).
4) That they will live because Jesus lives, and abide with and in Jesus (6:56; 15:4–7).
5) That they have been cleansed by Jesus's word (15:3).

They would also have heard that they need to keep the commandments as a token of their love for Jesus (14:15), that they must abide in Jesus (15:4), and they must love the others in her group (15:12); that they have been appointed to bear fruit (15:16) and to testify to Jesus (15:27); that they will face the hatred and persecution of the world (15:18; 16:2) and even expulsion from the synagogue (16:2). Finally, they would have been reassured that their sorrow at Jesus's death will be erased by the joy that will follow (16:22–24). By using the second person pronouns, the lengthy farewell discourses address the disciples but also look beyond the disciples to address also "those who will believe in me through their [the disciples'] word" (17:20).

The promises of the farewell discourses are sealed by the prayer to the Father in John 17. In this chapter, the second person singular pronoun is used to address God, and the third person plural is used to refer to the disciples, and, by extension, all believers: "I have made your name known to those whom you gave me from the world. They were yours, and you gave them to me, and they have kept your word" (17:6). This prayer was surely for Alexandra's benefit, in the same way that Jesus's prayer in 11:41 was "for the sake of the crowd standing here, so that they may believe that you sent me" (11:42). Jesus prays for the unity of the believers (17:21) and expresses the desire that they may be with him and see his glory (17:24). Similar use of the third person can be found in John 20:29, in which Jesus looks past Thomas to speak directly to the readership as a prelude to 20:30–31: "Have you believed because you have seen me? Blessed are those who have not seen and yet have come to believe."

LOVE

Finally, the strong and intimate bond among members of the community of believers is mandated by the so-called love commandment that appears throughout the farewell discourses. In 15:17, Jesus declares to his disciples: "I am giving you these commands so that you may love one another" (15:17). Their love for each other reflects Jesus's love for them: "As the Father has loved me, so I have loved you; abide in my love. If you keep my commandments, you will abide in my love, just as I have kept my Father's commandments and abide in his love" (15:9–10). But their love for one another also completes a circle of love: between God and Jesus, between Jesus and the disciples, and now, between the disciples and God: "They who have my commandments and keep them are those who love me; and those who love me will be loved by my Father, and I will love them and reveal myself to them" (14:21). This love constitutes a new commandment, fitting for this new phase of their relationship with God: "I give you a new commandment, that you

love one another. Just as I have loved you, you also should love one another"
(13:34). The love between Father and Son, between the Son and those who
believe, and among believers themselves, places the individual believer at
the center of the cosmological drama enacted through the incarnation of the
Word, his works in the world, and his glorification and return to the Father.

The love commandment is often seen as evidence of the universal, expansive, even pluralistic worldview of the Gospel and indeed of Jesus himself.[32]
But the plain meaning of the passages is more specific and circumscribed
than some might care to admit. In the first place, the commandment is given
to the disciples alone, not to the crowds or indeed to anyone outside their
immediate circle. Second, and more important, the commandment does not
instruct them to love everyone, but to love one another: the group present at
dinner and whose feet were washed. This group excluded Judas, as the commandment was given after his departure. The love command of the Johannine
Jesus stresses that this command, far from being universal, applies only to the
small group of faithful disciples gathered around Jesus: "love one another as I
have loved *you*" (emphasis added).[33] In emphasizing the love for another, the
Gospel implies separation, even estrangement, from outsiders to their group.

A NEW IDENTITY

As a compliant listener, Alexandra will join with others to constitute a group
bound by love for one another, for Jesus, and, through Jesus, for God. Although scholars often refer to this group as the "Johannine church,"[34] it is important to note that John does not use the term *ekklesia*. Nor does he describe
an already-existing Johannine community,[35] or a full-fledged Johannine
Christianity.[36] Terms such as "Christ-confessors,"[37] "Christ-believers,"[38] or
"Christ-followers"[39] describe the sort of people that John hopes his audience
will become, but such labels do not emerge as community designations in the
Gospel's own usage. Although John describes Jesus as "the way" (e.g., 14:6)
he does not use this term to describe those who follow Jesus along this path.[40]
The images of the sheepfold and the vine, while rhetorically important, do
not extend throughout the Gospel but are limited to portions of chapters 10
and 15 respectively. "Disciples" is used primarily to refer to the small group
of followers that accompanied Jesus, though in John 6 it appears to be used
more broadly.[41]

Believers as the Children of God

Although John does not reveal whether, when, and how a group formed
around his Gospel, he provides abundant evidence for how he wanted his

audience members to understand themselves: as children of God (1:12; 11:52; cf. 1 John 3:1, 10; 5:2) who participated in the cosmic realm rather than the earthly realm of existence.[42] These children of God, believers in Jesus as the Messiah and Son of God, "do not belong to the [everyday] world" (17:14, 15) that hates Jesus (7:7; 15:18) but rather, Jesus prays, will be with Jesus where he is (17:24).

John was not the first to describe believers as God's children. In Deuteronomy 14:1, the Israelites are told: "You are children of the LORD your God." In Hosea 1:10, the prophet promises that "the number of the people of Israel shall be like the sand of the sea, which can be neither measured nor numbered; and in the place where it was said to them, 'You are not my people,' it shall be said to them, 'Children of the living God.'" The term appears in Second Temple Jewish literature (e.g., Wis 5:5; Bar 4:37, 5:5; 3 Macc 6:28, 7:6) and is also implied in the use of "Abba," a familiar Hebrew term for father ("daddy"), to refer to God, evoking the emotional attachment of fathers and children, the responsibility of fathers to care for their children, and the duty of children to obey their fathers.[43] The Johannine Jews too refer to God as their father (8:41).

Nor is John's usage unique within the New Testament. "Children of God" appears in the Synoptic Gospels (Matt 5:9; 10:14; Luke 18:16, 20:36), Ephesians (5:1), Hebrews (12:7), and frequently in the Pauline letters, especially Romans (8:14–21; 9:8, 26; cf. Gal 3:26, 4:6; Phil 2:15). In much of this literature, "children of God" emphasizes the spiritual intimacy between God and Israel (in the case of biblical and Second Temple Jewish literature) or among God, Jesus, and believers.

For John, this spiritual intimacy has a material foundation. Those who are persuaded by the Fourth Gospel to engage in a process of transformation are reborn as the children of God and the siblings of one another. Like the Father-Son relationship between God and Jesus, this identity as God's children is described using the language of Aristotle's theory of epigenesis.

The Telos of Generation: The Next Generation

In John, as for Aristotle, generation has a divinely-given goal or purpose. According to Aristotle, the purpose of generation is the perpetuation of the species through the cyclical process of genesis and decay (GA 731b35).[44] The male is *"homo faber,* the maker, who works upon inert matter according to a design, bringing forth a lasting work of art. His soul contributes the form and model of the creation. Out of his creativity is born a line of descendants that will preserve his memory, thus giving him earthly immortality" (cf. GA 731b30–732a1).[45]

The Gospel of John describes a species of sorts. Although Jesus is the only one begotten directly of God, he "begets" future generations.[46] The model and first son of this second generation is the disciple whom Jesus loved. Just as Jesus, the only begotten Son of God, rests in the bosom of his father (εἰς τὸν κόλπον τοῦ πατρός; 1:18), so does the Beloved Disciple rest in Jesus's own bosom (ἐν τῷ κόλπῳ τοῦ Ἰησοῦ (13:23; 13:23).

As Jesus tells Nicodemus, others can, and should, become God's children by being reborn "from above" or "again" (ἄνωθεν 3:3) through water and the spirit (γεννηθῇ ἐξ ὕδατος καὶ πνεύματος, Jn. 3:5). The idea of being born through the spirit echoes 1:12–13, in which the children of God are begotten by God, and this notion can therefore to be understood as birth through the *divine* spirit. But what does it mean to be born ἄνωθεν? Is one to be born a second time, as Nicodemus presumes (3:4), or is one to be born from above? Relevant here may be the fact that ἄνωθεν also appears in the GA in reference to the upper cosmos which is the source of the generative abilities of animal species (GA 731b25).

A second problematic element in Jesus's words to Nicodemus is the reference to water, which is often understood as amniotic fluids and/or baptismal waters.[47] Yet it too has a striking parallel in the Aristotelian vocabulary of epigenesis. According to GA 735b10, semen, that is, the fluid of generation that provides the sentient soul of the offspring, is said to be made of water and spirit.[48] Thus John 3:5 can be read as a declaration that a child of God is one who is begotten of the divine seed that originates in the upper cosmos.[49]

That the disciples achieve this rebirth is implied in 20:22, when the risen Jesus breathes the Holy Spirit upon them. In Aristotelian terms, the *pneuma* is carried by the male seed that gives form to the offspring. The giving over of Jesus's *pneuma* to the disciples therefore might imply that Jesus is now, upon the completion of his earthly sojourn, "begetting" them, molding them in his shape and form. Just as the divine father begot and sent Jesus into the world through the process of divine *pneuma* and generation, so does Jesus beget and send his disciples into the world. As Jesus says to God, "As you have sent me into the world, so I have sent them into the world" (17:18; cf. 20:21). With this spiritual rebirth, the disciples inherit the abilities that Jesus had, namely, the ability to forgive or retain the sins of others (20:23), just as Jesus acquired the abilities of the father to judge and to give life.[50] They will do the works that Jesus does and even greater works than these (14:12). The relationship that the father and son enjoyed will now be entered into by the disciples, "that they may all be one. As you, Father, are in me and I am in you, may they also be in us, so that the world may believe that you have sent me" (17:21).

Another suggestive detail is the outpouring of water and blood from Jesus's pierced side. John 19:31 explains that those crucified on the eve of Passover had to be removed from their crosses prior to sundown. Soldiers broke the legs of the two men crucified alongside Jesus but as Jesus was already dead they merely pierced his side, "and at once blood and water came out" (19:34). This detail was so unusual that John provided authentication: "He who saw this has testified so that you also may believe. His testimony is true, and he knows that he tells the truth" (19:35). An outpouring of water and blood is unusual in a wound such as piercing, but it is inevitable during childbirth.[51] Perhaps, then, the outpouring at this point in the narrative stresses that the rebirth of the believers can occur only with Jesus's death. To put it otherwise, in dying, Jesus also gives birth to the new species; only at this hour can believers become God's children: "Very truly, I tell you, unless a grain of wheat falls into the earth and dies, it remains just a single grain; but if it dies, it bears much fruit" (12:24). The children of God, like the only-begotten son, will receive the benefits of dwelling with God, as Jesus goes to prepare a place for them in his Father's house (14:2–3).

The infusion of the Holy Spirit, through which the new species is born, is a one-time event in contrast to other processes, which are temporary events that require repetition. This is emphasized particularly in John 4 and 6. In 4:13–14, Jesus tells the Samaritan woman: "Everyone who drinks of this water will be thirsty again, but those who drink of the water that I will give them will never be thirsty. The water that I will give will become in them a spring of water gushing up to eternal life." In 6:35 Jesus declares to the crowd, "I am the Bread of Life. Whoever comes to me will never be hungry, and whoever believes in me will never be thirsty" (see also 6:48–58.)

No Death

Rebirth as a child of God guarantees eternal life. In 5:24–26, Jesus declares:

> Very truly, I tell you, anyone who hears my word and believes him who sent me has eternal life, and does not come under judgment, but has passed from death to life. Very truly, I tell you, the hour is coming, and is now here, when the dead will hear the voice of the Son of God, and those who hear will live. For just as the Father has life in himself, so he has granted the Son also to have life in himself.

The decay and death that are part of the cyclical life process are no longer operative for this new species. Rather, hearing the word, imbibing the spirit, eating the flesh: all of these are necessary for spiritual rebirth that promises eternal life.

This promise of freedom from death, however, may have led some to be surprised at the death of the Beloved Disciple, the child of God par excellence. The problem is alluded to in John 21:20–23:

> Peter turned and saw the disciple whom Jesus loved following them. . . . When Peter saw him, he said to Jesus, "Lord, what about him?" Jesus said to him, "If

it is my will that he remain until I come, what is that to you? Follow me!" So
the rumor spread in the community that this disciple would not die. Yet Jesus
did not say to him that he would not die, but, "If it is my will that he remain
until I come, what is that to you?"

This enigmatic passage illustrates the uncomfortable relationship between the
cosmological understanding of the new family into which the transformed
hearers of the Gospel are reborn, and the still-inevitable fact of physical death.

The Next Generations

Later generations, who come to faith after the earthly sojourn of the Word, are
generated through the Paraclete, who is the Holy Spirit (cf. Genesis 2:7). In
John 6:63, Jesus declares: "It is the spirit that gives life; the flesh is useless.
The words that I have spoken to you are spirit and life." But for the Gospel's
audience, those who have not seen but yet believe (20:29), it is the Gospel
itself that functions as the source of the Holy Spirit through whom they can
become children of God. The Gospel therefore presents different means of
acquiring the Holy Spirit, experiencing transformative rebirth into the family
of God, and thereby fulfilling the profound human desire for eternal life.[52]

CONCLUSION

The presentation of the community as "the children of God" extends beyond
the death of Jesus and (of) the Beloved Disciple to include Alexandra and
all members of John's future audiences, all hearers of the book. It is John's
Gospel that breathes life into future believers, just as Jesus breathed the spirit
into the disciples before his ascension, and as God did to the first human in
Genesis 2:7. From the point of view of the community, the Paraclete is the
Holy Spirit and the agent through which rebirth occurs (15:26). But, for John,
the Gospel also fulfills this role, as the book that conveys Jesus's words and
the Holy Spirit to all.

The use of the Aristotelian concept of epigenesis to flesh out the idea that
believers constitute the family of God is a final step in the rhetoric of affiliation. Using such strategies, many of them based in Greek rhetoric, John
articulates the human desire to avoid death and seek eternal life, identifies
faith in Jesus as the fulfillment of that desire, and the use of the Gospel itself
as the vehicle for rebirth.

This is not the whole story, however. Through a rhetoric of affiliation,
John binds Alexandra together with other believers to create God's family

by virtue of their belief in Jesus as God's son. Along with this affiliation come numerous benefits, the most powerful of which is the promise of "life in his name." Just as families are bound together by an irreducible connection—effected for Johannine believers by their rebirth in the spirit—so too are they marked off from other families. Human families, created by the "will of the flesh, or the will of man" (1:13), do not necessarily have a negative stance towards all those outside their family. The members of the family that John describes, however, is an exclusive family of choice. Joining this family requires separating from other powerful, family or family-like affiliations.

Social psychologists and social identity theorists emphasize that any group affiliation requires connection to an in-group and difference from outsiders. Chad Kile draws on Steven Pinker's explication of "coalitional psychology," the human tendency toward group behavior, to explore this point: "Even when groups are chosen entirely at random (that is, when there is no criterion, and therefore no substantial 'reason' for their distribution), and even when subjects are fully aware of this fact, they still will readily identify themselves with their own group and oppose the other."[53]

As we shall see in the following section, John's powerful rhetoric of affiliation is matched by an equally strong rhetoric of disaffiliation that marks the boundary between the children of God and those who claim falsely (in John's view) to be the children of God, that is, the *Ioudaioi*. This rhetoric of disaffiliation has two distinct elements. Through what we might term a rhetoric of expropriation, the Gospel asserts that these children of God reborn through the spirit have exclusive access to the covenantal relationship between God and Israel and to the concrete manifestations of that relationship: the scriptures and the Temple. In that sense, they have expropriated these "properties" from the *Ioudaioi*. And through a rhetoric of vituperation, the Gospel constructs a profound chasm—or a high wall—between his compliant audience and those who reject his claims. No member of God's family can be a *Ioudaios*; no *Ioudaios* can be a child of God.

At this point, I confess to some concern about our imaginary Alexandra. Although her choices are not mine (if they were, I would not have needed to invent her), I have affection for her. She is a sincere seeker who may have found a way of life, faith, and community that can satisfy her spiritual longings. As a compliant audience member, however, she is by definition persuaded not only by John's positive rhetoric, but also by the underside of his message of faith, love, and eternal life. If so, regardless of her personal history or prior identification, she will soon begin to see the *Ioudaioi* not as friends, family, or respected members of society but as her spiritual or even physical enemies.

NOTES

1. As I will discuss at greater length in chapter 7, however, we do not know whether John succeeded in this goal during his own lifetime or the years that followed. The letters attributed to John do imply the existence of such a community, but we do not have the evidence that would allow us to say what this community was like and how long it persisted.

2. For discussion of the Beloved Disciple as author and authority, see Brown, *The Community of the Beloved Disciple*; R. Alan Culpepper, *John, the Son of Zebedee: The Life of a Legend (Studies on personalities of the New Testament)* (Columbia: University of South Carolina Press, 1994).

3. On 20:17, see Adele Reinhartz, "To Love the Lord: An Intertextual Reading of John 20," 56–69. See also Erin E. Benay, *Faith, Gender and the Senses in Italian Renaissance and Baroque Art: Interpreting the Noli Me Tangere and Doubting Thomas*, Visual Culture in Early Modernity (London: Routledge, 2016), https://login.proxy.bib.uottawa.ca/login?url=http://www.taylorfrancis.com/books/9781315094168. Reimund Bieringer, Barbara Baert, and Karlijn Demasure, eds., *"Noli me tangere" in interdisciplinary perspective: textual, iconographic and contemporary interpretations* (Leuven: Peeters, 2016).

4. The fifth-century CE Gospel of Mary imaginatively fills this gap. See Karen L. King, *The Gospel of Mary of Magdala: Jesus and the First Woman Apostle* (Santa Rosa: Polebridge Press, 2003).

5. Given the emphasis on believing oral testimony that is evident in 20:19–29, it seems that the disciples themselves should have believed Mary's words and not needed Jesus to come to them. Nevertheless, the narrative needs to recount the disciples' acquisition of the Holy Spirit in order to substantiate their role in carrying on the mission.

6. Melanie C. Green and Timothy C. Brock, "The Role of Transportation in the Persuasiveness of Public Narratives," *Journal of Personality and Social Psychology* 79, no. 5 (2000): 701–721, https://doi.org/10.1037/0022–3514.79.5.701. This power underlies the therapeutic approach of bibliotherapy. See Sarah J. Jack and Kevin R. Ronan, "Bibliotherapy: Practice and Research," *School Psychology International* 29, no. 2 (2008): 161–182, https://doi.org/10.1177/0143034308090058. This point also helps to explain why some narratives can be deemed dangerous. Green and Brock, "The Role of Transportation in the Persuasiveness of Public Narratives," 701. See also Richard J. Gerrig, *Experiencing Narrative Worlds: On the Psychological Activities of Reading* (New Haven: Yale University Press, 1993), 10–11. The fact that some modern readers consider the Fourth Gospel to be their favorite New Testament book suggests that the Gospel can create such a response in at least some of its audience. See, for example, Dwight A. Pryor, "The Most Jewish Gospel?," accessed January 1, 2017, http://jcstudies.com/the-most-jewish-Gospel/. "Though last in New Testament sequence, the Fourth Gospel surely holds first place in the hearts and minds of most Christians. Of all the Gospels, John's is the most read, cherished and oft-cited. If a single book of the Bible is to be distributed in pamphlet or tract form, invariably it

will be the Gospel of John. If any verse of the Bible is more memorized than John 3:16—"For God so loved the world . . ."—it is hard to imagine what it would be."

7. Green and Brock, "The Role of Transportation in the Persuasiveness of Public Narratives," 702.

8. Noël Carroll, *The Philosophy of Motion Pictures*, Foundations of the Philosophy of the Arts; (Malden: Blackwell Pub., 2008), 161.

9. Suzanne Keen, "A Theory of Narrative Empathy," *Narrative* 14, no. 3 (2006): 217–18, https://doi.org/10.1353/nar.2006.0015.

10. Keen, 218. See Wayne C. Booth, *The Rhetoric of Fiction*, 2nd ed. (Chicago: University of Chicago Press, 1983), 158.

11. Keen, "A Theory of Narrative Empathy," 217. This is the main point of Keith Oatley, "A Taxonomy of the Emotions of Literary Response and a Theory of Identification in Fictional Narrative," *Poetics* 23, no. 1 (1995): 53–74, https://doi.org/10.1016/0304-422X(94)P4296-S.

12. This perspective implicitly undergirds the expulsion theory, which reads the Gospel's references to the *aposynagogoi* as reflecting the experiences of its audience. See the discussion in chapter 6.

13. See here Cornelis Bennema, *Encountering Jesus: Character Studies in the Gospel of John* (Milton Keynes: Paternoster, 2009), 1. Some scholars view Jesus as a model for identification in his role as a martyr; his resurrection thereby proves reassurance to followers facing persecution and martyrdom themselves. See Paul S. Minear, *John, the Martyr's Gospel* (New York: Pilgrim Press, 1984). Others view Jesus as an ethical model. See, for example, the essays in J. G. van der Watt and Ruben Zimmermann, eds., *Rethinking the Ethics of John: "Implicit Ethics" in the Johannine Writings*, Wissenschaftliche Untersuchungen zum Neuen Testament 291 (Tübingen: Mohr Siebeck, 2012). For my own critique of the latter, see Adele Reinhartz, "Reproach and Revelation: Ethics in John 11:1–44," in *Torah Ethics and Early Christian Identity*, ed. Susan J. Wendel and David M. Miller (Grand Rapids: Eerdmans, 2016), 92–106.

14. Characters can also invite negative identification. The prime example is Judas, whose betrayal of Jesus is clearly not a model to be emulated.

15. This is a commonplace of Johannine interpretation. For one example, see Ruben Zimmermann, "Imagery in John," in *Imagery in the Gospel of John: Terms, Forms, Themes, and Theology of Johannine Figurative Language*, ed. Jörg Frey et al. (Tübingen: Mohr Siebeck, 2006), 40. On Mary Magdalene as a disciple, see Gerald O'Collins, "Mary Magdalene as Major Witness to Jesus's Resurrection," *Theological Studies* 48, no. 4 (1987): 631–46; Jane Schaberg, *The Resurrection of Mary Magdalene: Legends, Apocrypha, and the Christian Testament* (New York: Continuum, 2002); Antti Marjanen, "Mary Magdalene, a Beloved Disciple," in *Mariam, the Magdalene, and the Mother*, ed. Deirdre Joy Good (Bloomington: Indiana University Press, 2005), 49–61.

16. I understand John 21 to be an epilogue to the Gospel, but not necessarily written by a different author or authors. For one discussion of John 21, see Francis J. Moloney, "John 21 and the Johannine Story," in *Anatomies of Narrative Criticism*, ed. Tom Thatcher (Atlanta: Society of Biblical Literature, 2008), 237–52.

17. In the words of Robin Griffith-Jones, "John's listeners were being primed for rebirth." Robin Griffith-Jones, "Apocalyptic Mystagogy: Rebirth-from-Above in the Reception of John's Gospel," in *John's Gospel and Intimations of Apocalyptic*, ed. Catrin H. Williams and Christopher Rowland (London: Bloomsbury T & T Clark, 2013), 281.

18. The term is used again in 3:31 and 19:11, 23. In these cases the primary meaning seems to be "from above." Nevertheless, the double entendre ("from above," "again") would be consistent with Johannine style.

19. For a sample of differing approaches to Nicodemus as an ambiguous figure, see Jouette M. Bassler, "Mixed Signals: Nicodemus in the Fourth Gospel," *Journal of Biblical Literature* 108, no. 4 (1989): 635–46; Debbie M. Gibbons, "Nicodemus: Character Development, Irony and Repetition in the Fourth Gospel," *Proceedings (Grand Rapids, Mich.)* 11 (1991): 116–28; Terence L. Donaldson, "Nicodemus: A Figure of Ambiguity in a Gospel of Certainty," *Consensus* 24, no. 1 (1998): 121–24; Raimo Hakola, "The Burden of Ambiguity: Nicodemus and the Social Identity of the Johannine Christians," *New Testament Studies* 55, no. 4 (2009): 438–55, doi:10.1017/S0028688509990014.

20. On the betrothal motif, see Eslinger, "The Wooing of the Woman at the Well," 167–83.

21. On the pattern of refusal and fulfillment in the signs stories, see Adele Reinhartz, "Great Expectations: A Reader-Oriented Approach to Johannine Christology and Eschatology," *Literature Theology Literature and Theology* 3, no. 1 (1989): 61–76.

22. Whether the delay was intended to ensure Lazarus's death—so that he might be raised—is not stated in the story but has been suggested by numerous commentators. See, for example, Keener, *The Gospel of John*, 839. For discussion, see Reinhartz, "Reproach and Revelation."

23. Robin Griffith-Jones states that hearing the Gospel drew the hearer progressively deeper and deeper into the experience of transformative rebirth. Griffith-Jones, "Apocalyptic Mystagogy: Rebirth-from-Above in the Reception of John's Gospel," 282. By the time the narrative reaches John 11, the raising of Lazarus, "the listeners were to be ready to hear the voice of the Son of God, and so to be born again from above. . . . [T]he story of the raising of Lazarus was designed to realise the rising of the listeners from the dead." Griffith-Jones, 296–97. Griffith-Jones argues that this hearing took place in a ritualized, liturgical context and that the Gospel was written for catechumens who were neophytes in a religious community.

24. Keen, "A Theory of Narrative Empathy," 224.

25. Raimo Hakola, *Reconsidering Johannine Christianity: A Social Identity Approach* (New York: Routledge), 2015.

26. On communal prayer at Qumran, see Esther G. Chazon, "Prayers from Qumran and Their Historical Implications.," *Dead Sea Discoveries* 1, no. 3 (1994): 265–84. On the importance of the prayer quorum or minyan in the rabbinic period, see Mishnah Megillah 4:3. See also Shaye J. D. Cohen, "Were Pharisees and Rabbis the Leaders of Communal Prayer and Torah Study in Antiquity? The Evidence of the New Testament, Josephus, and the Church Fathers.," *The Echoes of Many Texts: Reflections on*

Jewish and Christian Traditions: Essays in Honor of Lou H. Silberman, eds. William G. Denver, J. Edward Wright, (Atlanta: Scholars Press, 1997), 89–105. On the Jewish and pagan origins of Christian communal practices, see Valeriy A. Alikin, *The Earliest History of the Christian Gathering Origin, Development and Content of the Christian Gathering in the First to Third Centuries*, Supplements to Vigiliae Christianae; v. 102 (Leiden: Brill, 2010), http://www.jstor.org/stable/10.1163/j.ctt1w76wv6.

27. Nussbaum, *The Therapy of Desire,* 63–64. See Martha C. Nussbaum, "Aristotle on Human Nature and the Foundations of Ethics," in *World, Mind, and Ethics: Essays on the Ethical Philosophy of Bernard Williams*, ed. J. E. J. Altham and Ross Harrison (Cambridge: Cambridge University Press, 1995), 86–131, https://www.cambridge.org/core/books/world-mind-and-ethics/aristotle-on-human -nature-and-the-foundations-of-ethics/28C561667CF0A244E2FDBFE20265ED89.

28. Nussbaum, *The Therapy of Desire*, 40.

29. For discussion, see Adele Reinhartz, *The Word in the World: The Cosmological Tale in the Fourth Gospel* (Atlanta: Scholars Press, 1992).

30. This metaphor will be discussed in greater detail in chapter 7.

31. This is the term proposed by Brubaker and Cooper as a substitute for the problematic term "community." Rogers Brubaker and Frederick Cooper, "Beyond 'Identity,'" *Theory and Society* 29, no. 1 (2000): 1–47, https://doi.org/10 .1023/A:1007068714468; Rogers Brubaker, *Ethnicity without Groups* (Cambridge, MA: Harvard University Press, 2004). See also Stanley K. Stowers, "The Concept of 'Community' and the History of Early Christianity," *Method & Theory in the Study of Religion* 23, no. 3–4 (2011): 238–56.

32. See, for example, Francis J. Moloney, *Love in the Gospel of John: An Exegetical, Theological, and Literary Study*, (Grand Rapids: Baker, 2013).

33. John P. Meier, *A Marginal Jew: Rethinking the Historical Jesus. Volume 4, Law and Love* (New Haven: Doubleday, 2009), 560.

34. For "Johannine church" see, for example, Johan Ferreira, *Johannine Ecclesiology* (Sheffield: Sheffield Academic Press, 1998), http://search.ebscohost.com/login .aspx?direct=true&scope=site&db=e000xna&AN=378316.

35. "Johannine community" is used through Martyn's work. Martyn, *History and Theology in the Fourth Gospel*.

36. For "Johannine Christianity" see, for example, D. Moody Smith, *Johannine Christianity: Essays on Its Setting, Sources, and Theology* (London: T & T Clark, 2006).

37. E.g., Smith, *Johannine Christianity*; Hakola, *Reconsidering Johannine Christianity*.

38. Mikael Tellbe, *Christ-Believers in Ephesus: A Textual Analysis of Early Christian Identity Formation in a Local Perspective* (Tübingen: Mohr Siebeck, 2009).

39. Fredriksen, "How Later Contexts Affect Pauline Content," 17–51.

40. Paul Trebilco stresses that "the way" is used as a formal group label only in Acts. Paul R. Trebilco, *Self-Designations and Group Identity in the New Testament* (Cambridge: Cambridge University Press, 2011), 247–71.

41. For an overview of New Testament usage, see Trebilco, 208–46.

42. See Jörg Frey, "Temple and Identity in Early Christianity and in the Johannine Community: Reflections on the 'Parting of the Ways,'" in *Was 70 CE a Watershed in*

Jewish History? On Jews and Judaism before and after the Destruction of the Second Temple, ed. Daniel R. Schwartz and Zeev Weiss (Leiden: Brill, 2012), 447–507. See also van der Watt and Zimmermann, *Rethinking the Ethics of John*. Jan Gabriel van der Watt, *Family of the King: Dynamics of Metaphor in the Gospel According to John* (Leiden: Brill, 2000).

43. For detailed and helpful discussion, see Mary Rose D'Angelo, "Theology in Mark and Q: Abba and 'Father' in Context," *The Harvard Theological Review* 85, no. 2 (1992): 149–74; Mary Rose D'Angelo, "Abba and 'Father': Imperial Theology and the Jesus Traditions," *Journal of Biblical Literature* 111, no. 4 (1992): 611–30, https://doi.org/10.2307/3267435.

44. A. Preus, "Science and Philosophy in Aristotle's Generation of Animals," *Journal of the History of Biology* 3 (1970): 51.

45. Mary Horowitz, "Aristotle and Woman," *Journal of the History of Biology* 9, no. 2 (1976): 197, https://doi.org/10.1007/BF00209881.

46. A similar argument with respect to Paul's understanding of the Gentile believers' biological or genealogical relationship to Abraham has been made convincingly by Caroline Johnson Hodge, *If Sons, Then Heirs: A Study of Kinship and Ethnicity in the Letters of Paul* (New York: Oxford University Press, 2007), http://www.myilibrary.com?id=116252; Matthew Thiessen, *Paul and the Gentile Problem* (New York: Oxford University Press, 2016).

47. Margaret Pamment, "John 3:5: 'Unless One Is Born of Water and the Spirit, He Cannot Enter the Kingdom of God.,'" *Novum Testamentum* 25, no. 2 (1983): 189–190, https://doi.org/10.1163/156853683X00249. Ben Witherington, "The Waters of Birth: John 3. 5 and 1 John 5. 6–8," *New Testament Studies* 35, no. 1 (1989): 155–160, https://doi.org/10.1017/S0028688500024565.

48. Preus, "Science and Philosophy in Aristotle's Generation of Animals," 26.

49, Hugo Odeberg, *The Fourth Gospel: Interpreted in Its Relation to Contemporaneous Religious Currents in Palestine and the Hellenistic-Oriental World.* (Amsterdam: B.R. Grüner, 1968), 48–71 also calls attention to this range of meaning, citing parallels in Jewish and Christian texts from the first several centuries CE, but does not call attention to the Aristotelian parallels.

50, We might suggest that the Johannine author is here playing with the double notion of pneuma, as motivating life force and as breath, drawing on both the Aristotelian and biblical notions of human generation.

51. Sebastian A. Carnazzo, *Seeing Blood and Water: A Narrative-Critical Study of John 19:34* (Eugene: Pickwick Publications, 2012).

52. That a family could include or even be composed of individuals who are not related biologically was accepted in the Roman Empire, paving the way for metaphorical or other types of family configurations. See Suzanne Dixon, *The Roman Family* (New York: ACLS History E-Book Project, 2005), 30.

53. Kile, "Feeling Persuaded: Christianization and Social Formation," 233. See Steven Pinker, *How the Mind Works* (New York: Norton, 1997).

Part II

THE RHETORIC
OF DISAFFILIATION

Chapter Three

"Casting off the withered branch"

The Rhetoric of Expropriation

John's story of Jesus emphasizes the role of the Jews in persecuting both Jesus and his followers. If she does not already know the story, Alexandra might be alarmed to learn that the Jews hounded Jesus, tried to stone him, and eventually plotted his death (11:8, 49–52). Those who might have testified in his favor, such as the blind man's parents (9:21–22), feared repercussions. Jesus warned the disciples that they may be put out of the synagogues or even killed (16:2), a warning that made Peter's later denial of Jesus all the more understandable (18:17, 25, 27). The Gospel's cosmological framework, however, reassures Alexandra and her group that, from the broad perspective of salvation history, it is they, not the Jews, who have the upper hand. Their belief in Jesus as the Messiah, Son of God, has caused them to be reborn as children of God. As God's children they enjoy an intimate, covenantal relationship with the divine, marked, on their part, by their faith and obedience, and on God's part by God's love and protection (3:16; 17:15).

The main benefit of being counted among the children of God is the promise of "life in his name." In itself, this promise need not affect other aspects of personal and communal identity such as ethnic identification or liturgical practice. For this Gospel, however, membership in God's family entails not only a guarantee for the future but also an entitlement to specific benefits that, prior to Jesus's earthly sojourn, were reserved for the Jews alone.

In contrast to Paul's letter to the Galatians, the Gospel is silent on Jewish practices such as circumcision and the dietary laws. Nor does John suggest that believers should not observe the Sabbath or holidays. On the contrary. Jesus's acts of healing on the Sabbath do not advocate desecration of the Sabbath but rather demonstrate his filial relationship with God: "My Father is still working, and I also am working" (5:17). Similarly, Jesus's participation in the Jewish festivals confers importance on these practices.[1] And while

Jesus's act of "cleansing" in 2:13–22 criticizes activities taking place in the Temple's vicinity, it does not challenge the Temple's existence or importance as an institution but rather stresses the importance of keeping "his Father's house" untainted by commerce.

Nevertheless, John's account of Jesus's words and deeds implies a redefinition of some of these same identity markers: whereas they were formerly centered on Jewish law and practice, they now revolve around Jesus and are subject to Jesus's authority. Exactly what this redefinition entails is a matter of considerable debate. Does the Gospel promote a replacement theology or a fulfillment theology, or something else altogether?

John Townsend argues that as divine revelation, Jesus replaces the Torah, including major symbols for Torah such as bread, light, water, and wine, and his death replaces the Passover sacrifice.[2] In Townsend's view, John's replacement motif reflects the post-70 context of the Gospel's composition, in which Christ-believers and non-Christ-confessing Jews alike needed a theology that did not depend on Temple and sacrifices.[3] Andrew Brunson too identifies a subtle and widespread replacement structure evident in the Gospel's use of biblical quotations, and, in particular, its use of Psalm 118.[4] Brunson argues that, for John, Jesus replaces, or, better, fulfills, embodies, or gives new significance to the manna, the Exodus, the Temple, and numerous other important symbols, stories, and institutions.[5] Nevertheless, Brunson continues to use the term replacement because of its usefulness for his broader analysis.[6] Mary Coloe, by contrast, prefers the term displacement to either replacement or fulfillment, particularly when speaking about the Temple. She argues that in 2:13–22 the Temple as such is not replaced. Rather, it is emptied of its Jewish meaning and mode of worship—mediated by the priests and the sacrificial cult—and replaced with a new meaning, focused on Jesus.[7] For Alan Kerr, the question of whether we see Jesus as replacing or fulfilling Jewish identity markers depends on emphasis and definition. For John, Jesus does indeed replace the Temple, but he fulfills the scriptures.[8] Some avoid the terms such as displacement or replacement because of their supersessionist associations. As Kåre Fugleseth points out, however, none of these terms is free from supersessionist nuances.[9]

My own goal in this chapter is not to search for more delicate language in order to cover up John's supersessionism but to attempt to understand its place in the Gospel's overall rhetorical program. I go further than Townsend and other scholars to suggest that what the Gospel presents is not only replacement, fulfillment or displacement, but expropriation. In the Gospel's rhetoric, the Jews are no longer God's children but have relinquished their entitlement to that identity by refusing to believe that Jesus is God's son. Through his rhetoric, John argues that the Jews' stake in the divine estate—

scriptures and Temple—has been expropriated by God and granted to those who do believe. The Jewishness of the Gospel, or rather, the Gospel's use of Jewish scriptures, modes of reasoning, and theological concepts such as divine love does not reflect its positive stance towards Jews or Judaism, but the appropriation—expropriation—of Jewishness, a self-understanding grounded in covenantal relationship with God.

COVENANT

The Greek term, διαθήκη, -ης, ἡ, meaning covenant, does not appear in the Fourth Gospel. Nevertheless, the intimate relationship that, for John, binds God and human beings through belief in Jesus as God's Son is best described as covenantal in that it involves an exclusive and highly-prized contract that is binding on both parties. Second Temple Jewish literature testifies amply to the centrality of covenant to Jewish self-understanding. For Jews, a covenantal relationship to God originates with God's promises to Abraham and Moses in the Torah. The relationship is governed by mutual love and obligation, and is sealed in the Torah, God's gift to the Jewish people, the revelation of his will, and the blueprint for the Jewish way of life.[10]

John argues vigorously that, at this moment in history, God has redrawn the terms of the covenantal contract by sending his Son into the world as an expression of his love (3:16). In this new reality, covenantal relationship with God belongs only to those who believe that Jesus is truly God's son and the Messiah of Israel (20:30–31). Underlying the notion of covenant is election; election, in turn, implies exclusivism. A group that defines itself as elected or chosen by God necessarily differentiates itself from others who, in its view, are not so chosen. In Second Temple Jewish texts the excluded group are the Gentiles; for John, in an ironic twist, they are the *Ioudaioi*.[11]

The *Ioudaioi* and Covenantal Identity

This claim pervades Jesus's discourses but its most concentrated and detailed expression occurs in John 8:31–59. This passage recounts a confrontation between Jesus and a group of Jews who had believed in him but apparently no longer do so (8:31). The brief comments attributed to the *Ioudaioi* in this section assert their covenantal relationship with God by emphasizing three key points: that Abraham is their father (8:33, 39), that they have never served or been enslaved to anyone or anything (8:33), and that they are children of God (8:41). Together these elements proclaim their profound commitment to monotheism, a tenet that is central in the Hebrew Bible, Jewish theology, and Jewish liturgy.[12]

Children of Abraham. In claiming to be children of Abraham, the *Ioudaioi* draw attention to Abraham's status as the patriarch of the Jewish people. As the first monotheist, Abraham is known in Jewish tradition as the first person to recognize the one God as the creator of the world.[13] The *Ioudaioi* are Abraham's children insofar as they too maintain a firm commitment to monotheism.

This claim depends upon Genesis 15 and 17, in which God explicitly pledges his covenant with Abraham's descendants. In Genesis 15:18–21, "the LORD made a covenant with Abram, saying, 'To your descendants I give this land, from the river of Egypt to the great river, the river Euphrates, the land of the Kenites, the Kenizzites, the Kadmonites, the Hittites, the Perizzites, the Rephaim, the Amorites, the Canaanites, the Girgashites, and the Jebusites.'"

Genesis 17 in its entirety concerns the covenant. In 17:1–2 the Lord appears to Abram and declares: "I am God Almighty; walk before me, and be blameless. And I will make my covenant between me and you, and will make you exceedingly numerous." These verses outline the foundation of the relationship: Abram's "blamelessness" and the promise that Abram will father a multitude of nations. The deal is sealed in two ways: God changes Abram's name to Abraham, which encodes the promise of many descendants and requires Abraham to circumcise himself and the male members of his household (17:5, 10–14). God promises that the covenant will be everlasting, extending to Abraham and his offspring for all their generations (Gen 17:7).

Enslavement. The claim that the *Ioudaioi* have never served or been enslaved to anyone is more ambiguous. In a literal sense, the *Ioudaioi* certainly were once enslaved, in Egypt under the Pharaohs. But the verb normally translated "to be enslaved" has another, well-established meaning, namely, "to serve," as in, to serve many gods. In many places in the Septuagint, this verb specifically refers to worship of God or gods. For example, LXX Psalm 106:36 accuses the Israelites of being ensnared (ἐδούλευσαν) by the idols whom they served. In his letter to the Galatians, Paul uses this verb in a way that implies both worship and slavery (4:9; cf. LXX Jeremiah 5:19). He chastises the Galatians, who are of Gentile background, by asking, "Now, however, that you have come to know God, or rather to be known by God, how can you turn back again to the weak and beggarly elemental spirits? How can you want to be enslaved [δουλεύειν] to them again?" Against this background, the claim that they have never "served" anyone or anything, expresses their profound commitment to monotheism (8:33). They have never served any being other than God; indeed, to serve another "divine" being would be tantamount to slavery.

God's children. Finally, and most telling for our purposes, John's *Ioudaioi* claim that covenantal relationship with God identifies them as God's children. This claim too is supported in the Torah. In Exodus 4:22–23, for example, God coaches Moses on what to say to the Pharaoh as he tries to secure Israel's release from slavery: "Then you shall say to Pharaoh, 'Thus says the LORD: Israel is my firstborn son. . . . Let my son go that he may worship me.'" Thus the three major claims attributed to the *Ioudaioi*—that they are children of Abraham, have never served any other beings, and that they are children of God—all make the same point: Jews are in an eternal covenantal relationship with God.

Loss of Covenantal Identity

The Johannine Jesus, in turn, insists that the *Ioudaioi* can no longer lay claim to this special relationship. For Jesus, their rejection of his Messiahship proves that, while they may be descended from Abraham (σπέρμα Ἀβραάμ— the seed of Abraham; 8:33) they cannot be the children of Abraham (τέκνα Ἀβραάμ; 8:39).[14] Whereas Abraham accepted God's messengers (cf. Genesis 18), the *Ioudaioi* try to kill God's son (8:40). Despite their boasts to the contrary, the *Ioudaioi* were and continue to be enslaved as long as they refuse to believe. In 8:34, Jesus proclaims: "Everyone who commits sin is a slave to sin. The slave does not have a permanent place in the household; the son has a place there forever. So if the Son makes you free, you will be free indeed." Finally, for John, the *Ioudaioi* cannot be the children of God: "If God were your Father, you would love me, for I came from God and now I am here. I did not come on my own, but he sent me" (8:42).

Their rejection of Jesus has ousted the *Ioudaioi* from their covenantal relationship with God, and, so John's Jesus asserts, has revealed their true ancestry as children of the devil (8:44). Having turned away from God's son, they have forsaken God himself.

TORAH

In 8:17 and 10:34, John's Jesus seems to dissociate himself from the Torah by referring to "your law" when speaking to the *Ioudaioi*. Nevertheless, throughout the Gospel as a whole, Jesus, and those who believe in him, are in fact the ones who have rightful access to the scriptures, or, at least, to their correct, that is, Christological, interpretation. Even though the Torah was given to the *Ioudaioi*—a point that the Gospel does not deny—they themselves have failed to understand it, for they have never known God (5:38–47; 7:28; 8:19, 24–27, 47; 15:21; 16:3).

The centrality of Torah to John's rhetorical message is evident throughout, beginning with the first few verses of the Prologue:

> In the beginning was the Word [ὁ λόγος], and the Word was with God, and the Word was God. He was in the beginning with God. All things came into being through him, and without him not one thing came into being. What has come into being in him was life, and the life was the light of all people. The light shines in the darkness, and the darkness did not overcome it. (John 1:1–5)

Whether John drew directly on a pre-Johannine wisdom hymn is difficult to say. There is little doubt, however, that John's Prologue draws on wisdom traditions for at least some aspects of its depiction of the Logos.[15] This tradition appears in numerous texts, but perhaps most clearly in Proverbs 8:22, the Wisdom of Ben Sira (Sirach) 24, and the Wisdom of Solomon. Three elements of the biblical and Second Temple Jewish depiction of Wisdom are directly relevant to John's Prologue.

Pre-existence. Proverbs 8:22–23 has Wisdom declare: "The LORD created me at the beginning of his work, the first of his acts of long ago. Ages ago I was set up, at the first, before the beginning of the earth." Similarly, Ben Sira's Wisdom figure: "Before the ages, in the beginning, he created me, and for all the ages I shall not cease to be" (Sirach 24:9). The parallels with John 1:1–2—"In the beginning was the Word, and the Word was with God, and the Word was God. He was in the beginning with God"—are irrefutable.

Creation. In Wisdom 7:21–22, Wisdom is referred to as "the fashioner of all things." Proverbs 8:27–31 has a more expansive description:

> When he established the heavens, I was there, when he drew a circle on the face of the deep, when he made firm the skies above, when he established the fountains of the deep, when he assigned to the sea its limit, so that the waters might not transgress his command, when he marked out the foundations of the earth, then I was beside him, like a master worker; and I was daily his delight, rejoicing before him always, rejoicing in his inhabited world and delighting in the human race.

John 1:3 telegraphically conveys this same idea about the *Logos*: "All things came into being through him, and without him not one thing came into being."

The manifestation of wisdom within God's covenant people. In Sirach 24:8–9, Wisdom describes how she came to reside within Israel: "Then the Creator of all things gave me a command, and my Creator chose the place for my tent. He said, 'Make your dwelling in Jacob, and in Israel receive your inheritance.'" Similarly, John 1:14a declares that "the Word became flesh and lived among us."[16]

John's *Logos* also has some similarities to the *logos* in Philo. For Philo, the *logos* is a highly complex concept; in developing this idea Philo is greatly indebted to both Platonic and Stoic philosophy.[17] Like Sophia or wisdom, and like John's *Logos*, Philo's *logos* was the medium of creation and continues to mediate between God and the world.[18]

Ben Witherington III suggests that "the evangelist simply uses the term Logos to better prepare for the replacement motif—Jesus superseding Torah as God's Logos."[19] But the Prologue ties the *Logos* to the Torah in several ways. In the first place, *logos*, in the sense of "word," recalls biblical and postbiblical reflection on God as the one who speaks the world into being. This follows the pattern of the creation narrative in Genesis 1, whereby light, the sky, the sea, and all other worldly, including humankind, elements are brought into being by God's speech.

A second and related point concerns the connections among wisdom, *logos*, and scripture as the embodiment of divine wisdom, and the record of divine speech. The identification of Wisdom as Torah is implied in Ben Sirach 24:3: "I came forth from the mouth of the Most High, and covered the earth like a mist." The Prologue uses this same language of the divine *Logos* who becomes incarnate in Jesus (1:14). Furthermore, the grace and truth that accompanies God's only begotten son (1:17) is in Exodus 33:18–20 associated with the giving of the Torah.[20]

At the same time, the Torah as well as the books of the prophets retain their authoritative status insofar as they are witnesses to Jesus (5:39–47). The witness of scripture would not be meaningful unless the scripture itself retained the divine authority ascribed to it within Jewish circles.[21] The Gospel does not explicitly say that the Jews have lost their access to scripture. But it does state that in refusing to see Jesus as the fulfillment of scripture, they fail to understand its true meaning (5:39–40). This failure in effect means that they no longer believe the scriptures themselves (5:47).

For John, Jesus, like Torah, is both the content and the vehicle of revelation. At the same time, Jesus, his words, and his deeds, also constitute the fulfillment of Torah, which retains its role and status a trustworthy and authoritative witness to the workings of the divine in the world. Two things have changed. The first is the centrality of Torah in the covenantal relationship between God and God's people, the children of God, those who believe and who orient their lives towards the divine. Jesus, the *Logos*, has nudged the Torah aside, and now occupies its place as the centerpiece in God's relationship to humankind. The second is the demotion of the Jews from their privileged relationship to Torah and their role as its authoritative interpreters.

Finally, the covenant through God's Son, like the covenant through Torah, includes not only the past history of God's elect people (the patriarchs; the Exodus) and the words of the prophets but also the intertwined ideas of commandment and obedience. For Jews, the Torah constitutes the contract in their relationship with God. The Israelites, whom first-century Jews saw as their ancestors, promised that "everything that the LORD has spoken we will do" (Exodus 19:8) even before Moses ascended Mount Sinai to receive the Decalogue. God, in turn, promises that "if you obey my voice and keep my covenant, you shall be my treasured possession out of all the peoples." Although the whole earth is mine, you [Israel] shall be for me a priestly kingdom and a holy nation" (Ex 19:5–6; cf. also Deut 28).

The Fourth Gospel casts Jesus as both the message and the medium of the covenant relationship from the moment of his incarnation, but it too sees commandment, obedience, and love as constitutive of the relationships among God, Jesus, and the believers. Jesus does as the Father has commanded him, "so that the world may know that I love the Father" (14:31). All that Jesus says and does fulfills God's commandment, "for I have not spoken on my own, but the Father who sent me has himself given me a commandment about what to say and what to speak. And I know that his commandment is eternal life. What I speak, therefore, I speak just as the Father has told me" (12:49–50). This includes the most difficult command of all: to lay down his life and take it up again (10:18).

TEMPLE

A rhetoric of expropriation can also be seen in the Gospel's stance towards the Temple. This motif is introduced in John 2:13–22 when, at the time of Passover, Jesus chases the merchants and money changers out of the Temple precinct, saying (or perhaps yelling): "Take these things out of here! Stop making my Father's house a marketplace!" (2:14–17). Here Jesus ascribes to himself authority over the Temple and the arbiter of which activities may take place in its vicinity. If the Temple is God's house, and if Jesus is God's son, then surely Jesus has the right to drive out those who, in his judgment, are turning a place of worship into a marketplace.

The Jews' response to this act—"What sign can you show us for doing this?" (2:18)—conveys their disapproval. In asserting his authority he is challenging theirs; it is he, and not they, who determines what is permitted in the Temple and what is forbidden. This point is affirmed later on, in 8:31–34, in which Jesus urges the *Ioudaioi* "who had believed in him" to continue in his word and thereby free themselves from their enslaved state. He then adds that

"The slave does not have a permanent place in the household; the son has a place there forever" (8:35). As God's son, he has already removed access to the Temple from the (unbelieving) Jews, who remain slaves of sin due to their unbelief.

Jesus's response to the *Ioudaioi* in 2:19 introduces the replacement theme: "Destroy this temple, and in three days I will raise it up" (2:19). They scoff but John draws our attention to Jesus's true meaning: "but he was speaking of the temple of his body" (2:21), foreshadowing his death and resurrection but also declaring that he has displaced the Temple as the locus of worship of the divine.

This same point is evident in the exchange between Jesus and the Samaritan woman in 4:20–21. After being convinced that Jesus is a prophet, the Samaritan woman tells him: "Our ancestors worshiped on this mountain, but you say that the place where people must worship is in Jerusalem" (4:20). Indirectly, of course, she is asking a question: Which of these competing views is correct? Jesus's response is: Neither. Rather, "the hour is coming when you will worship the Father neither on this mountain nor in Jerusalem" (4:21). 4:23 clarifies that the "you" in question are not only Samaritans but all "true worshippers" who "will worship the Father in spirit and truth." Within the story world, Jesus's prophecy in 2:21 and 4:21 is fulfilled at least provisionally in John 6. Contrary to his usual practice, Jesus does not go up to Jerusalem for the Passover but spends it on a mountain in the Galilee. A multitude of Galilean Jews flock to him there; he nourishes them with bread, fish, and his teachings. For those Galileans, worship has already shifted from Jerusalem to wherever Jesus is.[22] If Alexandra knew that the Temple was destroyed during the first Jewish revolt (66–73 CE), she may well have understood these passages (2:18–21; 4:21; 6:1–5) as prophetic. If so, she may also have understood John as saying that the absence of the Temple is not an impediment for Christ-confessors, whose devotion in any case is localized not in a building but in a person.[23]

Like the Torah, however, the Temple retains a positive significance within the Gospel as one of the places where, as Jesus tells the high priest, he speaks openly to the people (cf. 18:20). Two things have changed, however. First, both Torah and Temple are now rightfully under Jesus's jurisdiction, ousting the *Ioudaioi* from their privileged positions with regard to these markers. Second, the Gospel decenters both Torah and Temple from their place in the first-century Jewish understanding of divine covenant. In his identity as the *Logos* or Word that proceeded from God before the world was created, Jesus displaces the Torah as God's preeminent and decisive revelation, even as the Torah remains revelatory insofar as it bears witness to Jesus and authenticates the claim that he is the Messiah and Son of God (see 1:1–3; 5:39–40).

And while the Gospel nowhere suggests that the Temple has lost its status as God's house, it is now Jesus who constitutes the preeminent locus for divine-human relationship.[24]

CASTING OUT THE WITHERED BRANCH

The verse that encapsulates the expropriation of Jewishness is John 15:6. This verse appears in the context of the so-called parable of the vine in which Jesus identifies himself as the true vine and God as the vinegrower. Jesus declares that all who abide in—believe in—Jesus as God's son will belong to and be nourished by the vine (15:1–5). But "whoever does not abide in me is thrown away like a branch and withers; such branches are gathered, thrown into the fire, and burned" (15:6).

The Greek term translated here as "thrown away" is βάλλω. In Greek, this word has a forceful connotation that is captured far better by the King James translation of the term as "cast forth" than by the milder-sounding "thrown away" of the New Revised Standard Version. The verse therefore states that, due to their failure to abide, these branches are cast aside by the vinegrower and severed from the vine.[25]

The entire passage refers to practices of viticulture that were familiar to all who lived in the Mediterranean basin. These practices included the pruning of branches to ensure the health of the vine.[26] In Second Temple Jewish literature, the metaphor refers to the Jews, who, like Jews today, identify with the Israel of whom the prophets spoke.[27] The vine could also be identified with divine wisdom and Torah (Sir 24:17; Philo *On Dreams* 2.171).

When John's Jesus identifies himself as the "true vine" and believers as the fruit-laden branches, he is appropriating this metaphor for himself. Jesus is the vine therefore both in his role as the divine *Logos* of the Prologue and as the corporate body in which believers must abide in order to bear fruit. As Raymond Brown put it, "Jesus is not the stalk but the whole vine, and the branches remain part of the vine.[28] Who, then, are the withered branches that are cast forth, gathered, and burned? Cyril of Alexandria knew: the Jews.[29]

John 15:1–6 also draws on the widespread use of the vine as a metaphor for Israel in the books of the prophets. Genesis 17:7 promises that God's covenant with Abraham and his descendants will be eternal. How then can those descendants—the children of Abraham—be removed from that covenantal relationship? Isaiah 5:1–9 provides the condition under which such an eviction could take place. The passage begins with a love song about the vineyard: "My beloved had a vineyard on a very fertile hill" (5:1). The vinegrower dug the field, cleared it of stones, planted it with the best vines, and built a watchtower to guard it, all in the expectation of a bountiful harvest (5:2). To his dismay, however, the vineyard yielded only wild grapes (5:2, 4). As punishment, the vinegrower laid waste to the vineyard, trampled it down, and allowed it to go to seed (5:5–6). Isaiah then explains—as if the meaning were not clear!—that God is the vinegrower, the house of Israel his vineyard. Where God expected justice and righteousness, he saw only bloodshed and cries (5:7).

A similar progression—from divine nurturing to divine punishment—occurs in Jeremiah 2:21, in which God, through the prophet, tells Israel: "I planted you as a choice vine, from the purest stock. How then did you turn degenerate and become a wild vine?" A few chapters later, the prophet conveys God's lament: "When I wanted to gather them, says the LORD, there are no grapes on the vine, nor figs on the fig tree; even the leaves are withered, and what I gave them has passed away from them" (Jer. 8:13). Here is a vine that had already died, forsaking the one who had nurtured them and given them everything they needed in order to thrive.

For Ezekiel, the mere withering of the vine is not enough. Israel's faithlessness must result in the utter destruction that only fire can accomplish: "Like the wood of the vine among the trees of the forest, which I have given to the fire for fuel, so I will give up the inhabitants of Jerusalem" (Ezek 16:6). And Ezekiel 9:12 contains the same elements as John 15:1–6: withering, gathering, and burning. Though Israel began as a fruitful vine (9:10), "it was plucked up in fury, cast down to the ground; the east wind dried it up; its fruit was stripped off, its strong stem was withered; the fire consumed it."

John 15:1–6 appropriates these prophetic motifs and applies them to the intertwined relationships among Jesus, God, and believers. In the Gospel, as in the books of the prophets, God is the vinegrower. For John, however, Jesus replaces Israel as the vine, of which believers are an integral part. Whereas the prophets describe a judgment on all Israel for faithlessness, John differentiates between the faithful (those who believe Jesus to be the Messiah, Son of God) and the faithless (those who reject such belief, that is, the Jews). The passage therefore declares that, on account of their refusal to believe in Jesus, Jews are no longer God's vine. God has removed them from divine covenantal relationship; like withered vine branches, God gathers them up, casts them into the fire, and burns them (15:6).

The differentiation that John enacts is not his innovation but, like the metaphor of the vine and branches, based on scripture. Zechariah 8:12 refers to a remnant that shall remain, promising a time when "the vine shall yield its fruit, the ground shall give its produce, and the skies shall give their dew; and I will cause the remnant of this people to possess all these things." Jeremiah 6:9 also describes the faithful remnant as a vine: "Glean thoroughly as a vine the remnant of Israel; like a grape-gatherer, pass your hand again over its branches."

The vine metaphor in John 15 therefore exemplifies the rhetoric of appropriation and expropriation that I have been tracing in this chapter. Here John appropriates a biblical motif of covenant and removal from the covenant—symbolized by the vinegrower's cultivation and then destruction of the vineyard—effectively declaring that the faithlessness for which God destroyed the vineyard in the past is matched by the faithlessness that the Jews display in their rejection of God's son. The believers are the righteous remnant of Israel that retains its covenantal relationship with God from which the faithless have been cast off to wither and die.[30]

CONCLUSION

The Gospel is thoroughly Jewish, in the sense that its narrative is structured around the Jewish Sabbath, the Jewish festivals, and Jewish institutions of synagogue and Temple; its hero draws on scripture in ways both obvious and subtle; it views God as a creator who offers loving care to the cosmos and humankind. These features, however, function rhetorically not to include Alexandra and the rest of John's audience within a broader Jewish corporate entity but, perhaps ironically, to exclude the *Ioudaioi* from the divine covenant. In appropriating the scriptures, the Temple, and covenantal language for its audience, the Gospel rhetorically casts the Jews out from that covenant. This expulsion is justified on the grounds that the *Ioudaioi* have failed to recognize that God has redrawn the terms of the covenantal contract. No longer is the covenant to be based on acceptance of and obedience to the Torah, but on the basis of belief in Jesus as God's Son. No longer do the leaders of the *Ioudaioi* control the Temple precincts. As God's Son, it is now Jesus who has jurisdiction over his Father's house. In other words, the Jewishness of the Gospel is not an antidote to its anti-Jewishness, but part and parcel thereof.

This also means, however, that the children of God have taken on some of the identity markers of the *Ioudaioi*. They are now the ones who have access to the Temple and Torah, and they are the ones in covenantal relationship with the God of Israel, and therefore have the status of God's elect or chosen. Thus they are like *Ioudaioi* without actually being *Ioudaioi*, "Jew-ish" without being Jewish. To be more precise, they stake their claim to the status and perhaps even the name of Israel but reject both the label *Ioudaioi* and the *Ioudaioi* themselves.[31] This repudiation of the *Ioudaioi* is accomplished by a rhetoric of vituperation, to which I now turn.

NOTES

1. On the feasts in John, see Aileen Guilding, *The Fourth Gospel and Jewish Worship: A Study of the Relation of St. John's Gospel to the Ancient Jewish Lectionary Sstem* (Oxford: Clarendon Press, 1960); Gale A. Yee, *Jewish Feasts and the Gospel of John* (Eugene: Wipf & Stock, 2007); Michael A. Daise, *Feasts in John: Jewish Festivals and Jesus's "Hour" in the Fourth Gospel* (Tübingen: Mohr Siebeck, 2007); Mary B. Spaulding, *Commemorative Identities: Jewish Social Memory and the Johannine Feast of Booths* (London: T & T Clark, 2009); Gerry Wheaton, *The Role of Jewish Feasts in John's Gospel* (New York: Cambridge University Press, 2015), http://ebooks.cambridge.org/ref/id/CBO9781139942034. It is tempting to imagine, on the basis of Jesus's behavior as described by John, that a community that formed around John's Gospel would have observed the Sabbath and festivals. There is no evidence, however, either to support or refute this supposition.

2. John T. Townsend, "The Gospel of John and the Jews: The Story of a Religious Divorce," in *Anti-Semitism and the Foundations of Christianity* (New York: Paulist Pr, 1979), 72–73.

3. Townsend, 83.

4. Andrew C. Brunson, *Psalm 118 in the Gospel of John: An Intertextual Study on the New Exodus Pattern in the Theology of John* (Tübingen: J.C.B. Mohr Siebeck, 2003), 149. See also Jerome Neyrey, who argues that John's Jesus systematically replaces Israel's great heroes, its cult, and its central religious symbols. Jerome H. Neyrey, *An Ideology of Revolt: John's Christology in Social-Science Perspective* (Eugene: Wipf & Stock Publishers, 2007), 131–32. This is part of Neyrey's sociological analysis of the Gospel, in which he assigns the replacement motif to Stage 2 of community development and proclamation. For discussion of Neyrey's views, see Kåre Fuglseth, *Johannine Sectarianism in Perspective: A Sociological, Historical, and Comparative Analysis of Temple and Social Relationships in the Gospel of John, Philo, and Qumran* (Leiden: Brill, 2005), 138–39.

5. See 2:18–21; John 6. Brunson, *Psalm 118 in the Gospel of John*, 147–49.

6. Brunson, 149.

7. Mary L. Coloe, *God Dwells with Us: Temple Symbolism in the Fourth Gospel* (Collegeville: Liturgical Press, 2001), 81.

8. Alan Richard Kerr, *The Temple of Jesus's Body: The Temple Theme in the Gospel of John* (Sheffield: Sheffield Academic Press, 2002), 131, 133 n. 80.

9. On the connection between replacement and supersessionism, see Fuglseth, *Johannine Sectarianism in Perspective : A Sociological, Historical, and Comparative Analysis of Temple and Social Relationships in the Gospel of John, Philo, and Qumran*, 137.

10. This point is documented at length by E. P. Sanders. Sanders, *Paul and Palestinian Judaism*; E. P. Sanders, *Judaism: Practice and Belief, 63 BCE-66 CE* (London: SCM Press, 2016).

11. On the importance of covenant and election, see Sanders, *Judaism*, 241–78.

12. Cf. Deuteronomy 6:4–6: "Hear, O Israel, the Lord our God the Lord is One" (Deuteronomy 6:4–6). The opening section of the Decalogue (Exodus 20:2–3) declares God's uniqueness and singularity: "I am the Lord your God, who brought you out of the land of Egypt, out of the house of slavery; you shall have no other gods before me. You shall not make for yourself an idol, whether in the form of anything that is in heaven above, or that is on the earth beneath, or that is in the water under the earth. You shall not bow down to them or worship them . . . ." Both of these texts assert God's uniqueness and call upon Israel to worship God alone. At the same time, the ancient Jewish notions of monotheism may also have allowed of a belief in "Two Powers in Heaven." See Alan F. Segal, *Two Powers in Heaven: Early Rabbinic Reports about Christianity and Gnosticism* (Leiden: Brill, 1977); Daniel Boyarin, *Border Lines: The Partition of Judaeo-Christianity* (Philadelphia: University of Pennsylvania Press, 2004), 112–27.

13. Cf. Apocalypse of Abraham 1, Jubilee 12:12–14.

14. For detailed discussion of this contrast, see Jeffrey S. Siker, *Disinheriting the Jews: Abraham in Early Christian Controversy* (Louisville: Westminster/John Knox Press, 1991), 136–39.

15. On the debate concerning the Prologue as a pre-Johannine hymn, see, for example, John Ashton, "The Transformation of Wisdom. A Study of the Prologue of John's Gospel," *New Testament Studies* 32, no. 2 (1986): 161–86, https://doi.org/10.1017/S0028688500013047. As noted in chapter 4, *logos* language also coheres with Aristotelian epigenesis. On wisdom imagery in the Prologue, see Martin Scott, *Sophia and the Johannine Jesus.* (Sheffield: JSOT Press, 2016).

16. If the Gospel identifies Jesus as divine wisdom, why the use of *Logos* rather than *Sophia*? One explanation is that Sophia, as a feminine noun (in both Greek and in Hebrew, hokmah), is not a suitable way to describe a male incarnation. *Logos*, a masculine noun, would be far more suitable. But this alone does not seem like enough to account for the use of Logos. For a postcolonial feminist perspective, see Mayra Rivera, "God at the Crossroads: A Postcolonial Reading of Sophia," in *Postcolonial Theologies Divinity and Empire*, ed. Catherine Keller, Michael Nausner, and Mayra Rivera (St. Louis: Chalice Press, 2004), 183–203.

17. For a detailed discussion of the *logos* in Philo, see David Winston, *Logos and Mystical Theology in Philo of Alexandria* (Cincinnati: Hebrew Union College Pr., 1985) and David Robertson, *Word and Meaning in Ancient Alexandria: Theories of Language from Philo to Plotinus* (Farnham: Ashgate Pub., 2008), 9–28, https://nls.ldls.org.uk/welcome.html?ark:/81055/vdc_100029263789.0x000001.

18. Peder Borgen, "The Gospel of John and Hellenism: Some Observations," in *Exploring the Gospel of John: In Honor of D. Moody Smith*, ed. R. Alan Culpepper, C. Clifton Black, and D. Moody Smith (Louisville: Westminster John Knox, 1996), 107–9.

19. Ben Witherington, *John's Wisdom: A Commentary on the Fourth Gospel* (Cambridge: Lutterworth Press, 1995), 53.

20. John Painter, "Rereading Genesis in the Prologue of John?" in *Neotestamentica Et Philonica: Studies in Honor of Peder Borgen*, ed. David E. Aune, Torrey Seland, and Jarl Henning Ulrichsen (Leiden: Brill, 2003), 197.

21. This point leads some interpreters to argue that the Gospel sees Jesus as supplementing rather than replacing Torah. Daniel Boyarin states that "For John, as for that other most 'Jewish' of Gospels, Matthew—but in a very different manner—Jesus comes to fulfill the mission of Moses, not to displace." According to Boyarin, 1:10–12—"He was in the world, and the world came into being through him; yet the world did not know him. He came to what was his own, and his own people did not accept him"—describes the "partial failure" of Israel to accept God's Word when they received it in the form of scripture. In response to this failure, God conceived of Plan B: to incarnate the *Logos* in flesh and blood. Says Boyarin, "The Torah simply needed a better exegete, the Logos Ensarkos, a fitting teacher for flesh and blood. . . . God thus first tried the text, and then sent his voice, incarnated in the voice of Jesus." Although he does not say so, Boyarin's analysis implies that, for John, Jesus not only fulfils and supplements Torah, Jesus *is* Torah, just as, for Second Temple Jewish wisdom literature, Sophia/Hokhma/Logos *are* Torah. Boyarin, *Border Lines*, 104. Boyarin's text refers to verses 12 and 13, but his discussion fits 1:10–11 more precisely.

22. Adele Reinhartz, "Jesus as Prophet: Predictive Prolepses in the Fourth Gospel," *Journal for the Study of the New Testament* 11, no. 36 (1989): 3–16.

23. As Mary Coloe and Alan Kerr both note, Temple symbolism extends to many other passages in addition to John 2 and 4. For detailed consideration, see Coloe, *God Dwells with Us*, Kerr, *The Temple of Jesus's Body*. For analysis of Temple language in John 4, see Stephen T. Um, *The Theme of Temple Christology in John's Gospel* (London: T & T Clark, 2016). For discussion of Temple imagery in John 14, see James McCaffrey, *The House with Many Rooms: The Temple Theme of Jn. 14, 2–3* (Rome: Editrice Pontificio Istituto Biblico, 1989).

24. On the connection to anti-Judaism, see R. Alan Culpepper, "Anti-Judaism in the Fourth Gospel as a Theological Problem for Christian Interpreters," in *Anti-Judaism and the Fourth Gospel: Papers of the Leuven Colloquium, 2000*, ed. R. Bieringer, Didier Pollefeyt, and F. Vandecasteele-Vanneuville (Assen: Royal Van Gorcum, 2001), 80–81.

25. This sense is captured in the The Murdock NT English Peshitta, first published in 1851. James Murdock, *The Syriac New Testament Translated into English from the Syriac Peshitto Version* (Piscataway: Gorgias Press, 2001). "And if a man abide not in me, he is cast forth as a withered branch; and they gather it up, and cast it into the fire to be burned. (John 15:6). Along these same lines, see Craig R. Koester, *Symbolism in the Fourth Gospel: Meaning, Mystery, Community*, 2nd ed. (Minneapolis: Fortress Press, 2003), 273.

26. The green harvesting technique involves pruning grapes that are still green on the vine. This forces the vine to focus its energy on the grapes that are closer to maturity. The technique also helps improve the quality of the grapes left on the vine.—See more at: Melissa Hardman, "Wine & Viniculture in Roman and Medieval History," *The Vine Daily* (blog), July 20, 2015, https://www.winebags.com/Wine-Viniculture-in-Roman-and-Medieval-History-s/2041.htm#sthash.qYel1LdP.dpuf.

27. See, for example, the Biblical Antiquities of Pseudo Philo 28:4. Daniel J. Harrington, "Pseudo-Philo," in *The Old Testament pseudepigrapha*, ed. James H. Charlesworth, vol. 2 (Garden City: Doubleday, 1985), 341.

28. Brown, *The Gospel According to John*, 2.669.

29. Cyril of Alexandria, *Commentary on John*, Book 10. http://www.tertullian.org/fathers/cyril_on_john_10_book10.htm (accessed October 9, 2017).

30. In the prophetic literature, the vine is Israel. This raises the question of whether the new vine that includes Jesus and the believers is also called Israel. The label "Israel" does not appear often in the Gospel, but it is generally used positively, or, at least, Jesus does not distance himself from the term. In 1:31, John the Baptist declares that he undertook his mission of water baptism in order that Jesus might be revealed to Israel. In 1:49, Nathanael declares Jesus to be the Son of God and King of Israel, which Jesus takes as an expression of his belief (1:50). In 3:10, Jesus criticizes Nicodemus for his lack of understanding as a "teacher of Israel." And when Jesus enters Jerusalem triumphantly, the people call out "Hosanna! Blessed is the one who comes in the name of the Lord—the King of Israel!" (12:13). Nevertheless, it is difficult to determine whether John envisioned the children of God as Israel.

31. I have chosen not to describe the new group implied by Johannine rhetoric as an "ethnic" or "racial" group, but my rhetorical analysis would be amenable to the sort of interpretation of ethnicity and race that is proposed by Denise Kimber Buell, *Why This New Race: Ethnic Reasoning in Early Christianity* (New York: Columbia University Press, 2005). The appropriate use of ethnic categories in reference to early groups of Christ-followers remains hotly debated. For a positive assessment of these categories, see David G. Horrell, "'Race', 'Nation', 'People': Ethnic Identity-Construction in 1 Peter 2.9," *New Testament Studies* 58, no. 01 (2012): 123–43, https://doi.org/10.1017/S0028688511000245; David G. Horrell, "Ethnicisation, Marriage and Early Christian Identity: Critical Reflections on 1 Corinthians 7, 1 Peter 3 and Modern New Testament Scholarship," *New Testament Studies* 62, no. 3 (2016): 439–460, https://doi.org/10.1017/S0028688516000084. And the response to the latter article in Steve Mason and Philip F. Esler, "Judaean and Christ-Follower Identities: Grounds for a Distinction," *New Testament Studies* 63, no. 4 (2017): 493–515, https://doi.org/10.1017/S0028688517000145.

Chapter Four

"The world has hated you"

The Rhetoric of Vituperation

Through his story of Jesus, John urges Alexandra to believe in Jesus as the Messiah and Son of God. This belief, he assures her, will fulfill her deep desire for eternal life and cause her to be reborn into the family of God, bound by love to her sisters and brothers. John presents this process as a gift, wrapped in love, spirit, light, and life, in order to entice her with the joy that she will experience if she is so reborn. But the rhetorical strategies he uses to describe this cohesive and loving community are matched by equally powerful and diverse tactics that emphasize the need for the children of God to separate themselves from those outside their group. One of these strategies, as we have seen, involves both appropriation and expropriation: the rhetorical appropriation of central markers of Jewishness and the ouster of Jews from their entitlement to them. Closely related to this strategy is a second rhetorical move: repudiation of the *Ioudaioi*. It seems inevitable that Alexandra and other compliant audience members will absorb this hostile rhetoric alongside the glowing promises of rebirth and life eternal.

The *Ioudaioi* present a major challenge to interpreters on several fronts. One concerns the external referent or referents of *Ioudaioi*. Does the term refer to all Jews? A subgroup of Jews? A related issue pertains to translation of the term into English. Should "Jews" be used or avoided? Are other terms—Judeans, Jewish authorities—preferable from a historical and/or ethical perspective? Underlying these matters is a fraught question: is the Gospel's portrayal of the *Ioudaioi* anti-Jewish?

These issues are important and not easily resolved, as the sheer volume of scholarly literature attests.[1] But for the moment, we will bracket them, to focus solely on the role of the *Ioudaioi* in Johannine rhetoric.[2] John both taps into an external phenomenon—the human dread of death—and also creates it and moulds it for his own rhetoric of affiliation. So too does he refer to a historical group known to have existed in the first century—the *Ioudaioi*—but he defines and describes this group in ways that serve his rhetoric of disaffiliation. Although the Gospel does not portray the *Ioudaioi* in a uniformly negative light, John uses the label *Ioudaioi* primarily to construct a group that is distanced from and hostile to both Jesus and the believers.

If the Gospel's rhetoric encouraged affiliation primarily by encouraging identification with the believers portrayed in the Gospel—the disciples and Mary Magdalene—it insists on disaffiliation by discouraging identification with the *Ioudaioi*, or, to put it another way, by presenting the *Ioudaioi* as negative models.

NEUTRAL *IOUDAIOI?*

To be sure, not all of the Gospel's approximately seventy references to the *Ioudaioi* express an explicitly hostile stance.[3]

Descriptive

Sixteen such occurrences are neutral in the sense that they convey neither a positive nor negative stance and call forth no emotional response whatsoever. Nor are the Jews actors in these passages; the term *Ioudaios/Ioudaioi* is simply used as an explanatory point or as a reference point.

In five of these verses, the term is used to describe a Jewish festival: Passover (2:13; 6:4; 11:55), an unnamed festival in 5:1, Tabernacles in 7:2. Jesus's own participation as stated in 2:13 and 5:1 helps to establish his own context and ongoing practice. Two passages refer to specific Jewish customs. The water that Jesus turns into wine at the wedding at Cana was held in "six stone water jars for the Jewish rites of purification [literally: the cleansing of the Jews], each holding twenty or thirty gallons" (2:6). After Jesus's death, Joseph of Arimathea and Nicodemus "took the body of Jesus and wrapped it with the spices in linen cloths, according to the burial custom of the Jews" (19:40). 3:22 refers to the "land of the Jews" ("Judean countryside" in the NRSV). John 4:9 refers to a social custom, according to which "Jews do not share things in common with Samaritans." Here John is explaining why the Samaritan woman is surprised at Jesus's request for water: "How is it that you, a Jew, ask a drink of me, a woman of Samaria?" These verses imply the audience's unfamiliarity with these festivals and practices.[4]

Seven passages describe Jewish individuals or groups. Nicodemus is described as a leader of the Jews (3:1). Jews come to mourn Lazarus's death alongside his sisters (11:19, 31, 33). Jesus refers to the Jews as his addressees in 13:33 ("as I said to the Jews"); he insists, to Pilate, that "I have always taught in synagogues and in the Temple, where all the Jews come together" (18:20). Finally, there is the enigmatic reference in 3:25 to "a discussion about purification . . . between John's disciples and a Jew." This *Ioudaios* is not identified, and his relationship to the Baptist, the disciples, or to the group labelled the *Ioudaioi* is impossible to determine.

By referring to Jewish practices and festivals, these verses remind the audience of the Jewish context of John's Jesus story. They also stress Jesus's own participation in Jewish religious and communal life, even when his practices do not conform to the norms and expectations of other Jews, as when he heals a lame man (5:6–9) and a blind man (9:6–7) on the Sabbath (5:18; 9:14,16). Jesus's Jewishness is also noted when others call him "rabbi," a quintessentially Jewish title meaning teacher (1:38; 49; 3:2, 26; 4:31; 6:25; 9:2; 11:8), and Mary Magdalene calls him *Rabbouni*, meaning, "my teacher" in Aramaic (John refers to this language as Hebrew [20:16]).

John's overall Jewish context is evident also in its conceptual framework and vocabulary. John describes the cosmological significance of Jesus, his relationship with God, his pre-existence and his role in the creation of the world using language drawn from the Jewish wisdom tradition (1:1–18), and expresses the belief that Jesus is the fulfillment of the prophecies in the Jewish scriptures (e.g., 18:9). Most important, John presumes that salvation for all of humankind will arise through the intervention of the one God of Israel, who has sovereignty over the entire cosmos, including the created world and all of humankind. These neutral and descriptive occurrences of *Ioudaioi* contribute to the appropriation of Jewishness that we discussed in the previous chapter by associating Jesus uncritically with specific Jewish observances and adopting and adapting Jewish ideas and language for the Gospel's own theological discourse.

Salvation is of/from the Jews

This last point is relevant for understanding 4:22, which is often viewed as an unambiguously positive reference to the Jews.[5] John 4 describes Jesus's encounter with a Samaritan woman whom he meets at a well in Samaria. In the course of their lengthy conversation, Jesus tells the Samaritan woman: "You worship what you do not know; we worship what we know, for salvation is from the Jews" (4:22).

The precise meaning of this declaration, however, is unclear. This passage begins with a contrast between Samaritans and Jews; both the Samaritan woman and the narrator emphasize that "Jews do not share things in common with Samaritans" (4:9). John 4:20–21 continues this contrast. In 4:20

the Samaritan woman contrasts Samaritan and Jewish worship with regard to its focal point, saying "Our ancestors worshiped on this mountain, but you say that the place where people must worship is in Jerusalem." In response, Jesus promises a time in the future when such differences will be irrelevant, because "the hour is coming when you will worship the Father neither on this mountain nor in Jerusalem" (4:21).

John 4:22a resumes the contrast; Jesus declares that "You worship what you do not know; we worship what we know." In the Fourth Gospel, knowledge is generally a reference to knowledge of God. Here, then, Jesus is declaring that "we" (Jews? Jesus and his followers?) worship the God whom they know whereas the Samaritans do not. The conjunction ὅτι (because or for) in 4:22b, "for salvation is from [or of] the Jews," implies that this clause explains the first. In other words, the fact that "salvation is from [or of] the Jews" is meant to bolster the debate over against the Samaritans. Yet the conversation does not end here but climaxes in Jesus's self-revelation to the Samaritan woman as the Messiah (4:26). John's point here is not to emphasize that the Jews are the origin of salvation but that Jesus is the one through whom salvation comes. In other words, Jesus, the Jew who, by rights, should not have been speaking to a Samaritan woman, is the salvation that comes from the Jews. This analysis supports the idea that, while *Ioudaioi* is a positive term here, the point of the verse is not to stress Jesus's Jewish origins so much as to draw attention to Jesus himself.

This reading is supported by a play on words. In 4:22, Jesus tells the Samaritan woman that salvation is from or of the Jews (ἡ σωτηρία ἐκ τῶν Ἰουδαίων ἐστίν); in 4:42, the Samaritans tell her that through their encounter with Jesus, they now know that Jesus is truly the savior of the world (ἐστιν ἀληθῶς ὁ σωτὴρ τοῦ κόσμου). As the savior, Jesus himself *is* the salvation that comes from the Jews, to Samaritans, Jews, and, one presumes, others as well.

The elusive nature of 4:22 is due in great measure to one small word: the Greek preposition ἐκ (ἐξ). This preposition can mean "of," as in "a part of" or "can be found within." It can also mean "out of," or "emerging from." In claiming that "salvation is ἐκ τῶν Ἰουδαίων" Jesus is not declaring that salvation is "of" the Jews in the sense of belonging to or reserved for Jews only.

The ambiguity of this seemingly simple preposition leads to rather complex interpretations. C. K. Barrett, for example, states:

> The saying [4:22b] does not mean that Jews as such are inevitably saved, but rather that the election of Israel to a true knowledge of God was in order that . . . at the time appointed by God, salvation might proceed from Israel to the world, and Israel's own unique privilege be thereby dissolved. As the next verse shows, this

eschatological salvation is in the person of Jesus in process of realization and the Jews are losing their position to the Church.[6]

Schnackenburg views this statement as an affirmation "that the Jews still have precedence in the history of salvation. The Samaritans . . . do not possess true knowledge of God; their worship rather grew out of national and political ambitions. The Jews . . . are the legitimate worshippers of God, and salvation, that is, the Messiah, stems from the Jews. . . . In the situation as he found it, Jesus had to overcome the woman's repugnance to the "Jews" (v.9)."[7] Michael Theobald argues that the phrase ἐκ τῶν Ἰουδαίων means from the Jewish scriptures, rather than Samaritan scriptures.[8]

Edward Klink comments that "as much as Jesus must embrace his Jewishness, for salvation is from the Jews, he is also correcting what it means to be Jewish. He is the true Jew, through whom all people on earth will be blessed (Gen 12:3). Jesus is the 'blessing' given to the Jews, and it is through the Jewish Jesus that the rest of the world is blessed."[9] For Klink, Jesus is simply asserting that the one whom the Samaritan woman has identified as a Jew is offering salvation to those whom the Jews have excluded.

Despite the differing nuances attributed to 4:22, there is general agreement that the verse is not intended primarily to re-assert Jewish superiority over Samaritans (though there is a hint of that) but to emphasize that the one whom the Samaritan woman has called a Jew is in fact the savior whom the Samaritans expect and for whom they long. Although Jesus fulfills Samaritan messianic expectations (4:25, 29),[10] he does so in a Jewish trope, consistent with the rhetoric of expropriation discussed in the previous chapter. In declaring that salvation is of or from the Jews, John's Jesus is promising the Samaritans the salvation through covenantal relationship that the Jews alone had previously enjoyed as God's elect people. The one who provides salvation is a Jew; the salvation that he promises is the one that comes to God's covenant people. The Samaritans have an opportunity to benefit from the Jewish covenant with God without becoming Jews, but that covenant is still seen as primary, and better than, more authentic, truer, than the Samaritan beliefs. Furthermore, not only Samaritans, but now also the Jews themselves, can be in relationship with God only by worshiping the Father in spirit and truth, that is, through faith in Jesus.

The immediate and broader context rule out the idea that Jesus is after all declaring that only Jews will be saved.[11] Here John's Jesus is simply asserting that the one whom the Samaritan woman has identified as a Jew is offering salvation to those whom the Jews have excluded. The question then remains: is this indeed a positive usage of the term *Ioudaioi* or is it rather neutral or even, in the context of the Gospel's rhetorical program, negative?

The history of interpretation testifies to the uneasiness that 4:22 has generated. The verse was excised by some 19th and 20th century exegetes on redaction-critical grounds. Gilbert Van Belle traces this move as far back as Ernst Renan's *La vie de Jésus* in the mid-nineteenth century.[12] In the twentieth century, the main proponent of this view was Rudolf Bultmann. Bultmann excised 4:22 from the reconstruction of the Gospel's original form in his 1941 commentary on the Gospel of John, and relegated the explanation to a footnote: "In spite of 4:9, it is hard to see how the Johannine Jesus, who consistently dissociates himself from the Jews, . . . could have made such a statement."[13]

This view was taken up by the Nazi scholar Walter Grundmann, in a 1938 article.[14] Grundmann views John's depiction of the Jews as "those who reject the claim to the dominion of Jesus" as historically accurate. For that reason, 4:22 could not have been original to this (in Grundmann's estimation) thoroughly and correctly anti-Semitic Gospel, but emanated from the author of Revelation, who expressed a positive view of Jews in 2:9 and 3:9.[15] In 1940, the de-Judaized version of John in *Die Bottschaft Gottes* (The Message of God), published under the auspices of the Institute for the Study and Eradication of Jewish Influence on German Church Life in Jena, Germany, changed the text to echo a famous anti-Semitic slogan: "The Jews are our misfortune."[16] By contrast, another Nazi scholar, Gerhard Kittel, considered 4:22 to be part of the Gospel, although the positive statement about the Jews apparently did not affect his overall approval of John as an anti-Semitic text.[17]

In more recent years, the verse has been called into service to counteract the anti-Jewish tone of other Johannine references to the *Ioudaioi*. Van Belle, for example, stresses that "no other New Testament text places greater emphasis on the value of the Jewish religion."[18] For Rudolf Schnackenburg, this verse shows that "Judaism as such is not rejected, but only the unbelieving Jewish leaders of the day."[19] Raymond Brown comments that "Here, speaking to a foreigner, . . . the term [οἱ Ἰουδαῖοι] refers to the whole Jewish people. This line is a clear indication that the Johannine attitude to the Jews cloaks neither an anti-Semitism of the modern variety nor a view that rejects the spiritual heritage of Judaism."[20] For Keener, the verse demonstrates that the Johannine community had not broken with its Jewish heritage.[21]

Others, however, strongly disagree with using the verse to exculpate John's otherwise anti-Jewish stance. Bieringer and Pollefeyt argue that John 4:22 cannot be used as a counterpoint to such blatantly anti-Jewish statements as 8:44: "For one thing, however positive the content of 4:22 might be considered, it cannot make 8:44 go away."[22] Johannes Beutler bluntly disputes the interpretation of 4:22 as a positive expression: "We need to ask ourselves whether the sense of Jn 4:22 consists in respect for Judaism or rather in the preparation of the Samaritan Woman for a new form of faith which surpasses the institutions both of Israel and of the Samaritans."[23]

I agree with Bieringer, Pollefeyt, and Beutler, and would further suggest that while 4:22 seems to contradict the anti-Jewish statements in the Gospel, it in fact stems from the same set of ideas and impulses. The Gospel's stance towards the Jews is explicitly based on (the Gospel's own claims concerning) their persecution of, rejection of, and blindness to Jesus as the Son of God. Although the *Ioudaioi* were not the only ones who did not accept Jesus—the same was true of Samaritans and Gentiles—they are singled out due to the rhetoric of expropriation explored in the previous chapter. In rejecting Jesus, the Jews have forfeited their status as God's elect people. They have nullified their covenantal bond with the divine and instead demonstrated that the devil, not God, is their true father. The Gospel explicitly grounds its anti-Jewish statements precisely in the point that "salvation is from the Jews" yet the Jews rejected him. The Samaritans, however, who come to Jesus and now "know that this is truly the Savior of the world" (4:42), are now children of God because they believe in his name.

Wavering Jews: Positive or Negative?

Although it is not overtly hostile to Jews, John 4:22 is consistent with the anti-Jewish rhetoric that pervades John's Gospel. The same can be said of the thirteen occurrences in which crowds of *Ioudaioi* ponder the christological claims made by or about Jesus among themselves and express ambivalence about Jesus's identity. In the Bread of Life discourse (6:26–59), the Jews complain about the claim that "I am the bread that came down from heaven" (6:41) whose flesh they must eat (6:51–52). At the Feast of Tabernacles, the Jews search for him (7:11) and are then puzzled about his learning (7:15), his possible intentions to travel to the Diaspora and teach the Greeks (7:35), his promise that "where I am going, you cannot come" (8:22), and his very Messiahship (10:19; 24). After Lazarus's death, the Jews who mourn with Mary and Martha of Bethany are struck by Jesus's love for Lazarus (11:36); after witnessing Lazarus's resurrection, some of these Jews believe (11:45; 12:11) or at least are very interested in him (12:9), while others raise the alarm (11:46).

These passages point to differences of opinion among the Jews and leave open the possibility that at least within the narrative, some will become believers. The Johannine Jesus himself holds out hope for the Jews in 8:31 by promising that "If you continue in my word, you are truly my disciples"—an opportunity that, in the view of this Gospel, they proceed to squander. In 13:33 Jesus repeats a point that he had said earlier to the Jews (cf. 8:21).

Susan Hylen suggests that the *Ioudaioi* function as an ambiguous group character that is often undecided as to their stance towards Jesus, and as such, they can constitute a point of positive identification for an audience faced with a similar set of choices.[24] Christopher Skinner argues that the implied reader (implied audience) is not always called upon to identify with the believers and against the *Ioudaioi* or specific characters like Nicodemus, but rather must weigh each case.[25]

Even those who are tempted to believe, however, are not quite among the faithful followers that the Gospel presents as worthy of eternal life. In each case, Jesus comes to the encounter with the undecided Jewish crowds having already decided that they fall short. When the multitude that had enjoyed the meal of loaves and fishes finds Jesus again after a search, Jesus tells them: "Very truly, I tell you, you are looking for me, not because you saw signs, but because you ate your fill of the loaves. (6:26). He punctuates the Bread of Life discourse that ensues with statements expressing his lack of confidence in their willingness to believe:

> Jesus said to them, "I am the Bread of Life. Whoever comes to me will never be hungry, and whoever believes in me will never be thirsty. But I said to you that you have seen me and yet do not believe" (6:35–36).

Later he declares to them:

> "It is the spirit that gives life; the flesh is useless. The words that I have spoken to you are spirit and life. But among you there are some who do not believe." For Jesus knew from the first who were the ones that did not believe, and who was the one that would betray him (6:63–64).

In John 7, at the Feast of Tabernacles, Jesus goes on the offensive, telling the crowd: "Did not Moses give you the law? Yet none of you keeps the law. Why are you looking for an opportunity to kill me?" (7:19). Although one might view his words as being directed at the Jewish authorities, the context specifies that he is addressing the crowd (7:20). Later, as the crowd is weighing the question of his Messiahship, Jesus mocks them. The crowd ponders that Jesus cannot be the Messiah as "we know where this man is from; but when the Messiah comes, no one will know where he is from" (7:27). Jesus then cries out: "You know me, and you know where I am from. I have not come on my own. But the one who sent me is true, and you do not know him. I know him, because I am from him, and he sent me" (7:28–29).

The pattern continues in John 8. In 8:31–32 Jesus offers an opportunity to "the Jews who had believed in him:" "If you continue in my word, you are truly my disciples; and you will know the truth, and the truth will make you free." They have trouble understanding this (8:33), but Jesus impatiently jumps to a negative conclusion: "I know that you are descendants of Abraham; yet you look for an opportunity to kill me, because there is no place in you for my word" (8:37). The same is true in John 10. When the Jews ask whether he is the Messiah, he is again on the offensive: "I have told you, and you do not believe. The works that I do in my Father's name testify to me; but you do not believe, because you do not belong to my sheep" (10:25–26). Finally, in John 11, there are many Jews who believe but some "of them"— whether "of the Jews" or of those who believed—told the Pharisees (11:45–46), and in this way sparked the Council's plot against his life.

In these passages Jesus prejudges the waffling crowds, as it seems he did also in 2:23–24 when he did not entrust himself to the believing crowds after cleansing the Temple, and in 6:15 when he hid from those who proclaimed him a prophet and wished to make him king. Much as we might hope that John's Jesus would give these wavering Jews a chance, their rejection of Jesus seems to have been a foregone conclusion.

HOSTILE *IOUDAIOI*:
THE RHETORIC OF VITUPERATION

The majority of occurrences of the term *Ioudaios/Ioudaioi*, are less coy than 4:22 and the "wavering" passages. Approximately 40 verses are unambiguously negative, expressing the Jews' hostility towards Jesus and/or Jesus's hostility towards the Jews.[26] These express a rhetoric of vilification, or, in classical terms, a rhetoric of vituperation. Vituperation, referring to slander, blame, or vilification, was a standard aspect of epideictic rhetoric.[27] The rhetoric of vituperation thematizes the commonplace "human tendency to uplift the self by vilifying the other"[28] and was "aimed at destroying the social and political *persona* of one's adversary."[29] In classical Greek rhetoric, vituperation was aimed at "lowlifes" and "hot shots." Lowlifes were accused of "embarrassing lineages (mother a whore, father a Scythian), low-class occupations (sausage-seller, cobbler), ugliness, uselessness to the city, and lack of refinement."[30] Hot shots were charged with "violent and cruel actions, sexual perversion, drunkenness and gluttony, being supercilious, impiety, taking bribes, anti-democratic sympathies, and, in general, shamelessness."[31]

In modern legal terms, slander refers to a false accusation. For ancient rhetoric, however, the accuracy of the accusation was beside the point. Neither orators nor their audiences paid much attention to the facts or alleged facts brought to the argument. A "defamatory conjecture" was as good as historical fact if it would sharpen the point of invective.[32] While the goal was always persuasion, the point was not always to persuade the audience of the truth of the speaker's position, but often rather to persuade them that the speaker, rather than his/her opponent, has their best interests at heart.[33] For this reason, vituperation often worked together with the rhetoric of praise to assert, reinforce, and perform communal values.[34]

It is widely recognized that the Gospel uses vituperation in its portrayal of the *Ioudaioi*.[35] Freyne describes John's form of vituperation as "irony which flows over into caricature and parody."[36] David Rensberger notes that the Gospel's "vituperation against 'the Jews' produces a distancing effect that must not be underestimated."[37]

Narrative Vituperation

The main accusation against the *Ioudaioi* concerns their opposition to and pursuit of Jesus, culminating in his crucifixion. This opposition is hinted at in the Prologue—"He came to what was his own, and his own people did not accept him" (1:11)—and escalates from there.

The *Ioudaioi* first appear as actors in the story in 1:19–27, when they send priests and Levites to interrogate John the Baptist as to his identity. The Baptist immediately responds in the negative: he is not the Messiah—answering a question that they did not ask but was apparently implicit in their initial question: "Who are you?" (1:19). The conversation deteriorates from there. Although they exchange words and not blows, the underlying tone of the passage is antagonistic.

In John 2:18–21, the Jews challenge Jesus himself after he has "cleansed" the temple: "What sign can you show us for doing this?" Jesus then replies: "Destroy this temple, and in three days I will raise it up." The Jews take his words literally, and respond, in either mockery or wonder, "This temple has been under construction for forty-six years, and will you raise it up in three days?" But, as the narrator informs us, "he was speaking of the temple of his body."

After these introductory chapters, however, the Jews' antagonism towards Jesus and those associated with him proceeds beyond words to an intention to harm. From John 5 to the end of the Gospels, the Jews persecute Jesus for breaking the sabbath and making claims about God (5:16, 18); argue with him over their covenantal relationship with God (8:48, 52, 57); attempt to stone Jesus (8:59; 10:31–33), and, finally, orchestrate his death (18:14, 31, 35, 36, 38; 19:7, 12, 31).

Rhetoric of Binary Opposition

The relentless focus on the *Ioudaioi*'s intentions to kill Jesus identifies them as the enemies of Jesus and all believers. The same point is made through the pervasive rhetoric of binary opposition, in which the behavior, attitudes, and attributes of the Jews are contrasted to the ones that the Gospel is trying to promote to its audience. The Gospel's Prologue explicitly contrasts the "children of God" (1:12)—the group to which, the Gospel argues, all hearers should belong—with those born of "blood or of the will of the flesh or of the will of man" (1:13). The contrast between those who are born of God and those who are born of man, that is, of blood and flesh, is a prime example of the strategy that I refer to as the rhetoric of binary opposition. This rhetoric is expressed in the Gospel's use of contrasting metaphors. One set of metaphors describes opposing states of being, such as light/darkness, life/death, above/below, from God/not from God. Another set describes opposing activities, such as believing/disbelieving, accepting/rejecting, doing good/doing evil, loving/hating.

The positive element of each pair is associated with Jesus, the negative element of each pair with those who oppose Jesus and reject the claim that Jesus is the Christ, the Son of God. In 1:4 and 8:12, for example, the Gospel describes Jesus as the light of the world. The light challenges the darkness that has tried but not succeeded in overcoming it (1:5). The light, as Jesus, came into the world in order that believers not remain in darkness (12:46). Some, however, love darkness rather than light because their deeds are evil (3:19).

In the Gospel, it is the *Ioudaioi*, the Jews, who exemplify and concretize the negative pole of these binaries. For example, although "darkness" is an abstract metaphor, it characterizes the Johannine Jews both as a group and individually. In 8:12, Jesus promises the Jews that "Whoever follows me will never walk in darkness but will have the light of life." But the Jews' absolute rejection of Jesus excludes them from this promise (12:37). In 3:2, Nicodemus, a Pharisee and leader of the Jews (3:1), comes to Jesus "by night" (3:2); in 13:30 night falls immediately upon Judas's departure from the disciples to betray Jesus to the authorities.

The rhetoric of binary opposition is also evident in behavior. A consequence as well as a cause of the Jews' existence in darkness is their inability to see. Their blindness is contrasted with the new-found vision of the man born blind who declares Jesus to be the Son of Man (9:39–41). The one who sees Jesus also sees God (12:45). Similarly, belief in Jesus as the Messiah and Son of God is evidence of faith in God (12:44); The Jews, *hoi Ioudaioi*, on the other hand, do not see or believe in God because they do not see and believe in Jesus as the Christ and Son of God (5:38). Accepting Jesus demonstrates a love for God, for Jesus, and for fellow believers (15:12–17). Rejecting Jesus is tantamount to hating God. Jesus accuses the Jews of not having the love of God in them (8:42) and tells the disciples that his enemies hate both himself and his Father (15:23–24).

The most insidious contrast, however, is between the children of God and children of the devil (8:44). The identification of the Jews as children of the devil situates them firmly within the cosmological tale alongside the villain whom the Word must defeat: the "ruler of this world" (14:30), "the evil one" (17:15), Satan (13:27), or the devil (13:2). Just as the positive language serves the purpose of pathos, by enticing the audience to take the path that leads to light, life, and joy, so does the negative usage encourage them to view the *Ioudaioi* in a negative light and for that reason to distance themselves from these children of Satan.

The confrontation between the Johannine Jesus and the Johannine Jews in 8:31–59 revolves around competing genealogical assertions. The Jews initially claim Abraham as their father (8:39). In 8:41 they trace back their genealogy even further, to God, declaring: "We are not illegitimate children (literally: begotten out of fornication, ἐκ πορνείας οὐ γεγεννήμεθα); we have one father, God himself" (8:41). To this Jesus responds: "If God were your Father, you would love me, for I proceeded and came forth (ἐκ τοῦ θεοῦ ἐξῆλθον) from God; I came not of my own accord, but he sent me" (8:42).

Because their behavior does not resemble that of Abraham or of God, Jesus denies their claim to be children of Abraham and of God. Jesus's argument in this case rests on the Aristotelian claim that paternity can be attested by the likeness or similarity between father and son. As Neyrey notes,

> Aristotle expresses the common expectation that "children will be chips off the old block" (see Deut 23:2; 2 Kings 9:22; Isa 57:3; Hos 1:2; Eccl 23:25–26; 30:7), either like father, like son (e.g., Matt 11:27) or like mother, like daughter (e.g., Ezek 16:44). If the parents or ancestors were "landed" or citizens of a free *polis*, then the root stock of the family was noble; virtuous ancients should be expected to breed virtue. Plato says: "They were good because they sprang from good fathers" (*Menex.* 237). Confirmation of this is found in the endless introduction of biblical characters as "son of so-and-so." To know the father is to know the son. The honor rating of the father indicates the honor rating of the son.[38]

Conversely, the qualities of the child confirm the identity of the father. According to Quintillian, "Persons are generally regarded as having some resemblance to their parents and ancestors, a resemblance which leads to their living disgracefully or honorably, as the case may be" (*Inst. Orat.* 5.10.24).

In identifying the devil as the father of the *Ioudaioi*, John is drawing on the Aristotelian theory of epigenesis, just as he did in identifying God as the father of Jesus. Epigenesis, therefore, provides not only a background against which to understand the Word's entry into the world, but also a rationale for the boundary that John draws between his audience and the *Ioudaioi*. Those within the elect group belong socially and even organically, that is, by means of divine generation, to the children of God. Those outside, though they may claim to be divinely begotten, are in fact children of the devil, as evidenced by their behavior towards Jesus, the Son of God.[39]

John's rhetoric of binary opposition does not necessarily point to a thoroughgoing dualistic worldview. Beneath and around these dichotomous categories, we can detect some nuance, irony, and, as in the formulation, "the hour is coming and now is," paradox. Binary opposition functions rhetorically, however, to contribute to the Gospel's construction of two opposing groups—the children of God and the children of Satan—and the boundary between them—faith in Jesus as Messiah, the Son of God, and rejection of that faith.

The Rhetoric of Fear

One of the most powerful ways that John encourages dissaffilation from the *Ioudaioi* involves a rhetoric of fear. This rhetorical strategy runs as an undercurrent in the depiction of the *Ioudaioi* as violent in both their intentions and their behavior.

Fear of the *Ioudaioi* is implicit in several scenes. It may be implied in Nicodemus's decision to approach Jesus by night rather than by day (3:1). Jesus's decision to leave Judea for the Galilee after learning that the Pharisees were aware of his baptizing activity implies that Jesus fears retribution (4:1–3). His concern emerges more overtly in the narrator's comment that Jesus preferred to stay in the Galilee rather than return to Judea in 7:1 "because the Jews were looking for an opportunity to kill him" (7:1). The disciples express fear on Jesus's behalf after learning of his plans to go to Bethany upon hearing of Lazarus's dire illness: "Rabbi, the Jews were just now trying to stone you, and are you going there again?" (11:8).

"Fear of the *Ioudaioi*" (τὸν φόβον τῶν Ἰουδαίων) is explicit in three passages. 19:38 specifies that Joseph of Arimathea remained a secret disciple of Jesus "because of his fear of the Jews." 20:19 asserts that the disciples hid after Jesus's crucifixion "for fear of the Jews," to explain why Jesus visited them in a closed room. Most ominous, perhaps, is 7:13. John 7 is set in the area of the Jerusalem Temple during the Feast of Tabernacles. The *Ioudaioi* were searching for Jesus, and the crowds were divided as to whether Jesus is a good person or deceitful one. The narrator then explains that "no one would speak openly about him for fear of the Jews" (7:13). The passage as a whole creates an ominous atmosphere that becomes intensified when Jesus eventually does show up at the festival and speaks openly to the crowd. Some Jerusalemites then wonder: "Is not this the man whom they are trying to kill? And here he is, speaking openly, but they say nothing to him!" (7:25–26).

These passages emphasize that not only Jesus but also those who believed in him or even expressed interest in him feared the Jews' retribution. This fear is concretized in the three passages that express fear of expulsion from the synagogue. The parents of the man born blind are afraid to answer questions about their son "because they were afraid of the Jews [ἐφοβοῦντο τοὺς Ἰουδαίους]; for the Jews had already agreed that anyone who confessed Jesus to be the Messiah would be put out of the synagogue" (9:22). Many of the Jewish authorities believed in Jesus but "they did not confess it, for fear that they would be put out of the synagogue; for they loved human glory more than the glory that comes from God" (12:42–43). And finally, in the Farewell discourses, Jesus warns his disciples that "They will put you out of the synagogue. Indeed, an hour is coming when those who kill you will think that by doing so they are offering worship to God" (16:2). Although "their" identity is not specified, an expulsion from the synagogue could only have been carried out by *Ioudaioi*.

These three passages have been construed by J. L. Martyn and the many scholars who followed him as references to the historical experience of the "Johannine community."[40] But whether we read these passages as primarily rhetorical or as a direct reference to a past trauma, the exclusion implied by the term *aposynagogos* cements the fear of the Jews that the Gospel is attempting to inculcate.

The Rhetoric of Repetition

Finally, it must be noted that the sheer repetition of *hoi Ioudaioi*, seventy times in this Gospel, coupled with the predominance of the passages that reflect a hostile stance, contributes to the rhetorical force of John's usage, and the creation of a rhetorical chasm between Christ-confessors and *Ioudaioi*. The impact of this repetition may be lost on those who read the Gospel piecemeal, but it would surely have been felt by those who were listening to the entire Gospel being read or recited aloud, as I imagine our Alexandra would have done in the agora.

Summary

The division of verses among neutral, positive, and hostile is summarized in Figure 4.1. But this chart does not tell the whole story. The hostile verses, in particular, are embedded in lengthy narrative or discursive contexts that contribute to the overall characterization of or stance towards the *Ioudaioi*, whereas the other usages are primarily short references, with the exception of chapter 11. In addition, the *Ioudaioi* are associated with other concepts or terms that further convey a negative stance.

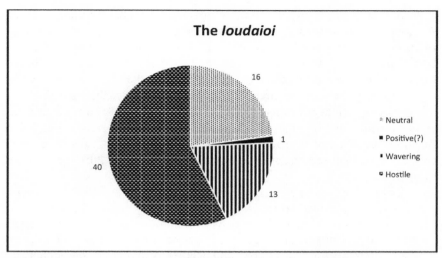

Figure 4.1. Occurrences of *Ioudaios/Ioudaioi* in the Gospel of John

WIDENING THE CIRCLE

The survey thus far shows that the term *Ioudaios/Ioudaioi* is not used mono-lithically simply to denote Jesus's opponents. This usage might then suggest that John's rhetoric would impress Alexandra and the rest of his audience with the diversity among the *Ioudaioi* in their response to Jesus.[41] Neverthe-less, the overall impression is negative. John's depictions of the *Ioudaioi* provide narrative support for the claim that "He came to what was his own, and his own people did not accept him" (1:11). This is not only because the majority of references are hostile, as are virtually all of the exchanges between Jesus and the wavering Jewish crowds. The negative portrayal of the *Ioudaioi* is evident in three more subtle ways: the blurring of boundaries among various Jewish subgroups; the association of the *Ioudaioi* with the negative aspects of the world (cosmos); and the Gospel's ambivalence about Jesus's own status as a *Ioudaios*.

Are there Subgroups among the *Ioudaioi*?

Like the Synoptic evangelists, John knows that the first-century *Ioudaioi* were not a monolithic undifferentiated group. Unlike the Synoptics, John does not refer to Sadducees or scribes,[42] but he frequently refers to Pharisees (on their own: 1:24; 3:1; 4:1; 7:47; 8:13; 9:13; 9:15; 9:40; 11:46; 12:19; 12:42) and chief priests (on their own: 12:10; 18:35; 19:6; 19:15; 19:21), oc-casionally in combination (7:32; 7:45; 11:47; 11:57; 18:3).

Nevertheless, these groups are not clearly differentiated from one another. At several points, for example, "the Pharisees" give way to "the Jews," thereby blurring the distinctions between these groups. The interrogation of the man born blind in John 9 provides a good example. In 9:15, "the Pharisees . . . began to ask him how he had received his sight." In 9:16, the Pharisees are divided as to whether Jesus comes from God, with some of the Pharisees doubting this possibility while others seem ready to accept it. In 9:18, however, it is the Jews who do not believe the son's testimony that he had been born blind. The functional equation of Pharisees and Jews is evident in 12:42, which refers to the fear of the Pharisees in the same way as 7:13, 19:38, and 20:19 refer to fear of the Jews.

In 19:14–15 a similar pattern occurs with respect to the priests. In 19:14, Pilate said to the Jews, "Here is your King!" "They"—that is, the Jews— "cried out, 'Away with him! Away with him! Crucify him!' Pilate asked them, 'Shall I crucify your King?' The chief priests answered, 'We have no king but the emperor.'" Had John intended to differentiate the authorities from the Jews as a whole, as some argue, he could easily have referred to the former as leaders of the Jews, a term he uses in 3:1 to describe Nicodemus.[43]

The *Ioudaioi*, the People, and the World

The differentiation among the *Ioudaioi*, the "people," and the "crowds" is also blurred in many passages. This blurring extends the rhetoric of vituperation beyond the *Ioudaios* passages as such. In John 6, for example, Jesus's interactions are primarily with "a" or "the" crowd to whom he feeds bread and fish. The metaphor of the manna, which dominates this interaction, indicates that these people are *Ioudaioi*. John 6:31 acknowledges this explicitly, as the crowd (ὁ ὄχλος) says: "Our ancestors ate the manna in the wilderness; as it is written, 'He gave them bread from heaven to eat'" (6:24).

In John 7, the people in the Temple area at the time of the Feast of Tabernacles are also referred to as the crowd (ὁ ὄχλος; e.g., 7:20, 31, 32, 40, 43) and the *Ioudaioi* (7:11; 15). During this exchange, Jesus accuses the crowd of the actions that elsewhere are associated with the *Ioudaioi*. In 7:19, Jesus declares: "Did not Moses give you the law? Yet none of you keeps the law. Why are you looking for an opportunity to kill me?" The reference to Moses shows that the crowd are *Ioudaioi*, and the reference to killing Jesus clearly has its antecedent in 5:18, which continues to be Jesus's frame of reference in speaking to the crowd in 7:21–24:

> I performed one work, and all of you are astonished. Moses gave you circumcision (it is, of course, not from Moses, but from the patriarchs), and you circumcise a man on the sabbath. If a man receives circumcision on the sabbath in

order that the law of Moses may not be broken, are you angry with me because I healed a man's whole body on the sabbath? Do not judge by appearances, but judge with right judgment.

In 11:42, Jesus prays to God for Lazarus's healing "for the sake of the crowd [διὰ τὸν ὄχλον] standing here." The chapter as a whole specifies that those who came to mourn with Mary and Martha were *Ioudaioi* (11:19). Verse 12:9 refers to "the great crowd of the Jews" who learned that Jesus was dining with the Bethany siblings.

The world. Finally, there is partial overlap between the *Ioudaioi* and "the world," ὁ κόσμος.[44] The world is often a spatial category, as in 1:9–10a, which refer to the true light coming into the world (see also 9:32; 9:39; 10:36; 13:1; 16:28; 17:5; 17:18; 17:24; 21:25). Other possible examples are 3:19, which refers to the light that has come into world, and 6:14, which refers to the "prophet who is to come into the world" (see also 11:27; 12:25).

"World" can also refer to humankind, as in 1:29, in which John the Baptist welcomes Jesus as "the Lamb of God who takes away the sin of the world," and in 3:16, which attributes Jesus's death to God's love for the world (see also 3:17, 4:42; 6:33; 6:51; 7:4; 8:12; 8:26; 12:19; 17:18; 17:23; perhaps 9:5 though this has a spatial connotation as well). In these verses, "world" is a neutral and generalizing term. Elsewhere, however, the world is portrayed negatively. The world hates Jesus (7:7) and its works are evil (7:7).

The relationship between Jesus and the world is ambiguous. On the one hand, the Prologue states that Jesus, as the *Logos*, was involved in the creation of the world, and was sent into the world in order to save it. On the other hand, Jesus sometimes strongly differentiates himself from the world (8:23). His kingdom is not of this world (18:36) but he has conquered the "ruler of this world" (12:31; 14:30–31; 16:11; 16:33). In the future, the world will not see Jesus but the disciples will (14:19; 14:22). Jesus does not give as the world does (14:27); furthermore, the world does not know God (17:25; cf. 16:8; 14:17) and hates those who believe (15:18).

The disciples too are separate from the world: "If the world hates you, be aware that it hated me before it hated you. If you belonged to the world, the world would love you as its own. Because you do not belong to the world, but I have chosen you out of the world—therefore the world hates you" (15:18–19). While the disciples mourn Jesus, the world will rejoice, yet in the end, the disciples' pain will turn to joy (16:20–21). Indeed, "those who love their life lose it, and those who hate their life in this world will keep it for eternal life" (12:25). The disciples are sharply distinguished from "the world" in Jesus's prayer (John 17). God gave Jesus the disciples "from the world" (17:6); he asks on their behalf, not on behalf of the world (17:9). Like Jesus, they do not belong in the world (17:13–16) but unlike Jesus they must remain in the world, and for that reason require divine protection from the "evil one" (17:11; 17:15).

These passages are vague and open-ended, without a concrete referent for "world." But some verses invite an identification of the world as the *Ioudaioi*. In 12:19, the Pharisees lament: "You see, you can do nothing. Look, the world has gone after him!" Even more explicit is 18:20, in which Jesus tells Pilate: "I have spoken openly to the world; I have always taught in synagogues and in the temple, where all the Jews come together. I have said nothing in secret."

Finally, the idea that the believers need protection from the "evil one" (ἐκ τοῦ πονηροῦ; 17:15) or the "ruler of this world" (ὁ ἄρχων τοῦ κόσμου; 12:31, 14:30, 16:11) recalls 8:44, in which Jesus tells the Jews that they have the devil as their father. While it might seem appropriate for Jesus to ask God to protect believers from evil spirits, it may well be, as 16:2 implies, that they truly need protection from the Jews, who are set to persecute them as they did Jesus.

The association of *Ioudaioi* with what is negative about the world amplifies the overall hostile characterization of the *Ioudaioi* in the Gospel narrative, just as their association with the "people" and the "crowd" magnifies their role in the Gospel as a whole.

IS JESUS A *IOUDAIOS*?

As we have seen, John portrays Jesus and his disciples as living in Jewish areas, engaging primarily, though not exclusively, with other Jews, observing the Jewish festivals and participating in Jewish practices. For some commentators, this point undermines or at least softens the Gospel's anti-Judaism. After all, Jesus's closest followers and associates were Jewish!

It is true, of course, that John would have looked positively on Jews who, like the disciples, committed themselves to believing in and following Jesus. But this implies that Jews are only good if they accept John's perspective on Jesus's importance for humankind, which, as we have seen, includes the claim that believers in Jesus have replaced the Jews as God's covenantal partner. In John's rhetoric of binary opposition, anyone who becomes a follower, whether Jew or pagan, is no longer identified a *Ioudaios* because for John the *Ioudaioi* are those who reject the Gospel's claims about Jesus, belief, eternal life, and covenantal relationship with God. Therefore the fact that Jesus's earliest followers were ethnically Jewish does not mitigate the Gospel's anti-Judaism.

In support of this point, it is important to note that the disciples themselves—the role models for audience identification—are never referred to as *Ioudaioi*. This point in itself rhetorically implies that the disciples are *not* *Ioudaioi* and, therefore, that there must be another category that covers those who engage in Jewish behaviors and yet do not belong to the category of *Ioudaioi* as such. This idea seems illogical from a narrative perspective. But in the context of the Gospel's rhetoric, it makes perfect sense. For John, the boundary between *Ioudaioi* and not-*Ioudaioi* is not ethnicity, genealogy, or ritual practice, but belief in Jesus as Messiah and Son of God. This is amply demonstrated by the use of the term *Ioudaioi* to refer to Jesus's enemies and the absence of the term for those who follow Jesus. °

Jesus himself, though surely a Jew, is called a *Ioudaios* only in 4:9, in which the Samaritan woman remarks on the unusual fact that Jesus, as a Jew, is asking her, a Samaritan woman, for a drink. This remark shows that in the Gospel's social world, someone who is not a *Ioudaios* herself would categorize Jesus as a *Ioudaios* and judge his behavior on that basis: "How is it that you, a Jew, ask a drink of me, a woman of Samaria?" This category accords with those elements of the narrative that show Jesus as behaving like a *Ioudaios* with respect to the festivals and in other ways.

In his conversation with the Samaritan woman, Jesus does not explicitly deny that he is a *Ioudaios*. He does, however, reframe his identity in Christological terms: "If you knew the gift of God, and who it is that is saying to you, 'Give me a drink,' you would have asked him, and he would have given you living water" (4:10). The Samaritan woman does not quite grasp this point, for she continues to view him as a *Ioudaios* in her question about the locus of worship: "Our ancestors worshiped on this mountain, but you say that the place where people must worship is in Jerusalem" (4:20). Jesus again corrects her by redirecting the conversation away from his putative identity as a *Ioudaios* to a prophecy of where true worship will occur in the future: neither Gerizim, the mountain holy to the Samaritans, nor Zion, the mountain holy to the *Ioudaioi* (4:21). In this way, the exchange demonstrates both Jesus's Jewish origins and his transcendence of that identity.

The titulus that Pilate insists on placing on the cross, identifying Jesus as king of the Jews, walks the same fine line (18:33, 39; 19:3, 14, 19). While it is true that historically the Jews had some kings who were not ethnically Jewish, the titulus testifies to Pilate's identification of Jesus as a *Ioudaios*. This had already been implied in Pilate's reference to the Jews as Jesus's own nation (18:35) and his subsequent, but short-lived, insistence that the Jews take him and crucify him themselves (19:6). The chief priests reject this association, however, and demand that Pilate rephrase: "Do not write, 'The King of the Jews,' but, 'This man said, I am King of the Jews'" (19:21). In this they are mistaken: the Johannine Jesus never made this claim. By this point in the story, our Alexandra, and other members of the Gospel's extradiegetic audience surely understand that

° Not really correct, as per chapts. 11, 12 (there is ambiguity as to whether "many" of the *Ioudaioi* continue as believers)

"King of the Jews" falls far short of describing Jesus's true identity. The entire episode, far from fixing Jesus as a *Ioudaios*, testifies to Jews' utter rejection of Jesus, and Pilate's complete misunderstanding of who he really is.

One could argue, of course, that the absence of *Ioudaios/Ioudaioi* as an unambiguous label for Jesus or his disciples simply shows that John, and his audience, took their Jewishness for granted. This seems unlikely, however, in light of the overwhelmingly negative connotations of *Ioudaioi* throughout the Gospel.

VITUPERATION AND EMOTION

John's rhetoric of vituperation turns *Ioudaios/Ioudaioi* into a label for the opponents of Jesus and, by extension, the enemies of the disciples and all later Christ-believers. In this sense, the Gospel conforms to the conventions of classical rhetoric, in which vituperation served precisely to establish clear sides in a given debate.[45] John's vituperation of the *Ioudaioi* would therefore signal to listeners experienced in the art of listening that the *Ioudaioi* are the enemies of Jesus and all who believe in him.

The conventional use of vituperation to differentiate the two sides in a debate has led some to argue that, in classical rhetoric, vituperation was not intended to arouse a negative emotive response on the part of the listener. Thomas Conley, for example, describes vituperation as a "standard aspect of the game of politics; it was not an attempt to arouse the audience's emotions, but . . . a *performance* of communal values."[46] Luke Timothy Johnson agrees, stating that "the slander of the NT is typical of that found among rival claimants to a philosophical tradition and is found as widely among Jews as among other Hellenists . . . the way the NT talks about Jews is just about the way all opponents talked about each other back then."[47] Indeed, Johnson describes the New Testament anti-Jewish slander as "remarkably mild" in comparison with other ancient texts.[48] The important thing about the slander is that it identified the opponent *qua* opponent.[49] Johnson attributes the vituperation in John and other New Testament texts to the gap in power between the "messianists" and the Jews. Some "non-messianist" Jews, Johnson notes, had a hand in executing Jesus and persecuting the leaders of the movement. Whether this is a factual rendition is irrelevant; what matters is that for "messianists," it is the "non-messianist" Jews who were to blame.[50] In such circumstances, Johnson implies, slander on the part of the persecuted party was only natural and does not necessarily express the hatred that we normally associate with the terms anti-Judaism and anti-Semitism.

Whether John's vituperative rhetoric had emotional force for its historical first-century audience is not possible to determine. If Johnson is right, our fictional Alexandra would have understood that the Gospel's hostile comments about the *Ioudaioi* were not meant to condemn them but simply to identify them as opponents in a debate. But we should hesitate before subscribing to the view that convention and emotion are mutually exclusive. If slander and blame can be conventional and connotative rather than denotative, it does not necessarily follow that audiences, then and since, would not respond emotionally. The reception history of John's Gospel suggests that, on the contrary, its depiction of the *Ioudaioi* could indeed arouse strong negative emotions and be used to justify violence against real live *Ioudaioi*, Jews.[51] This is not to say that the Gospel is *responsible* for the violence done in its name, only that its vituperative rhetoric made it amenable for those who hated and persecuted Jews.

JOHANNINE RHETORIC AND THE "PARTING OF THE WAYS"

The rhetorical analysis above suggests that the Gospel is advocating, at the very least, that Christ-confessors see themselves as separate from the *Ioudaioi*. This is not to say that Christ-confessors could not have been ethnically or genealogically Jewish, as were Jesus and the disciples. In undergoing the transformative process proposed and facilitated by the Gospel, however, they become children of God and thereby cease being *Ioudaioi* who, having rejected Christ, have the devil as their father.

Whether or not the Gospel is reflecting a process of self-identification that would ultimately create a "Christianity" that saw itself as completely outside and in some sense opposed to the *Ioudaioi* is impossible to say. But it is clear that for this Gospel, such a "parting" is not only imaginable but also essential. The divide that the Gospel constructs between believers and *Ioudaioi* marks a boundary wall that is built up brick by rhetorical brick. On one side of the wall stand the rhetorical "children of God" who are persuaded by the Gospel that belief in Jesus as Messiah, Son of God, and affiliation with others who believe the same, will fulfill the innate and universal desire for eternal life. On the other side stand the "children of Satan" whose rejection of this world-view is marked by their violence towards Jesus and his followers.

CONCLUSION

These remarks highlight that the distinction between rhetoric and reality that I have been maintaining thus far is easily blurred. The rhetorical "parting of the ways" may or may not have corresponded to the historical process by which Christianity eventually developed an identity separate from and over against Jewishness. It would be tempting for a minimalist scholar such as myself to refrain from drawing historical conclusions on the foundations of rhetorical or any other kind of analysis. It feels far safer to remain in the realm of literary theory, according to which all concepts, including Jesus, belief, *Ioudaioi*, and the "parting of the ways" remain the constructions by and of the Gospel. Is it not enough to point out the persuasive purposes which are served by these constructs? Jesus, for example, is obviously a *Ioudaios* and is seen as such by some of those he encounters (the Samaritan woman and Pilate, also the crowds who have no sense of his true identity) but he is constructed as a not-*Ioudaios* by this Gospel, which defines a *Ioudaios* as someone who should have accepted Jesus but did not.

At the same, given the central role that historical constructions have played in Johannine scholarship over the last half century or more, it is cowardly not to try. In the next section of this book, then, I address what George Kennedy referred to as the rhetorical situation that may have prompted the rhetorical aims and strategies described in the previous chapters.

In chapters 6 and 7, I will consider two models. The first is the so-called expulsion theory, based on the work of J. L. Martyn, according to which the Gospel is addressed to an already-existing Johannine community that had experienced a traumatic and forceful exclusion from the Jewish community—the "synagogue." The second is my own "propulsion" theory, according to which the Gospel of John constructed the rationale and foundation for the rejection of Jews and separation from Jewish identity as an attractive and indeed necessary move for its compliant audience.

Before doing so, however, I will turn to the difficult question of whether John's rhetorical *Ioudaioi* have a historical referent. Would Alexandra have associated this label with a particular group of real people in her own social milieu?

NOTES

1. The literature on this topic is vast, reflecting its importance in the field as much as the central role that the Fourth Gospel has played in the development of Christian theology, identity, and history. The following are some of the most influential works on this question: Culpepper, *Anatomy of the Fourth Gospel*; Urban C. von Wahlde, "The Johannine Jews: A Critical Survey," *New Testament Studies* 28, no. 1 (1982); Urban C. von Wahlde, "'The Jews' in the Gospel of John," *Ephemerides Theologicae Lovanienses* 76, no. 1 (2000): 30–55. Also: Malcolm F. Lowe, "Who Were the 'ΙΟΥΔΑΙΟΙ?'" *Novum Testamentum* 18, no. 2 (1976): 101–30; Philip F. Esler, "From *Ioudaioi* to

Children of God: The Development of a Non-Ethnic Group Identity in the Gospel of John," in *In Other Words: Essays on Social Science Methods and the New Testament in Honor of Jerome H. Neyrey*, ed. Jerome H. Neyrey et al. (Sheffield: Sheffield Phoenix Press, 2007), 106–36; Ruth Sheridan, "Issues in the Translation of Οι Ἰουδαῖοι in the Fourth Gospel," *Journal of Biblical Literature*, 2013, 671–95. Also Bennema, *Encountering Jesus*. General studies of the term are also numerous. Examples include Daniel R. Schwartz, *Judeans and Jews: Four Faces of Dichotomy in Ancient Jewish History* (Toronto: University of Toronto Press, 2014); Mason, "Jews, Judaeans, Judaizing, Judaism." Cynthia Baker, "A 'Jew' by Any Other Name?" *Journal of Ancient Judaism* 2, no. 2 (2011): 153–80; Seth Schwartz, "How Many Judaisms Were There?" *Journal of Ancient Judaism* 2, no. 2 (2011): 208–38; David Miller, "The Meaning of *Ioudaios* and Its Relationship to Other Group Labels in Ancient 'Judaism,'" *Currents in Biblical Research* 9, no. 1 (2010): 98–126; David M. Miller, "Ethnicity, Religion and the Meaning of *Ioudaios* in Ancient 'Judaism,'" *Currents in Biblical Research* 12, no. 2 (2014): 216–65; David M. Miller, "Ethnicity Comes of Age: An Overview of Twentieth-Century Terms for *Ioudaios*," *Currents in Biblical Research* 10, no. 2 (2012): 293–311. My own treatment can be found in the following publications: Adele Reinhartz, "John 8:31–59 from a Jewish Perspective," in *Remembering for the Future 2000: The Holocaust in an Age of Genocides*, ed. John K. Roth and Elisabeth Maxwell-Meynard, vol. 2 (London: Palgrave, 2001), 787–97; Adele Reinhartz, "'Jews' and Jews in the Fourth Gospel."

2. See chapter 5 for detailed discussion.

3. Most studies of the *Ioudaioi* begin by considering the different categories, though the categories, and, to some extent, the assignments of verses to categories, vary. Compare, for example, Ruben Zimmermann, "'The Jews': Unreliable Figures or Unreliable Narration?" in *Character Studies in the Fourth Gospel: Narrative Approaches to Seventy Figures in John*, ed. Steven A. Hunt, D. F. Tolmie, and Ruben Zimmermann (Grand Rapids: Eerdmans, 2016), 71–109; Stanley E. Porter, *John, His Gospel, and Jesus in Pursuit of the Johannine Voice* (Grand Rapids: William B. Eerdmans Publishing Company, 2015).

4. This sense is reinforced by 10:22, which refers to the holiday of Hanukkah or Dedication but without specifying that it is a festival "of the Jews:" "At that time the festival of the Dedication took place in Jerusalem. It was winter." The reference to the season, however, like the phrase "of the Jews" in the other examples, suggests an audience that does not have close familiarity with the festival. Otherwise the detail that "it was winter" would be extraneous.

5. Some of the material in this section was prepared for a meeting of the Colloquium Iohanneum, in Jerusalem, September 2017. It will appear in a chapter entitled "Of Mountains and Messiahs: John 4:19–23 and Divine Covenant" in the volume of papers from that conference.

6. Barrett, *The Gospel According to St. John*, 198.

7. Schnackenburg, *The Gospel According to St. John*, 1.435–36.

8. Michael Theobald, *Das Evangelium nach Johannes* (Regensburg: Friedrich Pustet, 2009), 324.

9. Edward W. Klink, *John* (Grand Rapids: Zondervan, 2016), 244.

10. Edwin D. Freed, "Did John Write His Gospel Partly to Win Samaritan Converts?" *Novum Testamentum* 12, no. 3 (1970): 241–56.

11. One may ask whether it is essential that 4:22 be consistent with its immediate narrative context. Our usual mode of synchronic reading is generally predicated on this assumption though in the case of the Gospels one might always resort to a source-critical solution in order to explain narrative inconsistencies. For a summary of positions, see Benny Thettayil, *In Spirit and Truth: An Exegetical Study of John 4:19–26 and a Theological Investigation of the Replacement Theme in the Fourth Gospel* (Leuven: Peeters, 2007), 79–105.

12. Gilbert Van Belle, "'Salvation Is from the Jews': The Parenthesis in John 4:22b," in *Anti-Judaism and the Fourth Gospel: Papers of the Leuven Colloquium, 2000*, ed. R. Bieringer, Didier Pollefeyt, and F. Vandecasteele-Vanneuville (Assen: Royal Van Gorcum, 2001), 373. For a detailed survey, see Van Belle, 371–76, and Thettayil, *In Spirit and Truth*, 79–105.

13. Rudolf Bultmann, *The Gospel of John: A Commentary* (Philadelphia: Westminster Press, 1971), 189–90, n. 6.

14. Anders Gerdmar speculates that Grundmann had access to the print proofs of Bultmann's commentary. Anders Gerdmar, *Roots of Theological Anti-Semitism: German Biblical Interpretation and the Jews, from Herder and Semler to Kittel and Bultmann* (Leiden: Brill, 2010), 394, 558, n. 100.

15. Gerdmar, 558. It is difficult to see, however, why Grundmann considered the references to "synagogue of Satan" in 2:9 and 3:9 as positive towards Jews. On Grundmann, see also Susannah Heschel, *The Aryan Jesus: Christian Theologians and the Bible in Nazi Germany* (Princeton: Princeton University Press, 2010), 106.

16. Susannah Heschel, "Nazifying Christian Theology: Walter Grundmann and the Institute for the Study and Eradication of Jewish Influence on German Church Life," *Church History: Studies in Christianity and Culture* 63, no. 4 (1994): 595, https://doi.org/10.2307/3167632. The anti-Semitic phrase seems to have been coined by Heinrich von Treitschke (1834–1896). It became the motto for the Nazi newspaper *Der Stürmer*.

17. Gerdmar, *Roots of Theological Anti-Semitism*, 463–64.

18. Van Belle, "Salvation is from the Jews," 370.

19. Schnackenburg, *The Gospel According to St. John*, 1.435.

20. Raymond Edward Brown, *The Gospel According to John*, 1.172.

21. Craig S. Keener, *The Gospel of John*, 610.

22. Reimund Bieringer and Didier Pollefeyt, "Wrestling with Johannine Anti-Judaism: A Hermeneutical Framework for the Analysis of the Current Debate," in *Anti-Judaism and the Fourth Gospel: Papers of the Leuven Colloquium, 2000*, ed. R. Bieringer, Didier Pollefeyt, and F. Vandecasteele-Vanneuville (Assen: Royal Van Gorcum, 2001), 36.

23. Johannes Beutler, *Judaism and the Jews in the Gospel of John* (Rome: Pontificio Istituto Biblico, 2006), 156.

24. Susan Hylen, *Imperfect Believers: Ambiguous Characters in the Gospel of John* (Louisville: Westminster John Knox Press, 2009), 129.

25. Christopher W. Skinner, *Characters and Characterization in the Gospel of John* (London: Bloomsbury T & T Clark, 2013), 108.

26. As Porter points out, different scholars have different ways of counting these "hostile" passages. Porter, *John, His Gospel, and Jesus in Pursuit of the Johannine Voice*, 156–57.

27. Thomas M. Conley, "Topics of Vituperation," 236. John Granger Cook, *The Interpretation of the New Testament in Greco-Roman Paganism* (Peabody: Hendrickson Publishers, 2003), 9. Cicero, *De Orat.* 2,43,182 and 2.11.45f. see also Ben Sirach 5:1106:17; 8:507; 28:14; 39:4.6.10.

28. Seán Freyne, "Vilifying the Other and Defining the Self: Matthew's and John's Anti-Jewish Polemic in Focus," in *"To See Ourselves as Others See Us": Christians, Jews, "Others" in Late Antiquity*, ed. Jacob Neusner, Ernest S. Frerichs, and Caroline McCracken-Flesher (Chico: Scholars Press, 1985), 118.

29. Freyne, 118.

30. Conley, "Topics of Vituperation," 232.

31. Conley, 234.

32. Donald Lemen Clark, *Rhetoric in Greco-Roman Education.* (Westport: Greenwood Pr., 1977), 198.

33. Conley, "Topics of Vituperation," 236.

34. Conley, 236–37.

35. Neyrey discusses praise and vituperation as represented in the Gospel itself, with the Jews and Jesus facing off as adversaries. The Jews deliver a vituperation about Jesus, which Jesus and the narrator counter with praise. Neyrey, "Encomium versus Vituperation," 530–31.

36. Freyne, "Vilifying the Other and Defining the Self," 131.

37. David Rensberger, "Anti-Judaism and the Gospel of John," in *Anti-Judaism and the Gospels*, ed. William R. Farmer (Harrisburg: Trinity Press International, 1999), 153.

38. Jerome H. Neyrey, *The Gospel of John in Cultural and Rhetorical Perspective* (Grand Rapids: William B. Eerdmans Pub. Co., 2009), 10.

39. John 8:44 generated considerable discussion by the Church fathers as to whether Jews were by their nature the children of the devil. For discussion, see Michael Azar, "The Eastern Orthodox Tradition, Jews, and the Gospel of John," in *The Gospel of John and Jewish Christian Relations,* ed. Adele Reinhartz, (Lanham: Lexington, 2018 forthcoming). April DeConick has argued that 8:44 should not be read appositionally as "you are of the father, the devil" but literally, as "you are from the father *of* the devil." This reading allows her to consider the differences between the "catholic" and "gnostic" readings of the verse, a conflict that she argues underlies 1 John. April DeConick, "Who Is Hiding in the Gospel of John? Reconceptualizing Johannine Theology and the Roots of Gnosticism," in *Histories of the Hidden God: Concealment and Revelation in Western Gnostic, Esoteric, and Mystical Traditions*, ed. April DeConick and Grant Adamson, Gnostica (Durham: Acumen, 2013), 13–29. DeConick's arguments are compelling. For our purposes, however, the differences between these two interpretations of 8:44 does not change the overall analysis concerning the rhetoric of binary opposition and the anti-Jewish stance of 8:42–44.

40. See chapters 6 and 7.

41. See, for example, Stephen Motyer, "Bridging the Gap: How Might the Fourth Gospel Help Us Cope with the Legacy of Christianity's Exclusive Claim over against Judaism?" in *The Gospel of John and Christian Theology*, ed. Richard Bauckham and Carl Mosser (Grand Rapids: William B. Eerdmans Pub., 2008), 143–67.

42. The exception is 8:3, in the story of the woman caught in adultery, which, however, is not originally Johannine. For discussion of the text-critical history, see Jennifer Wright Knust, "Early Christian Re-Writing and the History of the Pericope Adulterae," *Journal of Early Christian Studies* 14, no. 4 (2006): 485–536; Jennifer Wright Knust, "Too Hot to Handle? A Story of an Adulteress and the Gospel of John," in *Women of the New Testament and Their Afterlives*, ed. Christine E. Joynes (Sheffield: Sheffield Phoenix Press, 2009), 143–63.

43. See Urban C. von Wahlde, "The Terms for Religious Authorities in the Fourth Gospel: A Key to Literary-Strata?," *Journal of Biblical Literature* 98, no. 2 (1979): 231–53.

44. For detailed discussion of the congruence of the Jews and the world, see Lars Kierspel, *The Jews and the World in the Fourth Gospel: Parallelism, Function, and Context* (Tübingen: Mohr Siebeck, 2006).

45. Conley, "Topics of Vituperation," 236.

46. Conley, 236.

47. Johnson, "The New Testament's Anti-Jewish Slander," 429.

48. Johnson, 441.

49. Johnson, 433.

50. Johnson, 242.

51. This is acknowledged by Johnson, who also argues, however, that recognizing the conventional nature of New Testament vituperation can help to diffuse Christian anti-Semitism. Johnson, 421, 441.

Chapter Five

Rhetorical *Ioudaioi* and Real Jews

In writing his Gospel, John has constructed the *Ioudaioi*—as well as Jesus, the disciples, and all other characters—to suit an important rhetorical goal: to promote his audience's disaffiliation from those who do not believe and thereby to strengthen the mutual affiliation of those who do.

That *hoi Ioudaioi* refers to a group character that John has shaped to suit his literary, theological, and rhetorical purposes is broadly recognized.[1] Alan Culpepper, for example, comments that the Jews "represent the response to unbelief and rejection of Jesus's revelation . . . they legalistically maintain their observance of the festivals but do not recognize the reality they celebrate. At the festivals they are more concerned to catch Jesus in some offence. . . . Having now no king but Caesar, the world's king, they kill in order to defend their nation and their holy place."[2] Warren Carter refers to "deadly conflict" between the Johannine Jesus and the *Ioudaioi*.[3] Terence Donaldson comments that "John's indiscriminate and categorical use of 'the Jews'" in situations of conflict or opposition stands in sharp contrast to the more nuanced presentations of the Synoptics.[4]

As the previous chapters have demonstrated, John's rhetoric and its literary and symbolic universes can be analyzed in isolation from its historical context and from the history of its interpretation and reception.[5] Rudolf Bultmann famously advocated precisely that, in his insistence that the Gospel's *Ioudaioi* must be understood symbolically rather than historically.[6] But would a compliant audience member such as Alexandra have distinguished so systematically between rhetoric and reality?

There can be no doubt that John's stance towards the *Ioudaioi* contributed historically to Christians' attitudes towards Jews. In the discourse of Christian anti-Semitism, as Cynthia Baker notes, *"the Jews* functions foundationally as a kind of originary and constitutional alterity or otherness." She continues that the term:

> serves as the alpha to the Christian omega; the "Old" to the Christian "New"; the "particular" to the Christian "universal"; grounded and bound materialism to visionary, redeemed spirituality; deicide to self-sacrificial love—at best, the sainted or moribund "ancestor"; at worst, the evil "spawn of Satan" to a godly, good, and triumphantly immortal Christianity. *The Jews*, in other words, serves instrumentally to name the key *other* out of which *and* over against which the Christian *self* was and is constituted (emphasis in the original).[7]

Is the Gospel's rhetorical construction of the *Ioudaioi* culpable in the demonization of real Jews? The answer, in my view, is yes. By situating the story in a historical time and place, and populating it with undisputedly historical figures such as Caiaphas, Pilate, and Annas, John encourages Alexandra and others to postulate a historical referent for the *Ioudaioi* as well. The authoritative status that the Gospel acquired for Christians by virtue of its inclusion in the Christian scriptural canon extended not only to its uplifting Christology but also to its characterization of the *Ioudaioi*. Just as John's Christology could be taken as true, so too could its statements about the *Ioudaioi* be taken by hearers and readers as factual statements about the Jews among whom they lived. Of course, not every reading and every reader of the Gospel would take John's statements about the *Ioudaioi* as the literal truth about the Jews as a historical people. Many, perhaps most, faithful Christian readers of the Gospel, certainly since the mid-twentieth century, are not the thoroughly compliant readers that the implied author John might have hoped for, insofar as they give weight to the social and historical distance between John's time of writing and their own era.

Modern scholarship testifies to considerable concern about John's use of *Ioudaios/Ioudaioi*. This discomfort plays out in the ongoing debate about the referent and translation of the term *Ioudaios/Ioudaioi*. This is not to say that every entry into the debate is motivated by questions of anti-Judaism in the ancient world or today.[8] Nevertheless, the discussion as a whole is integrally related to scholars' judgments about John's attitudes towards Jews, and, often, to the scholars' own attitudes as well.

HISTORICAL REFERENTS

Many scholars have categorized and evaluated the different hypotheses concerning the historical identity of the *Ioudaioi*, often with the intention, explicit or implicit, of limiting its referent.[9] One strategy for mitigating the anti-Jewish potential of John's usage of *Ioudaios* is to limit its scope. The extensive use of *Ioudaios/Ioudaioi* in other ancient texts, such as the writings of Josephus, inscriptions, and papyri, supports the idea that *Ioudaios* was a widespread and well-known designation that had concrete meaning for those who used the term.[10] But some scholars argue that in the Johannine context *Ioudaios/Ioudaioi* does not denote the Jewish people as a whole but a specific subgroup.

Daniel Boyarin, for example, views the *Ioudaioi* as a group that originated in Judea. Some *Ioudaioi* may have migrated to areas outside of Judea, but they affiliated themselves ancestrally with the exiles who had returned from Babylonia in the fifth century BCE. The followers of Jesus, on the other hand, came from the residents who had stayed behind. These residents were not known as *Ioudaioi* (or, in Hebrew, *yehudim*), but as *'ammei ha'arets* (people of the land).[11] Those who had experienced exile in Babylon returned to the land with a sense of superiority over those who had remained. For Boyarin, the conflict in the Gospel of John is not between Jews and Christians, but between the *Ioudaioi* who trace their ancestry to the returnees from Babylonian exile, and the *'ammei ha'aretz* who believed Jesus to be the Messiah. This interpretation coheres with his overall view of the Gospel of John as a purely Jewish document, and the conflict it describes as an entirely inner-Jewish issue.[12]

Boyarin's theory is not implausible; the primary sources do bear witness to tensions between those who returned from the Babylonian exile and those who remained behind, as well as, in later periods, between some elite groups and the *'ammei ha'arets*.[13] But it is difficult to sustain the limited definition of John's *Ioudaioi* as the descendants of the Babylonian exiles when it comes to the Fourth Gospel. As we have seen, the Johannine *Ioudaioi* are directly connected to a range of other groups, including both the elite (the Pharisees, the chief priests), and the crowds of presumably *'ammei ha'arets* who debated Jesus's words among themselves at various feasts and festivals. In contrast, for example, to the Dead Sea community, who had distinctive beliefs and practices, John's *Ioudaioi*—authorities and crowds alike—shared the beliefs and behaviors such as a firm commitment to monotheism, an association with Abraham as the ancestral progenitor, the observance of the Sabbath and pilgrimage festivals, and a view of the Jerusalem Temple as the locus of the sacrificial cult.[14]

Cornelis Bennema too proposes a narrow referent for John's *Ioudaioi*. In his view, the Gospel applies the term to a particular religious group of Torah and Temple partisans that is not coextensive with the people as a whole, but constitutes a group alongside the Pharisees and chief priests, with whom they align against Jesus.[15] Urban von Wahlde, on the other hand, constructs the

Ioudaioi not alongside but precisely *as* the Jewish authorities, as distinct from the crowds. For support, he draws on John 11:49–52, in which the high priest Caiaphas provides the Council with a rationale for pursuing Jesus lest the "whole nation" be destroyed, as well as the role accorded to the chief priests in leading the call for Jesus's crucifixion (19:6).[16]

Stephen Motyer takes a multi-layered approach.[17] He distinguishes among three levels of meaning: a primary sense, according to which *Ioudaioi* refers to "those who identify themselves as Jews and adhere to the religion of Judea, whether living in Judea or not"; a derived reference, designating "adherents of the particularly strict, Torah- and Temple-centered religion found especially (but not exclusively) in Judea and Jerusalem"; and finally a derived metaphorical reference, according to which "'the Jews' stand for 'the world.'" Motyer specifies that the derived reference does not make *Ioudaioi* a synonym for Pharisees, although the Pharisees are the core and leading members of this group. Further, the metaphorical connotation does not supplant "the word's basic sense (it never comes to *mean* unbelievers), and only in the later stages of the narrative are examples found in which *Ioudaioi* clearly contributes a pejorative force *to* its co-text rather than merely deriving from it (e.g., 19:7, 38)."[18]

Stanley Porter dismisses the hypotheses proposed by other scholars, on the grounds that they "take a literalistic view and then read this throughout the entire Gospel and, as a result, condemn the biblical text."[19] Porter argues that "when the word group [*hoi Ioudaioi*] is used in John's Gospel, it has as its monosemous sense a group of people (two or more) who are to be identified by beliefs and practices, with the Jewish people as a religious-ethnic group." This usage is confirmed by references to Jewish festivals and practices, what we have called the neutral occurrences of the terms.[20]

Porter seems to opt for a generalized understanding of *Ioudaioi* as the Jewish people. At the same time, however, he argues, the sense of the term varies contextually.[21] The variations of meaning are signaled by the presence of the definite article. Porter argues that the definite article (*hoi*; "the") is a "structural indicator that has various contextually based functional uses. The article serves to define or disambiguate the sense relations of the words or phrases in construction with it." The definite article in the phrase *hoi Ioudaioi*—"the Jews"—far from signaling a generic sense, as in "all the Jews," actually means "these Jews," that is, these particular Jews in contrast to other Jews (e.g., the Pharisees) or other groups (e.g. the Gentiles).[22] For Porter, this linguistic analysis supplements the logical point that the *Ioudaioi* cannot possibly be generic given that Jesus and his disciples are also Jewish.[23]

In his conclusion, however, Porter appears to return to the monosemous sense with which he began: "In their opposition to Jesus, these opponents indicate a fundamental split between Judaism and what was to become Christianity, grounded in the language of the Gospel."[24] Yet this is precisely the point: that the Gospel uses a term that fundamentally denotes a monosemous group to denote the enemies of Jesus. Porter is explicitly motivated by the need to absolve the Gospel of anti-Judaism. He argues that those who claim that John is anti-Jewish are just as guilty of "abusing" the Gospel as are those who use John to justify anti-Judaism. In his view, the Gospel of John did not have strong anti-Jewish tendencies but "merely employed clear terms and used reasonable linguistic means to depict Jesus's opponents." [25] For Porter, then, the Jews' enmity towards Jesus may simply be historical fact. Nevertheless, declaring it so does not truly neutralize John's presentation of the Jews, which, whether historical or not, is nevertheless anti-Jewish in the sense that it has the potential to foster negative views of Jews.

Departing from the majority of Johannine scholars, Ruben Zimmermann resists the drive to pin John's *Ioudaioi* to one consistent meaning, sense, or referent.[26] After summarizing the various hypotheses, he proposes that we embrace the ambiguities and inconsistencies of the Gospel's use of *Ioudaioi* and ascribe them to "unreliable narration," and therefore to refrain from passing judgment on "the Jews."[27]

Zimmermann acknowledges that this vagueness may fail to satisfy. It is decidedly better, however, than an unambiguously anti-Jewish interpretation of "the Jews," which, he argues, has been the norm in the history of interpretation.[28] This comment suggests that Zimmermann does not view anti-Judaism as inherent in the Gospel's presentation of the *Ioudaioi*. Rather, anti-Judaism inheres in readers' interpretations; if we resist the temptation to harmonize or subsume the neutral and questioning uses under the negative or hostile ones, we will also avoid anti-Judaism.

Zimmermann and the other scholars mentioned above are correct that the Gospel uses *Ioudaioi* in a number of different ways. The term can refer to a group united by similar practices ("the festival of the Jews"), or it can be a means to differentiate the *Ioudaioi*, from the followers of John the Baptist (3:25) or from the Samaritans (4:9). Such variation, however, does not necessarily mean that the term as such refers to a particular, clearly differentiated historical subgroup. The term retains its generalized meaning even if a more specific nuance is foregrounded in a particular verse or passage, as when, for example, a specific Jew was discussing purification with the Baptist's disciples (3:25), or when the Jews who were interrogating the man born blind are also referred to as Pharisees (cf. 9:18). Taken together with the rhetorical blurring of distinctions outlined in chapter 4, these reflections support the views of those who argue for a generalized meaning.[29] They also, I would argue, justify the view that the Gospel is anti-Jewish in the sense that it fosters negative views of Jews as a group.

JEW? JUDEANS? JEWISH AUTHORITIES?
THE PROBLEM OF TRANSLATION

Closely related to the question of referent is the problem of translation.[30] Numerous factors affect translation choice, including the target audience (scholars, worshippers, or the general public), and one's philosophy of translation. As Steve Mason observes, "Every translator knows that there is no correct rendering for all conditions, and each of us is likely to make different choices at different times."[31] Whether we are aware of it or not, our translation choices have ideological implications that may override other considerations.[32]

In the face of both a generalized meaning and variations of emphasis, one possibility is to translate each occurrence contextually. Norman Beck suggests, for example, that one could use "they" in 2:18, "some people in the temple" in 2:20; and omit "Jew" or the textual variant "Jews" altogether in 3:25; similarly, one might opt for "the people from Jesus's home area" in 6:41, and "Jesus's enemies" in 19:38.[33] This approach falls short, however, because it dilutes the rhetorical force which in part depends upon the seventy-or-so-fold repetition of *Ioudaioi*. For this reason most prefer a uniform translation.

The default practice has been to use Jew/Jews as the translation for *Ioudaios/Ioudaioi*, as in the New Revised Standard Version. This default position has been challenged periodically since the 1970s, on both historical and ethical grounds. Historical issues focus primarily on the ways in which ancient Jews and other groups would have understood the designation. The ethical issues pertain to the impact that one translation or another might have on contemporary attitudes towards Jews.[34]

The complex and partial nature of the extant evidence makes it very difficult to determine how ancients would have understood this term. And while many continue to use "Jew" to translate *Ioudaios*, several scholars have mounted a case for "Judeans." Although some recent publications have adopted this usage,[35] the "best" translation of *Ioudaioi* remains a matter of debate. Despite the complexity of translation as an enterprise, as noted above, when it comes to John, the choice comes down to "Jew" or "Judean."[36] In what follows, I will briefly describe the case for "Judeans," before arguing in favor of using "Jews" uniformally to translate *Ioudaioi* . Finally, I will reflect on how this debate does, or does not, mesh with the rhetorical analysis undertaken in this book.

THE *IOUDAIOI* AS JUDEANS

The Greek *Ioudaios/Ioudaioi* was originally a primarily geographical term referring to residents of Judea. In a 1976 article, Malcolm Lowe argued that this geographical meaning remains primary in the Fourth Gospel. For that reason, *Ioudaios/Ioudaioi* should be translated "Judean/Judeans" throughout.[37] He accounted for exceptions, such as 6:4, which mentions a feast of the *Ioudaioi* that Jesus and thousands of others celebrate in the Galilee, and 6:41, 52, which refers to *Ioudaioi* who are living in the Galilee, on text-critical grounds.[38]

Other scholars note, however, that by the first century, non-geographical meanings had accreted. Josephus and other first-century authors used *Ioudaios/Ioudaioi* also to refer to those of Judean origin who now lived elsewhere; those who adhered to a particular ethno-political entity; and those who shared a common set of beliefs and practices. Nevertheless, some scholars continue to argue for "Judean" on various grounds.

Steve Mason argued that we must overcome our tendency to view "Judean" as a primarily geographical designation. Instead, Judean should be used consistently as the translation for *Ioudaios* in Josephus, in the Gospel of John, and indeed, in all ancient sources: "Just as 'Roman,' 'Egyptian,' and 'Greek' (etc.) had a wide range of associations beyond the geographical . . . so too 'Judaean' should be allowed to shoulder its burden as an ethnic term full of complex possibilities."[39] To support this position, he provides a succinct description of how Greek/Roman writers such as Strabo, Pliny, Tacitus, and Josephus understood the *Ioudaioi* empire-wide: "as a people connected with Jerusalem's laws and customs."[40]

In his influential 2007 article, Mason did not address directly the question of which English word comes closest to the complex meaning of the Greek term. In this article, however, it seems clear that he viewed "Jews" as incorrect. Despite the fact that it is etymologically derived from *Ioudaios*, Mason argued that the English word "Jew" disrupts the relationship with the land that is inherent in the term "Judean," because it does not sound like *Ioudaios* (presumably because of the absence of "d").[41] It seems that Mason discounted "Jew" because it does not evoke the geographical meaning of "Judean," while at the same time urging that "Judean" take on a meaning that goes far beyond geography. In his 2014 contribution to the Marginalia Forum on "Jews and Judeans," Mason clarified that in his view "'Jew' is *not incorrect*; it simply does not reflect as clearly the connection with place-bound identity that ancient writers assumed."[42]

Mason's 2007 article suggests another important reason for preferring Judean, beyond its resonances with "place-bound identity": the religious connotations of the word "Jew." To be sure, by the first century, the *Ioudaioi* are no longer merely the residents of a certain geographic area but members of an ethno-political entity. Although they share a set of ancestral traditions and customs involving priests, Temple, and sacrifices, and shared a number of foundational narratives (the Bible), the *Ioudaioi* did not constitute a religious community, because, according to Mason, religion, as a concept and as a type of institution, did not yet exist.[43] It is therefore misleading to use a term commonly associated with a religion—Judaism—to translate a term found in a text from the period prior to the time when "religion" first appeared.

A different argument for preferring Judean is put forward by Philip Esler. Esler argued that there is no persistence of identity between the *Ioudaioi* of John's time and the Jews of ours. In his view, the identity of the *Ioudaioi* of John is so different from the Jews of the modern period that only by "gross moral and intellectual confusion can we impute to the latter any responsibility to the former."[44]

Esler's analysis explicitly makes reference to the ethical issue, a matter that Mason and Lowe do not address. The ethical argument in favor of "Judeans" is articulated most succinctly in Frederick Danker's brief lexical note on the term *Ioudaios* in the third edition of the classic reference work *A Greek-English Lexicon of the New Testament and Other Early Christian Literature*. Danker commented that: "Incalculable harm has been caused by simply glossing *Ioudaios* with 'Jew,' for many readers or auditors of Bible translations do not practice the historical judgment necessary to distinguish between circumstances and events of an ancient time and contemporary ethnic-religious-social realities, with the result that anti-Judaism in the modern sense of the term is needlessly fostered through biblical texts."[45]

THE *IOUDAIOI* AS JEWS

Danker and Esler would argue that rendering *Ioudaioi* as "Judean" lessens the likelihood that readers of or listeners to the Fourth Gospel would absorb anti-Jewish or anti-Semitic sentiments. There is no evidence, however, that merely altering the translation would have this salutary effect. To my knowledge, no one has tested the hypothesis that using "Judeans" instead of "Jews" works to deflect attention from Jews as guilty of Jesus's death. Jews do not have to be present, physically or linguistically, in order for anti-Judaism to exist. °

Further, eliminating the "Jews" lets the Gospel of John off the hook for its role in the history of anti-Judaism and anti-Semitism. To be sure, using "Jews" risks perpetuating the rhetorical hostility of the Gospel itself. But to use "Judean" instead of "Jew" whitewashes the Gospel of John and relieves us of the difficult but necessary task of grappling with this Gospel in a meaningful way.

° Given the historical consequences of the translation "Jews," it just might be worth testing the hypothesis! (Why reject a hypothesis without testing it?)

As Amy-Jill Levine notes: "The Jew is replaced with the Judean, and thus we have a *Judenrein* ('Jew free') text, a text purified of Jews. . . . So much for the elimination of anti-Semitism by means of changing vocabulary."[46] Continuing to use "Jews" as a translation of *Ioudaioi* allows readers to see the link between the Johannine Jews that are vilified by the Fourth Gospel and those who fell victim to anti-Semitism that arose out of long habits of vilification. °

Finally, to use "Judeans" for all occurrences of *Ioudaioi* writes the Jews out of both the history and the geography of Israel. To be sure, not all advocates for the Johannine "Judeans" deny the continuity between the ancient *Ioudaioi* and rabbinic, medieval, and modern Jews.[47] And some of those who deny such continuity, such as Esler, do so in the hope that anti-Semitism will thereby be alleviated. The argument as such, however, is problematic. Denying the connection between modern Jews (and medieval and rabbinic Jews) and ancient *Ioudaioi* makes it difficult to account for the importance of Jerusalem, the Temple, the Pharisees, and other staples of ancient "Judaeanism" in the construction of Jewish identity. Furthermore, how might we account for the actual existence of Jews from late antiquity to the present? Where did they come from and how did they come into being?

Bruce Malina, who argued strongly against using "Jew" to translate *Ioudaios*, believed he knew the answer: "Most of those Central European Jews and hence most U.S. Jews from Central Europe are descended from Khazars, a people who accepted the Jewish religion in the eighth century AD. They did so, it seems, to be unencumbered by either Byzantine Christendom or Islam. . . . Thus most U.S. Jews are essentially Khazar Americans rather than "Jewish" Americans. The same is true of the majority of people living in the Jewish State."[48] The Khazar theory, however, has long been debunked as anti-Semitic fiction. Indeed, Malina's writings on the Gospel of John and ancient Christianity have numerous dubious, offensive, and extraneous comments about modern American Jews as well as Israelis.[49] Such comments discredit the scholarly legitmacy of his publications on John and the Jews.

I stress that the other proponents of the Judean translation discussed here do not follow Malina's lead in using this translation issue as a way of denying Israel's legitimacy and disparaging Jews. But the fact that Malina bases his argument about modern Jews and Israel on the same sorts of arguments made by Lowe, Mason, and Esler illustrates the potential negative implications of denying that ancient Judeans were also Jews. As Jonathan Klawans has bluntly stated,

I suppose one could—and perhaps should—always be mindfully skeptical about the historical truth of any claim of descent. But let's face it: there are two ideologies that are well-served by disconnecting contemporary "Jews" from ancient "Judeans." The first ideology is anti-Zionism and the second is anti-Semitism.

° Not a sound scholarly basis for choosing the translation of a word in an ancient text. (See note, next page)

(To be clear: to my perception, neither ideology is necessarily at work in any of these academic debates, but that's not the point.) While I grant, in theory, that these two ideologies are potentially separable, the fact is they often bleed one into the other, precisely on the issue discussed: one can more easily oppose the existence of a Jewish state of Israel by denying any connections that contemporary "Jews" claim to those "Judeans" who lived there in the Roman era. (To wit, the Khazar hypothesis.)[50]

Whether it is wrong to speak about religion in antiquity, as Mason asserts, is a matter of debate.[51] Nevertheless, Mason is surely correct that *Ioudaios* was a complex term that carried ethnic, political, cultic, and many other dimensions. But the question remains: Why broaden the referent of "Judean" from its primary geographical meaning when there is a perfectly good English word— Jew—ready to hand? Mason and others seem to assume that Jewish identity is primarily a religious identification. But, as Leora Batnitzky has shown, "Judaism" is not, and has never, been comfortably defined as a "religion."[52]

Population surveys and other studies have demonstrated what is or should be obvious to anyone who is Jewish or who knows Jews: many Jews do not understand their Jewishness in religious terms at all. While all would agree that Judaism broadly includes elements that we construe as religious (belief in one God, sacred scripture, synagogues, prayer, and so on), many strongly self-identified Jews do not believe in God, never attend synagogue, and do not participate in Jewish worship or any form of Jewish practice. For some, identity is based on allegiance to family and to Jewish history; to others, on cultural elements such as foods, songs, and politics (e.g., the Jewish Labor Bund). With the possible exception of certain ultra-Orthodox groups, it would be difficult to find many Jews who share precisely the same understanding of what it means to be a Jew, or for whom that understanding remains stable throughout their entire lives. Indeed, Jewish identity includes the same elements—ethnic, political, cultural, genealogical, and, yes, geographical—that, in Mason's view, are conveyed by the Greek terminology.[53]

Ironically, the usage of Judean, intended to be more precise, often introduces vagueness, ambiguity, and even confusion. To describe Josephus as a Judean historian, or the revolt of 66–74 as the Judean War, strikes me as excessively narrow given the broad importance of the event and its chronicler for Jewish history. Nevertheless, such usage, in my view, is acceptable, given that Josephus lived for the most part in Judea and the first Jewish revolt against Rome was centered in Judea. But on what grounds is Philo of Alexandria a Judean philosopher?[54] How did the Hebrew Bible become the Judean Scriptures and Judaism the Judean religion?[55] And why, *pace* Mason, refer to Josephus's grand history of the Jews as "The Judean Antiquities" when the narrative covers far more geographical and chronological ground?[56]

[Handwritten marginal note:] The main problem: For the term "Jews," residents of ancient Judea is a (genuine but) fairly minor denotation, and it doesn't "work" when that specific denotation is called for in John's Gospel (several times). For the term "Judeans," residents of ancient Judea is a primary, major denotation and it works very well in those same passages

As Daniel Schwartz notes, both terms, Judean and Jew, are useful for translations and studies of the ancient world:

> Thus, for example, when we wish to write about the first-century rebellion against Rome that culminated with the destruction of the Second Temple of Jerusalem, once we note that it was in Judea . . . it is not difficult to decide to write about it as a Judean revolt, and about the rebels as "Judeans." In contrast, when we want to write about those ancient Judeans' cousins in Alexandria or Sardis or Rome, who did not participate in the rebellion, and whose synagogues, and right to live according to their ancestral traditions, continued to enjoy Roman protection, it is easy to decide that "Jews" is more appropriate.[57]

With respect to the Gospel, however, there is no perfect solution to the translation conundrum. As Tina Pippin has noted,

> If one changes the literal meaning of *Ioudaioi* to refer to Judeans or Jewish religious authorities, then one dilutes the force of the ethnic verbal warfare, and ignores that it was a warfare that turned into so much more than a first-century dispute. If one keeps the literal "the Jews" in the English translation, then one is perpetuating the hateful polemic.[58]

One option is to use the Greek term without translating. But in most cases, some sort of translation is called for. If so, "Jews" remains the most appropriate translation of *Ioudaioi*, as it reflects a complex construction of identity that parallels, even if it cannot precisely mirror, the ethnic-political, social, religious, and emotional identity to which the ancient term *Ioudaios* refers.[59]

CONCLUSION

The questions concerning the historical referent(s) and appropriate translation of *hoi Ioudaioi*, while important elements of the scholarly conversation, are not, in my view, germane to understanding the Gospel's *Ioudaioi*. As we have seen, the term does not correspond in a straightforward manner to a single referent; in some cases the referent is obviously the Jewish authorities or perhaps the people of Judea but in other cases it seems to be the people as a whole. Furthermore, there are no real traits associated with the Jews other than holidays and practices attributed to them, their lack of faith, their propensity for murder, and their association with Satan. These comments suggest that the Johannine *Ioudaioi* are not a specific historical group but rather a rhetorical and theological category. Although they have some affinities to "real" Jews their main importance lies in their role in the Gospel's rhetoric and theology. ❧

* Major reason: the denotation *residents of Judea* clashes with the term's more ~~important~~ portant denotation, *residents and members of the faith community of the (entire) Holy Land* (including Galilee, Idumea, Perea). (Cf. 7:1, 11:7-8; also 3:25-6; the first 2 passages clearly ref. to the Ioudaioi who reside in

The fact that Jews existed in the real world of the first century means, however, that in constructing its hermeneutic or theological Jew, the Gospel also creates distance between its ideal or intended audience and any Jews, or forms of Jewishness known to its real audiences.[60] In that sense, the Gospel rhetorically constructs a high wall between Christ-followers and *Ioudaioi* that had implications for the historical relationships between Christians and Jews over the course of millennia.

We can admire John's rhetorical impulse, and acknowledge how powerfully that impulse has shaped his story of Jesus's words and deeds, his friends, and his enemies. We can also accept that he himself is a construct of the Gospel—or rather, my own construct of the Gospel's implied author—and the same is true of Alexandra and other members of his implied audience. And yet the Gospel exists as a real object, or rather, hundreds, thousands, or more, real objects, and has done so at least since the mid-second century, when the Gospel was read and commented on by Heracleon and Origen.[61] As such, it must have had a real audience to which it was meaningful and persuasive. Who might our fictional compliant reader or hearer, Alexandra, have been in real life? With this question, we turn now to the rhetorical situation that might be constructed from John's account.

NOTES

1. Ultimately this is true of all the Gospel's characters. See Skinner, *Characters and Characterization in the Gospel of John*. See also, with regard to Christianity more generally, Boyarin, *Border Lines*, 30.

2. Culpepper, *Anatomy of the Fourth Gospel*, 129.

3. Warren Carter, *John: Storyteller, Interpreter, Evangelist* (Peabody: Hendrickson, 2007), 70.

4. Terence L. Donaldson, *Jews and Anti-Judaism in the New Testament: Decision Points and Divergent Interpretations* (Waco: Baylor University Press, 2010), 87.

5. The distinction between history of interpretation and reception history is understood differently by different scholars. On any definition, there is a fine line between them, and, potentially, considerable overlap as the argument can be made that every reuse of a text is implicitly an interpretation, whatever the main goal of the reuser happens to be. Here I wish only to distinguish between scholarly commentaries and analyses on the one hand, and, for example, the ongoing use of imagery associating Jews with the devil on white-supremacist websites. For discussion of the differences between interpretation and reception histories, see Brennan Breed, "Biblical Reception History: A Dangerous Supplement," October 2014, http://www.bibleinterp.com/articles/2014/10/bre388022.shtml.

6. Rudolf Karl Bultmann, *The Gospel of John A Commentary* (Oxford: B. Blackwell, 1971), 647, 655, and passim. Bultmann's analysis is problematic, however, for its anti-Jewish implications. For Bultmann the Jews represent the unbelieving world.

The term bears no relation to a particular historical group but rather refers to an existential rejection of Christ. But at the same time, he did not include Pilate, who is also of this world, in this category. For detailed discussion of the "world" and the *Ioudaioi,* see Lars Kierspel, *The Jews and the World in the Fourth Gospel: Parallelism, Function, and Context,* Wissenschaftliche Untersuchungen zum Neuen Testament 2, Reihe 220 (Tübingen: Mohr Siebeck, 2006).

7. Cynthia M. Baker, *Jew,* Key Words in Jewish Studies, 8 (New Brunswick: Rutgers University Press, 2017), 4.

8. Steve Mason, for example, denies that ethical concerns form any part of his own discussion of the term. See Reinhartz et al., "Jew and Judean," 13. Esler, by contrast, explicitly refers to the ethical dimension of the debate. Esler, "From *Ioudaioi* to Children of God," 110.

9. Here we may contrast Donaldson, who summarizes but does not pronounce on the matter, with Porter, who summarizes and then concludes that the major earlier views are all inadequate in that they are not comprehensive in scope, they ignore linguistic distinctions, and they are literalistic. Donaldson, *Jews and Anti-Judaism in the New Testament: Decision Points and Divergent Interpretations,* 108; Porter, *John, His Gospel, and Jesus in Pursuit of the Johannine Voice.* The most comprehensive discussion can still be found in R. Bieringer, Didier Pollefeyt, and F. Vandecasteele-Vanneuville, eds., *Anti-Judaism and the Fourth Gospel: Papers of the Leuven Colloquium, 2000* (Assen: Royal Van Gorcum, 2001). Also still relevant is the distinction between sense and reference made by John Ashton, "The Identity and Function of The Ἰουδαῖοι in the Fourth Gospel," *Novum Testamentum Novum Testamentum* 27, no. 1 (1985): 40–75. For other studies, see note 1 in chapter 4.

10. See, for example, the many primary sources cited in Daniel R. Schwartz, *Judeans and Jews.*

11. In other words, Common Judaism as described by Sanders, *Judaism Practice and Belief.*

12. Boyarin, "The IOUDAIOI of John and the Prehistory of Judaism," 216–39.

13. Dalit Rom-Shiloni, *Exclusive Inclusivity: Identity Conflicts between the Exiles and the People Who Remained (6th-5th Centuries BCE)* (London: Bloomsbury Publishing, 2015).

14. Sanders, *Judaism: Practice and Belief.*

15. Cornelis Bennema, "The Identity and Composition of Οι Ιουδαιοι in the Gospel of John," *Tyndale Bulletin* 60, no. 2 (2009): 239–63.

16. Von Wahlde, "The Johannine 'Jews,'"33–60.

17. Stephen Motyer, *Your Father the Devil: A New Approach to John and the Jews* (Carlisle: Paternoster Press, 1997), 46–57.

18. Motyer, 56–57.

19. Porter, *John, His Gospel, and Jesus,* 173.

20. Porter, 159, 163.

21. Porter, 160.

22. Porter, 161.

23. Stanley E. Porter, ed., *The Messiah in the Old and New Testaments* (Grand Rapids: William B. Eerdmans, 2007), 162. Porter does not comment on the fact that except for 4:9, *Ioudaios* is never used for Jesus or his disciples.

24. Porter, *John, His Gospel, and Jesus*, 173.

25. Porter, 173.

26. On the distinction between sense and referent and their relevance for this issue, see Ashton, "The Identity and Function of The Ἰουδαῖοι in the Fourth Gospel."

27. Ruben Zimmermann, "'The Jews': Unreliable Figures or Unreliable Narration?" 109.

28. Zimmermann, 109.

29. Graham Harvey refers to "All Jews, everywhere at any time." Graham Harvey, *The True Israel: Uses of the Names Jew, Hebrew, and Israel in Ancient Jewish and Early Christian Literature* (Boston: Brill Academic, 2001), 97. See also S. G. Wilson, *Related Strangers: Jews and Christians, 70–170 C.E.* (Minneapolis: Fortress Press, 1995), 76; Hakola, *Identity Matters*, 231.

30. The translation problem plays out differently in different languages. The discussion in this chapter pertains solely to English. See, briefly, the comments by Jonathan Klawans in Reinhartz et al., "Jew and Judean," 38.

31. Mason in Reinhartz et al., "Jew and Judean," 11.

32. On the ideological implications, see Sheridan 2013 and Forum; Annette Reed, Forum.

33. Norman A. Beck, *Mature Christianity: The Recognition and Repudiation of the Anti-Jewish Polemic of the New Testament* (Selinsgrove: Susquehanna University Press, 1985), 290–310.

34. Malcolm Lowe claims credit for initiating the proposal that "Judean" is a better translation for *Ioudaios* as used in John. See Lowe, "Who Were the IOYΔAIOI?" 101–30.

35. For example, Kristi Upson-Saia, Carly Daniel-Hughes, and Alicia J. Batten, *Dressing Judeans and Christians in Antiquity* (Farnham: Ashgate Publishing Group, 2014).

36. For a good introduction to the ins and outs of the debate, see Reinhartz et al., "Jew and Judean." Daniel Schwartz makes a good case for ancient texts where Jew is more appropriate and those in which Judean is to be preferred. Schwartz, *Judeans and Jews*.

37. Lowe, "Who Were the IOYΔAIOI?" 104, 115, though it could also refer to a broader region such as "the procurate of Pontius Pilate (i.e. Judea together with Idumea and Samaria) or the kingdom of Herod the Great and the last Hasmoneans (i.e. approximately the whole of the historic Land of Israel)." Lowe, 103.

38. Lowe, 117. A similar explanation is used, more tentatively, with regard to 7:1.

39. Mason, "Jews, Judaeans, Judaizing, Judaism:," 504. In the Forum, however, Mason seems to back away from this strong statement.

40. Mason, Reinhartz et al., "Jew and Judean," 16.

41. Mason, "Jews, Judaeans, Judaizing, Judaism," 489.

42. Mason, Reinhartz et al., "Jew and Judean," 16.

43. Mason, "Jews, Judaeans, Judaizing, Judaism," 48–88. See the Note on Terminology for further discussion about the term "religion."

44. Esler, "From *Ioudaioi* to Children of God: The Development of a Non-Ethnic Group Identity in the Gospel of John," 110.

45. William F. Arndt, Frederick William Danker, and Walter Bauer, *A Greek-English Lexicon of the New Testament and Other Early Christian Literature*, 3rd ed. (Chicago: The University of Chicago Press, 2000), 478. See also Daniel C. Ullucci, *The Christian Rejection of Animal Sacrifice* (New York: Oxford University Press, 2012), 103.

46. Amy-Jill Levine, *The Misunderstood Jew: The Church and the Scandal of the Jewish Jesus* (San Francisco: HarperSanFrancisco, 2006), 159.

47. Mason does not deny continuity between ancient Judeans and modern Jews. Mason, "Jews, Judaeans, Judaizing, Judaism," 510.

48. Bruce J. Malina, "Was Jesus a Jew? Was Aristotle a Greek-American? Translating 'Ioudaios,'" accessed February 19, 2017, http://assemblyoftrueisrael.com/Documents/Yahshuawasnojew%5B1%5D.htm.

49. For critique and examples, see Robert J. Myles and James G. Crossley, "Biblical Scholarship, Jews and Israel: On Bruce Malina, Conspiracy Theories and Ideological Contradictions," *The Bible and Interpretation*, December 2012, http://www.bibleinterp.com/opeds/myl368013.shtml. For detailed discussion of Malina's problematic work, see James G. Crossley, *Jesus in an Age of Neoliberalism: Quests, Scholarship and Ideology* (Cambridge: Cambridge University Press, 2014), 175–88, http://universitypublishingonline.org/acumen/ebook.jsf?bid=CBO9781844657384. For a thorough critique of the Khazar theory of Jewish origins, see Shaul Stampfer, "Did the Khazars Convert to Judaism?," *Jewish Social Studies* 19, no. 3 (2013): 1–72, https://doi.org/10.2979/jewisocistud.19.3.1.

50. Klawans, in Reinhartz et al., "Jew and Judean," 38–39.

51. For critique, see Baker, "A 'Jew' by Any Other Name?" 153–80; Seth Schwartz, "How Many Judaisms Were There?" 208–38; Daniel R. Schwartz, "'Judean' or 'Jew'? How Should We Translate *Ioudaios* in Josephus?" in *Jewish Identity in the Greco-Roman World = Jüdische Identität in Der Griechisch-Römischen Welt*, Ancient Judaism and Early Christianity (Leiden: Brill, 2007), 3–27. For previous studies, see especially S. J. D. Cohen, *The Beginnings of Jewishness: Boundaries, Varieties, Uncertainties* (Berkeley: University of California Press, 1999).

52. See Leora F. Batnitzky, *How Judaism Became a Religion: An Introduction to Modern Jewish Thought* (Princeton: Princeton University Press, 2013). The same is true of Islam, Hinduism, Buddhism and a host of other "world religions." On the other hand, Joan Taylor states that "We ourselves can rightly refer to it [Judaism] as a religion;" see Reinhartz et al., "Jew and Judean," 28. See also Annette Yoshiko Reed's comments in Reinhartz et al., "Jew and Judean," 24–25.

53. This is not to say that modern Jewish identity remains stable, only that it has components similar to those of the Greek term. On ongoing debate, see Baker, *Jew*.

54. David J. DeVore, "Eusebius' Un-Josephan History: Two Portraits of Philo of Alexandria and the Sources of Ecclesiastical History," in *Studia Patristica* (Leuven: Peeters, 2013), 161–79.

55. Ullucci, *The Christian Rejection of Animal Sacrifice*, 103.

56. I notice with interest that Mason's book on the first revolt is called "The Jewish War" and not "The Judean War" though the text itself does use Judeans. Steve Mason, *A History of the Jewish War, AD 66–74* (New York: Cambridge University Press, 2016).

57. Schwartz, in Reinhartz et al., "Jew and Judean," 18.

58. Tina Pippin, "'For Fear of the Jews': Lying and Truth-Telling in Translating the Gospel of John," *Semeia* 76 (1996): 93.

59. Mine is no lone voice crying in the wilderness. Others too have called for the restoration of the Jews to the Gospel of John, and to the study of antiquity more generally. In addition to the articles by Baker, S. Schwartz, D. Schwartz, and Miller cited above, see also Ruth Sheridan, "Issues in the Translation of οἱ Ἰουδαῖοι in the Fourth Gospel," 671–95.

60. On the Hermeneutical Jew in the Middle Ages, see Jeremy Cohen, *Living Letters of the Law: Ideas of the Jew in Medieval Christianity* (Berkeley: University of California Press, 1999), 5, http://hdl.handle.net/2027/spo.baj9928.0110.013. On Augustine's hermeneutical Jew, see C. C. Pecknold, "Theo-Semiotics and Augustine's Hermeneutical Jew, or, 'What's a Little Supersessionism between Friends?'" in *Augustine and World Religions*, ed. Brian Brown, John A. Doody, and Kim Paffenroth (Lanham: Lexington Books, 2008), 97–112, http://public.eblib.com/choice/publicfullrecord.aspx?p=1380481. On the hermeneutical Jew in patristics more generally, see the essays in Ora Limor and Guy G. Stroumsa, eds., *Contra Iudaeos: Ancient and Medieval Polemics Between Christians and Jews* (Tübingen: J.C.B. Mohr, 1996).

61. Exactly when the Gospel of John became broadly known and accepted as a foundation for Christian faith is a matter of dispute. Some argue that the compatibility of John's dualistic language with the ideas of groups labelled as heretical from the point of what became mainstream Christianity, as well as the fact that the earliest known commentary on John was written by a Valentinian named Heracleon caused "Johannophobia" among the fathers of the church, led the fathers to ignore or overlook the Fourth Gospel in the early second century. Culpepper, *John, the Son of Zebedee,* 131. Brown, *The Community of the Beloved Disciple,* 146–47.

This view has been strongly disputed by others, in particular, Charles Hill, who has argued convincingly that the Gospel of John was both known to and valued by the mainstream church by the mid-second century. For detailed discussion, see Charles E. Hill, *The Johannine Corpus in the Early Church* (Oxford: Oxford University Press, 2004). In his view, early evidence of the positive use of John can be found in the Epistle of Vienne and Lyons (177 CE); the anti-Christian apologist Celsus (160–180); Justin Martyr (1 Apol. 61.1); Tatian's *Diatesseron* (173 CE), among others.

(Some evidence for its use in the Dialogue with Trypho (ca. 155 CE)

Part III

IMAGINING THE RHETORICAL SITUATION

Chapter Six

"The Jews had already agreed"
J. L. Martyn and the Expulsion Theory

Most scholars agree that John 20:30–31 is the Gospel's statement of purpose and a conclusion to the narrative as a whole, and that John's aim is rhetorical. Some agree that John hopes to inspire his audience to believe in Jesus as the Messiah, Son of God, and that at least some of the Gospel's references to the *Ioudaioi* are hostile.[1] With regard to the Gospel's rhetorical situation, however—the historical context within which and/or for which the Gospel was written—my rhetorical analysis pulls in a different direction from the consensus.

Most New Testament textbooks assert that the Gospel of John was written for an existing "Johannine community" of Jewish Christ-confessors ("Christians") that had experienced a traumatic expulsion from the Jewish community.[2] This theory is based on the influential book by J. L. Martyn, *History and Theology in the Fourth Gospel*, in which he provides a masterful reading of John 9 and other passages as a two-level drama.[3] As Robert Kysar noted, Martyn's "proposal swept through Johannine studies and took deep and healthy roots that grew until it was regarded almost as a given fact."[4] Indeed, it is easy to forget that Martyn's theory *is* a theory, a particular construction of a set of historical events based on a particular reading strategy. The theory provides a hypothesis concerning John's historical audience and the circumstances that prompted him to write this Gospel. It also implies a particular way of understanding the Gospel's stance towards the Jews and Judaism, and its relevance for the "parting of the ways" between Judaism and Christianity.

THE NARRATIVE

According to Martyn, John wrote for a Johannine community that had already formed around the particular beliefs articulated in the Gospel itself. This community was composed primarily of ethnically Jewish believers in Christ who continued to participate in "the synagogue," that is, Jewish communal life, even as they also saw themselves as a subgroup within the Jewish collectivity.[5]

The synagogue did not initially prevent the participation of Jews who confessed Jesus to be the Messiah.[6] Nevertheless, there was considerable tension between Jews who believed the Christian message and those who did not. Over time, the tension grew to the point where the Jews expelled Christ-confessors from the synagogue.[7] This exclusion, accomplished through a formal mechanism initiated by a central Jewish authority, did not alleviate the tension. Discord increased to the point that Jews engaged in active persecution of the Johannine community (16:2).

According to this narrative, John wrote his Gospel in order to strengthen the faith of the Johannine Christians in this dire situation (20:30–31) and to provide them with arguments against their Jewish opponents. This traumatic event marked the Johannine "parting of the ways" from the Jewish mainstream, in this local area if not in the Roman empire as a whole, and resulted in two separate and rival communities of faith. This scenario attributes John's Jewishness to the ethnic identity of the Johannine community; John's often antagonistic language about the Jews is interpreted as the natural stance of the victims towards their oppressors.

THE ARGUMENT

Internal Evidence

The starting point for Martyn's narrative are the Gospel's references to the *aposynagōgos*. This term literally means "one who is apart from the synagogue" and it appears, in singular or plural, in three passages.[8] In 9:21–22, the parents of a blind man, whose sight had been restored by Jesus, deny knowledge of his healing "because they were afraid of the Jews; for the Jews had already agreed that anyone who confessed Jesus to be the Messiah would be put out of the synagogue." In 12:42–43, the Gospel narrator states that "many, even of the authorities, believed in him. But because of the Pharisees they did not confess it, for fear that they would be put out of the synagogue; for they loved human glory more than the glory that comes from God." Finally, in 16:2, Jesus warns his disciples that "they will put you out of the synagogues. Indeed, an hour is coming when those who kill you will think that by doing so they are offering worship to God."

These passages highlight two points that are incorporated into the expulsion theory. First, being put out of the synagogue is a dire and dreaded prospect, one which inhibits potential Christians from public adherence to Jesus (9:22; 12:42) and is linked strongly with the threat of physical persecution to the point of death (16:2). Second, exclusion from the synagogue was an official decree or declaration of the Jews (9:22) and/or one group among them (the Pharisees, 12:42).

What exactly were the consequences of being an *aposynagōgos?* In his study *The Law in the Fourth Gospel,* Severino Pancaro lists four possibilities: 1) exclusion from the synagogue building itself; 2) exclusion from synagogal gatherings; 3) exclusion from the local Jewish community; or 4) exclusion from the national-religious Jewish community of all Jews.[9]

While few if any scholars opt for the first possibility, the second option has a number of proponents. Notable among them is William Horbury, for whom these Johannine passages provide the clearest sign of the enforced separation of the Christ-confessors from Jewish worship: the exclusion marked the Christian loss of any right to synagogue membership.[10] More popular is the third option. Dwight Moody Smith argues that, at most, the evidence suggests local rather than universal measures against Christ-confessors in the synagogue and that these were a passing phase.[11] Martyn himself, somewhat reluctantly, recognizes this more limited scenario as a possible interpretation of 9:22.[12]

Most scholars, however, support Pancaro's fourth option, arguing that the consequences of being an *aposynagōgos* extended far beyond the local setting of the Johannine community. According to Brown, the *aposynagōgoi,* having been told that they could no longer worship with other Jews, ceased to consider themselves Jews despite the fact that many were of Jewish ancestry.[13] Barrett suggests that exclusion from the synagogue community marked them out, "not improperly," as apostates.[14] Schnackenburg declares that the exclusion to which 9:22 refers "is expulsion from the Jewish religious community, with serious personal and social consequences."[15] Sean Freyne goes even further, arguing that expulsion resulted not only in separation from the Jewish community but also in the loss of social and legal status within the larger Roman world.[16] Expulsion from the synagogue was therefore a traumatic experience that forced Christ-confessing Jews to leave the Jewish community. Though enacted by the authorities (12:42), its consequences were felt through social exclusion presumably through the cooperation, collusion, or acquiescence of the entire Jewish population.[17]

External Evidence

Crucial to Martyn's case was the claim that in about 85 CE the central Jewish authority, established at Yavneh (Jamnia), promulgated a decree that forbade

Jewish believers in Jesus from participating in synagogue services.[18] This authoritative body inserted a curse euphemistically called the Blessing on, or of, the Heretics (*Birkat ha-minim*) into the daily liturgy, in order to flush out Christ-confessors.[19] By recruiting suspected Christians as prayer leaders, Jewish leaders could observe whether and how they recited the twelfth benediction. Failure to do so would be seen as a sign of their allegiance to Jesus as the Christ and would result in their exclusion from the synagogue. Martyn argued that John 9:22, 12:42, and 16:2 reflect the effect of using *Birkat ha-minim* within the synagogues attended by Johannine Christ-confessors.[20]

METHODOLOGY: THE GOSPEL AS A TWO-LEVEL DRAMA

Martyn argued that it is anachronistic to imagine that Jesus's followers would have been excluded from the synagogue during his lifetime.[21] Instead, the three *aposynagōgos* passages must allude to a situation in the late first century, when the Gospel itself was written. For Martyn, these passages are characterized by an immediacy which suggests "that some of its elements reflect actual experiences of the Johannine community," particularly "the dramatic interaction between the synagogue and the Johannine church."[22] On the basis of this observation, Martyn described the Gospel as a two-level drama. The surface level is the story of Jesus in the first third of the first century CE. The second level is the story of the Johannine community in the last decade of the first century. To understand the Gospel's rhetorical situation therefore requires the interpreter to tease this second level out of John's story of Jesus.

The two-level reading strategy makes several assumptions: 1) that the Gospel was a central, perhaps foundational, document for a particular community that already existed at the time that the Gospel was written; 2) that the particulars of the community's history, specifically its relationship with the Jewish community, was encoded in the Gospel narrative and hence transparent to its earliest readers; 3) that this community read the Gospel both as a story of Jesus and as its own story.

By reading the Gospel in this way, Martyn asserted, the exegete could "take up temporary residence in the Johannine community," and "sense at l[e]ast some of the crises that helped to shape the lives of its members."[23] This approach also required the exegete to distinguish between pre-Johannine materials and those elements of the Gospel that have been shaped by the community's own interests and experiences.[24]

The exegetical arguments for Martyn's second-level reading are therefore both redactional and stylistic. These points, in conjunction with what Martyn took as evidence for the late-first-century institution of *Birkat ha-minim*, suggested that the second-level reading was not merely his own construction but actually constituted "seeing with the eyes" and "hearing with the ears" of the community.[25] It therefore corresponds to the way in which the intended audience would have read chapter 9, and, by implication, the Gospel as whole. This procedure implies that the Gospel should be read analogically or even allegorically, as a story pointing beyond itself.

Assumptions

The Gospel as a Window to the Past. For Martyn, the Gospel provided a window to the circumstances under which it was written and to its purpose: to use its story of Jesus, set in the early first century, to reflect back upon the past experience of its late-first-century audience.

The Audience and Aim. Central to Martyn's hypothesis is the conviction that the Gospel was written for an existing Johannine community. Raymond Brown fleshed out the contours and history of this community, using the expulsion hypothesis as his foundation. According to Brown, this community looked to the Beloved Disciple, the authority behind the Gospel if not its actual author, as their founder. It began as a group of Jewish Christ-followers in Palestine, and then moved to Asia Minor around the time of the first Jewish revolt (circa 70 CE). There it attracted Samaritan and, finally, Gentile adherents.[26] For both Martyn and Brown, this community was traumatized by its experience of expulsion. The aim of the Gospel was therefore to strengthen their faith and resolve in the face of persecution by reminding them that through belief in Jesus as the Messiah, Son of God, they would enjoy life in his name.

The Enemy. The role of the ordinary people is not directly addressed by Martyn. Martyn places the onus for enacting and carrying out the decree on Jewish political and religious leadership.[27] In Martyn's two-level reading of John 9, the Pharisees who interrogate the man and his parents are the Jewish authorities; the man and his parents are members of the Johannine community, and Jesus the healer is a Christian preacher.[28] While the dreaded decree *Birkat ha-minim* was imposed by "the Jews," the ones who enforce it are the Jewish authorities, or the synagogue.[29]

Appeal

The appeal of this theory rests on several factors. First, it has enormous exegetical utility insofar as it explicates John's anachronistic references to the Jews' expulsion of Christ-confessors from the synagogue. Perhaps even more important, it supplies a plausible context for the strident debate between Jesus and the Jews throughout the Gospel.[30] It also explains the portrayal of the Jews in the Passion Narrative,[31] and the pervasiveness of the designation *Ioudaios* as well as the confusion as to its precise referent or referents.[32] As David Rensberger suggests, the hypothesis "furnishes us with a definite social framework and polemic context within which John's highly developed theology could have taken shape, and it permits us to ask further questions about the social, as well as the theological, implications of Johannine thought."[33]

Second, the hypothesis is seen as a key for historical-critical investigation of the Gospel, the community within and for which it is thought to have been produced and, indeed, the relations between Judaism and Christianity in the first century.[34] As such, it provides a means by which the various stages in the history of the community can be distinguished and the different component groups may be discerned.[35] It also supplies the framework within which the relations between this community and other "borderline" groups—Galileans, Samaritans, secret Christians—are investigated.[36]

Third, the hypothesis is useful for homiletical purposes. In his 1980 article in *Dialog*, Robert Kysar argued that the frontal attack which John mounts upon the Jewish people of his time and place should be read as a "family feud," a consequence of the broken relationship to which the Gospel attests.[37] John intended to supply support for those Johannine Christians engaged in a struggle with the synagogue, but he never intended that his words about the Jews be taken as a sweeping condemnation of the Jewish people as a whole. By interpreting John's comments on Jews and Judaism as a response to Jewish rejection and exclusion, the hypothesis defuses the anti-Jewish potential of the Gospel and makes its expressions more acceptable to a post-Holocaust audience.[38]

CRITIQUE

Expulsion and John's Anti-Judaism

Notwithstanding the popularity of this hypothesis and its utility for exegetical, historical-critical, and homiletical purposes, it is not immune to criticism. In the first place, the homiletical uses to which the exclusion theory have been put are highly problematic. To a Jewish reader like myself, the tone of Jesus's exchanges with the Jews, the narrative role accorded to the Jewish authorities, and even the use of *Ioudaioi* to denote those hostile authorities are certainly grating. To neutralize this negative rhetoric on the grounds that it is a response to the Jewish act of exclusion does not alleviate the problem. Do we then suggest that such rhetoric is a reasonable response to hostility? Are not the Jews then still to blame for the exclusion of the Johannine Christians, which, according to this theory, led to the separation of Judaism and Christianity, and then, by extension, to the many difficult centuries in the history of Jewish-Christian relations?

That the consensus hypothesis does not in fact undo the anti-Jewish rhetoric of the Fourth Gospel has been recognized by some scholars over the years. In his 1987 work, *Anti-Semitism in the New Testament?*, Samuel Sandmel concluded that "one may . . . explain the historical circumstances [underlying the Fourth Gospel] but one cannot deny the existence of a written compilation of clearly expressed anti-Jewish sentiments."[39] Janis Leibig comments that many scholars fail to come to terms with the theological sources of John's polemic. In "understanding 'the anti-Jewish tenor of the Gospel as the unfortunate outgrowth of historical circumstances,'"[40] she argues, "they overlook the dialectical relation—in fact, the radical interpenetration—between John's theology and the concrete historical situation."[41] More recently, Robert Kysar argued that historical-critical investigation must allow room for literary-critical insights: "The fourth evangelist could tell the story of Jesus most powerfully only with a negative figure set over against the Christ figure in the dynamics of the narrative. The situation of the Johannine community provided such an antagonist ready at hand in the figure of the Jews."[42] The result is that "the community that was founded on the sacrifice of an innocent person for their salvation now sacrificed their former Jewish brothers and sisters for the sake of their self-identity."[43]

External Evidence

The homiletical use of Martyn's hypothesis to whitewash the Gospel's anti-Judaism may seem salutary to some and obnoxious to others; it does not, however, have direct bearing on the plausibility of the expulsion hypothesis per se. More to the point is the critique of Martyn's use of *Birkat ha-minim*. Martyn's own convictions notwithstanding, it is now acknowledged by most scholars that *Birkat ha-minim* was not yet incorporated into Jewish liturgy in the late first century. The first to blow the whistle on this aspect of the expulsion hypothesis was Reuven Kimelman, who drew on the extant primary sources to argue that "*Birkat ha-minim* does not reflect a watershed in the history of the relationship between Jews and Christians in the first centuries of our era," and, indeed, that "there never was a single edict which caused the so-called irreparable separation between Judaism and Christianity."[44] Kimelman's conclusion has been confirmed in Ruth Langer's definitive study of *Birkat ha-minim*, in which she concludes that there is no evidence for the existence of this "blessing" prior to the third century CE.[45] Furthermore, even had there been such a curse, it could not have been used to exclude Christ-confessors from the synagogue, unless those Christ-confessors were prepared to think of themselves as *minim* (heretics). As Steven Katz pointedly remarked, "As long as a person did not consider himself a *min* the benediction would be irrelevant and his participation in synagogue life would continue."[46]

Also problematic is the model by which Martyn understood the authority structure of post-70 Judaism. Like many other twentieth-century scholars, Martyn perceived the council of Yavneh (Jamnia) as the central authority of post-70 Judaism. The Rabbis at Yavneh were seen as preoccupied with the process of self-definition, which included the regularizing of prayer, the canonization of scripture, and the definition of who was "in" and who was "out."[47] This view has been challenged by numerous scholars, who argue that Yavneh itself may be a construct of later rabbis.[48] Even if Yavneh existed and operated in the ways described in rabbinic texts compiled centuries after the fact, no Jewish institution, then or now, exercised the unified central authority that Martyn and others ascribe to it.[49]

Most scholars now concede that *Birkat ha-minim* is a red herring in the discussion of the history of the Johannine community.[50] Some scholars still cling to it, as the only possible way to make sense of the Johannine data.[51] Others leave it aside altogether, but still maintain that an expulsion from the synagogue occurred, even if it was not due to a widespread policy emanating from a central authority.[52] In the third edition of his book, Martyn addressed the critique but maintained his conviction that *Birkat ha-minim* was behind the expulsion edict that he read into the Fourth Gospel.[53]

Further, Jesus was not the only person for whom messianic claims were made. Josephus recounts several "Messiahs" who achieved a following in the first century.[54] According to rabbinic literature, Rabbi Akiva identified Bar Kokhba as a Messiah.[55] The identification of certain individuals as Messiahs is attested from the ancient period through to the present day. Although none of these individuals was acclaimed by the majority of Jews, the often sizeable groups that formed around them were not, and are not, excluded from the larger Jewish collectivity.[56]

Finally, it is unclear that exclusion from the synagogue, even had it occurred in any formal way, would have had the wide-reaching consequences that scholars attribute to it. First, it seems unlikely that in the first century the "synagogue" would have been construed as the Jewish community writ large. Archaeological and textual evidence testifies to the activity of gathering together, at least for Torah reading, and to the existence of buildings ("synagogues") dedicated to such gatherings. But in the period before 70 CE the Jewish collectivity was not referred to as the synagogue but as "Israel," or "children of Israel"; it was still the Temple that constituted its symbolic gathering place.[57]

The absence of external evidence for the expulsion hypothesis, and the misconstrual of the nature of late first-century Jewish authority structures, removes the historical anchor for the expulsion hypothesis and leaves the field open for other hypotheses. Jonathan Bernier suggests that, contrary to Martyn, the expulsion from the synagogue could have happened in Jesus's lifetime.[58] Edward Klink draws on Daniel Boyarin's account of the gradual development of notions of heresy within Jewish circles to argue that the passages reflect intra-Jewish conflict prior to 70 CE.[59] More convincingly, John Kloppenborg situates the Gospel's *aposynagōgos* motif in the broader context of Greco-Roman voluntary associations and suggested that being excluded from the synagogue would not have been tantamount to expulsion from the Jewish community.[60]

From a historical perspective, one can only conclude, with D. Moody Smith, that "the sources available to us do not permit us to say exactly what transpired to produce the tension between Johannine Christianity and Judaism that is evident in the Fourth Gospel."[61] From a rhetorical perspective, as we have seen, the references to expulsion contribute to a rhetoric of fear that John used along with other strategies to construct a barrier or boundary between Christ-confessors and the *Ioudaioi*. By portraying characters who fear expulsion due to their faith, the Gospel conveys the message that Christ-confessors have good reason to stay away from the Jews. ○

Methodology: The Two-Level Reading Strategy

Like the reservations concerning the homiletical usage of the exclusion hypothesis, the possibility, or perhaps even the likelihood, that *Birkat ha-minim* was not the historical referent of the exclusion passages does not in itself refute the theory that the Johannine Christians experienced exclusion from the synagogue. After all, the theory was constructed neither to serve homiletical purposes nor to provide the historical context for a particular piece of Jewish liturgy. Rather, it emerged from the exegesis of the Johannine text itself, and, in particular, the application of the two-level reading strategy used so convincingly in Martyn's *History and Theology in the Fourth Gospel*.

Applying the two-level strategy to the entire Gospel. Although this strategy, like the expulsion theory which it supports, has become all but axiomatic in Johannine studies, it too is open to critical reexamination. One principal observation prompts this probing. The expulsion theory, as developed by Martyn and others, focuses primarily on a two-level reading of John 9, the healing of the man born blind. Yet, it is taken by most scholars to reflect the *Sitz-im-Leben* of the entire Gospel in its current form and to point to the central historical experience of the Johannine community. If this is the case, then

○ Thus, the Fourth Gospel as — in part — a polemic vs. Judaization.

we would expect that a two-level reading of the entire Gospel would paint a picture that supports, or at least is consistent with, the expulsion theory. If application of the two-level reading strategy yields a different or conflicting set of images, however, then the expulsion theory itself, as well as its historical-critical and homiletical ramifications, are called into question.

Other models. The Gospel itself includes at least two other stories that could in theory be read as two-level dramas of the relationship between Christ-confessors and the *Ioudaioi*. John 11:1–44 describes the sisters Mary and Martha in mourning after the death of Lazarus. Though their close connection to Jesus was no secret (11:36–37), these women have clearly not been excluded from the Jewish community, as evidenced by the fact that they are comforted in their mourning for Lazarus by "many of the Jews" (11:19). In a two-level reading of the Gospel, these sisters would represent Johannine Christians. If, as the consensus view asserts, such Christians had already been excluded from the synagogue and hence from the Jewish community as a whole, how is it that they are comforted by Jews?

John 12:11 presents yet a different scenario. This verse reports the chief priests' plan to execute Lazarus, as well as Jesus, "since it was on account of him that many of the Jews were deserting and were believing in Jesus." A second-level reading of this verse implies an incompatibility between believing in Jesus to be the Christ and maintaining membership in the Jewish community, yet it does not attribute this separation to an official Jewish policy of expulsion.

Reading these passages alongside John 9 as two-level dramas therefore yields three different models of the historical relationship between the Johannine community and the Jewish community among which it apparently lived. John 9 and the other *aposynagōgos* passages suggest that Johannine Christ-followers were excluded from the Jewish community for confessing Jesus to be the Messiah. The story of Mary, Martha, and Lazarus implies that known Christ-followers were comforted in their mourning by Jews who did not have prior faith in Jesus as the Messiah.❶ The comments of the Jewish leadership in 12:11 express alarm concerning those who were leaving the community—apparently of their own volition—in order to join the Johannine church.[62]

Gospel's Self-Presentation

As we have seen, in John 20:30–31 John presents the Gospel explicitly as a written record of some of the signs that Jesus did in the presence of his disciples, and in doing so he assigns to his Gospel an important role in the lives of its audience. On the basis of this self-reflexive conclusion, we would expect some sign that John meant his Gospel to be read as a two-level drama. Yet

❶ And comfort in mourning was a major role of associations — probably including synagogues

such a hint is nowhere to be found. Instead, the Gospel at two points insists that its record of Jesus's signs is factual, or, at least, true. After describing the piercing of Jesus's side on the cross, the narrator states: "(He who saw this has testified so that you also may believe. His testimony is true, and he knows that he tells the truth)" (19:35). John 21:24 makes a similar point in its reference to the implied author of the Gospel as a whole: "This is the disciple who is testifying to these things and has written them, and we know that his testimony is true."

More subtly, the Gospel evinces a pattern of prophecy and fulfillment which in itself imputes historicity to John's account. Several events, such as the triumphal entry into Jerusalem (12:12–16) and the casting of lots over Jesus's clothes (19:24), are described as a fulfillment of biblical prophecies whose import was not always understood at the time (12:16). Implicit in this view is the belief that the prophets' words are an expression of the divine will and that they forecast what will "really" happen at some future time. Some of Jesus's words too are introduced by fulfillment formulae. John 18:32, for example, describes the handing over of Jesus to Pilate as a fulfillment of what "Jesus had said when he indicated the kind of death he was to die."[63] This introduction identifies Jesus's words as prophetic and therefore as authoritative. Like the words of the biblical prophets, Jesus's words are the words of God and express the divine will (14:24; cf. 8:45–47, 14:10). The events in which they are fulfilled must therefore also be true, both as part of a divine plan for humankind and as an actual representation or reflection of human history. These points draw the reader's attention to the role of the Gospel not as a mirror for the community's own historical experience but precisely as the true story of the Son of God's sojourn in the human world.[64]

John's rhetoric therefore ascribes an extratextual reference point to its own story. This reference point, however, is not within the detailed historical experience of the Johannine community in the latter part of the first century CE but in the life of Jesus several decades earlier. John situates Jesus's life story in the context of God's eternal relationship with humankind, and thus gives it a seminal role in the spiritual journey of his audience. These comments suggest that Alexandra would have viewed the events recounted in the Gospel first and foremost as a story of Jesus, a story that is "true" historically (in the time of Jesus) and cosmologically (in the eternal relationship of God and the world).[65]

On the basis of these reflections, it seems to me that Alexandra and other members of John's implied audience would not have read the *aposynagōgos* passages as an allusion to their own experiences.[66] Rather, as I have suggested, they would have heard these passages as part of John's rhetoric of fear and accordingly distanced themselves from the *Ioudaioi*. The anachronisms that are so obvious to modern scholars of ancient Judaism and Christianity may not have been obvious at all to the intended audience.

Finally, the Johannine community is itself a hypothetical construct open to serious critique. While it is reasonable to assume that one or more groups may have formed in response to the Gospel, the fact that it circulated and was eventually canonized implies as much. There is no evidence for the prior existence of a Johannine community. In the expulsion theory, and, indeed, most discussions of the Gospel's aim and audience, a Johannine community is extrapolated from the Gospel itself and then used as a lens through which to interpret the Gospel as a window to that community's historical experience. While, as I have argued, circularity is unavoidable in any theory about John's historical context, the existence of a prior Johannine community has been reified and therefore all but axiomatic in Johannine studies.[67]

These points raise questions concerning the central conclusion of Martyn's two-level reading strategy, namely, that the Gospel preserves a specific memory of the experience of expulsion from the synagogue at the hands of the Jewish authorities, an experience that caused its separation from the Jewish community as a whole. The critique of Martyn's reading in itself does not prove that such an experience did not occur. The absence of external evidence, and the doubts about the internal evidence, however, draw attention to its hypothetical nature.

ONGOING APPEAL

Despite such concerns, the paradigm persists. Why? It is always possible, of course, that we critics are simply wrong and that Martyn was right. Absent convincing evidence, however, I suggest that the appeal of the expulsion theory lies in the rhetorical finesse of Martyn's book itself. Three elements of this rhetoric seem to me to be the most important: writing style, dramatic mode of presentation, and explanatory power.

Style

For those of us in New Testament doctoral programs in the late 1970s and early 1980s, Martyn's book, so clear, so easy to understand, and so engaging, was a breath of fresh air. We admired his audacity in departing from the usual thick prose of the era. Here, for example, is Werner Kümmel on the purpose of John's Gospel, from his *Introduction to the New Testament*: "If J[oh]n is not an expansion of, nor an improvement of, nor a substitute for the Synoptics, which it knows and can presuppose that its readers know, the only remaining possibility is that it presupposes (without directly saying so) knowledge of the existing Gospels and on that basis gives its own representation of Jesus, which seeks to reveal in a complete way that Jesus is the Anointed One, the Son of God (20:31)."[68] Compare now Martyn: "One thing, at least, is shared by all New Testament authors in this regard: none of them merely repeats the tradition. Everyone hears it in his own present and that means in his own way; everyone shapes it, bends it, makes selections from among its riches, even adds to it. Put in other terms, everyone reverences the tradition enough to make it his own."[69] Kümmel and Martyn are making the same point; Martyn's, however, is far more accessible, and more persuasive for that very reason.

Mode of Presentation

Martyn's use of the dramatic form also set him apart from other scholars of his time, and ours. The use of drama underscores the striking similarities between historiography and historical fiction, whether in the form of novels, drama, or film. Whereas we generally presume an opposition between history and fiction, philosophers of history have pointed out the degree to which historiography itself is an imaginative exercise not unlike that involved in writing historical fiction.

In his classic book *The Idea of History*, R. G. Collingwood notes that historical thought, by definition, is always about absence: "events which have finished happening, and conditions no longer in existence."[70] Historical thinking, therefore, is "that activity of the imagination by which we endeavor to provide 'the idea of the past' with detailed content."[71] The historical imagination entails reenactment, that is, a "perpetuation of past acts in the present."[72] The historian, concludes Collingwood, reenacts the past in his or her own mind.[73] The imagination plays a major role in such reenactment, and for that reason, the narratives constructed by historians have much in common with the narratives constructed by playwrights, novelists, and filmmakers.[74]

Martyn does not acknowledge the affinity between historiography and historical fiction, and indeed the mere suggestion might be seen as wrong-headed by the scholars who have accepted his hypothesis. Nevertheless, his use of the dramatic form gestures towards the role of the imagination in the very attempt to take up residence in the Johannine community, a point which must be acknowledged even by those who view his hypothesis as historical fact.

Detail

Most important, however, was the vivid detail that Martyn provided. Martyn's book was rhetorically persuasive not only because of the clear language and dramatic form, but because his imaginative reconstruction or reenactment of the historical situation of the Johannine community satisfied our own deep-seated desire to live in the past. He singlehandedly created the community, built its church, peopled it with preachers and parishioners, and shaped a dramatic narrative of conflict, ostracism, and resolution. In doing so, he satisfied the craving for detail that the Gospel itself denies us, and, like a good novelist, allowed us to inhabit this world while providing our scholarly selves with the reassurance that in fact it could have happened this way. Martyn's book not only urged us to "take up temporary residence in the Johannine community" but it became a means through which we could do so.

CONCLUSION

The expulsion theory provides a compelling way to "see with the eyes and hear with the ears" of the Gospel's audience, complete with hero, villain, conflict, and emotion. It envisions the Johannine community as victims who have suffered a traumatic expulsion from the synagogue at the hands of the Jewish authorities. It offers consolation and above all vindication to the victims, through the death and resurrection of God's son, who offers eternal life to those who believe. And it promises victory over their enemies who will suffer eternal condemnation on account of their rejection of God's son and their persecution of those who believe in him. Finally, it provides one way to account for the Gospel's Jewishness and anti-Judaism: the Jewishness as an indicator of the community's Jewish ethnic identification, and the anti-Judaism as the understandable rancor against those who had expelled them.

If Martyn is correct, our fictional Alexandra would have been a Jewish Christ-confessor who had herself been expelled from the synagogue and welcomed the Gospel as a narrative treatment for her trauma. The Gospel's hostile comments about the Jews, as well as the rhetorical expropriation of the Jews' scriptures, Temple, and covenant, would have seemed like a just response to their violent rejection.

Yet the expulsion theory suffers at three points: 1) the lack of external evidence for a formal expulsion; 2) the overlooking of other models within the Gospel of the relationship between Jesus's followers and the synagogue; 3) the lack of evidence that the intended audience read the Gospel as a story of their particular historical experience. Furthermore, while it has a place for the positive (faith-affirming) and negative (Jews-rejecting) aspects of the Gospel's rhetoric, the expulsion theory does not do justice to the emotional force of that rhetoric. Why would a Gospel intended for those who have already suffered for their faith engage in such a pervasive rhetorical campaign to encourage belief in the first place? And why would the Gospel's anti-Jewish rhetoric, which extends to the Jews in general, appeal to a Johannine community that was itself Jewish? Why not simply target the leaders responsible for enacting and enforcing the traumatic expulsion decree?

The adherents to the expulsion theory have found ways to address these objections, for example, by insisting that *Ioudaioi* does not refer to all Jews but just the authorities, or by positing the need to keep the traumatized believers within the community. But the historical and the rhetorical shortcomings of the hypothesis provide an opening for an alternative construction of the Gospel's rhetorical situation, to which I now turn.

NOTES

1. One should perhaps more cautiously say "most" instead of "all"; after all, it is impossible for any single individual to have read every work ever written on John in order to make such a blanket statement but I am not aware of any serious scholarship on the Gospel that would disagree with these basic points.

2. See, for example, Bart D. Ehrman, *The New Testament: A Historical Introduction to the Early Christian Writings* (New York: Oxford University Press, 2004), 172.

3. J. Martyn, *History and Theology in the Fourth Gospel*. Also important was Brown, *The Community of the Beloved Disciple*, which adopted Martyn's hypothesis as a basis for constructing the demography and history of the Johannine community. The earlier editions of Martyn's book were published in 1968 and 1979.

4. Robert Kysar, *Voyages with John: Charting the Fourth Gospel* (Waco: Baylor University Press, 2006), 238–39.

5. The history and nature of the first-century synagogue are extremely difficult to delineate with precision. Lee I. Levine notes that the synagogue was primarily a communal institution, in the sense that the full range of communal activities—"political meetings, social gatherings, courts, schools, hostels, charity activities, slave manumission, meals (sacred and otherwise), and of course, religious-liturgical functions" occurred there. Lee I. Levine, "The Nature and Origin of the Palestinian Synagogue Reconsidered," *Journal of Biblical Literature* 115, no. 3 (1996): 430–31, https://doi.org/10.2307/3266895.

6. Martyn, *History and Theology in the Fourth Gospel*, 47.

7. Martyn, 47.

8. These are the sole occurrences of this term in extant Second Temple literature. Arndt, et al., *A Greek-English Lexicon of the New Testament and Other Early Christian Literature*, 123.

9. Severino Pancaro, *The Law in the Fourth Gospel: The Torah and the Gospel, Moses and Jesus, Judaism and Christianity According to John* (Leiden: Brill, 1975), 247–48.

10. William Horbury, "The Benediction of the 'Minim' and Early Jewish-Christian Controversy," *The Journal of Theological Studies* 33, no. 1 (1982): 52–53.

11. D. Moody Smith, "Judaism and the Gospel of John," in *Jews and Christians: Exploring the Past, Present, and Future*, ed. James H. Charlesworth (New York: Crossroad, 1990), 85.

12. Martyn, *History and Theology in the Fourth Gospel*, 60, n. 69. But see also note 75, where he reasserts the first-century use of *Birkat Ha-Minim*.

13. Brown, *The Community of the Beloved Disciple*, 41.

14. Barrett, *The Gospel According to St. John*, 362.

15. Schnackenburg, *The Gospel According to St. John*, 2.239.

16. Freyne, "Vilifying the Other and Defining the Self," 129.

17. The role of the ordinary people is not directly addressed by Martyn, who places the onus for enacting and carrying out the decree on Jewish political and religious leadership. See Martyn, *History and Theology in the Fourth Gospel*, 50–62.

18. The relevant passage is Berachot 29b–29a.

Our rabbis taught: Simeon ha-Paquli organized the Eighteen Benedictions in order before Rabban Gamaliel in Yavneh. Rabban Gamaliel said to the sages: 'Isn't there anyone who knows how to fix the Benediction of the Heretics?' Samuel the Small stood up and fixed it, but another year he forgot it. And he thought about it for two or three hours, [and he did not recall it], but they did not remove him.—Why then did they not remove him? Did not R. Judah say that Rav said: 'If someone makes a mistake in any of the benedictions, they don't remove him, but if [he makes a mistake] in the Benediction of the Heretics, they do remove him, since they suspect that perhaps he is a heretic'? Samuel the Small is different, because he formulated it.

19. One version of this reads as follows:

למשומדים אל תהי תקוה
ומלכות זדון מהרה תעקר בימינו
והנצרים והמינים כרגע יאבדו
ימחו מספר החיים
ועם צדיקים אל יכתבו
ברוך אתה יי
מכניע זדים

For those doomed to destruction may there be no hope
and may the dominion of arrogance be quickly uprooted in our days
and may the Nazarenes and the heretics be destroyed in a moment
and may they be blotted out of the book of life
and may they not be inscribed with the righteous.
Blessed are you, O Lord,
who subdues the arrogant.

20. Martyn, *History and Theology in the Fourth Gospel*, 56–65.

21. This view has been critiqued extensively but, in my view, unconvincingly, by Jonathan Bernier, who wishes to argue that exclusion from the synagogue could indeed have taken place during Jesus'ss own lifetime. Jonathan Bernier, *Aposynagōgos*

and the Historical Jesus in John: Rethinking the Historicity of the Johannine Expulsion Passages (Leiden: Brill, 2013).

22. Martyn, *History and Theology in the Fourth Gospel*, 46.

23. Martyn, 29.

24. Martyn, 29 .

25. Martyn, 29.

26. Brown, *The Community of the Beloved Disciple*, 25–58.

27. Martyn, *History and Theology in the Fourth Gospel*, 56–65.

28. Martyn, 43.

29. Martyn, 45.

30. Barnabas Lindars, "The Persecution of Christians in John 15:18–16:4," in *Suffering and Martyrdom in the New Testament: Studies Presented to G.M. Styler by the Cambridge New Testament Seminar*, ed. G. M. Styler, William Horbury, and Brian McNeil (Cambridge: Cambridge University Press, 1981), 49. D. Moody Smith, "The Life Setting of the Gospel of John," *Review and Expositor* 85 (1988): 439. See also Robert Dean Kysar, "The Promises and Perils of Preaching on the Gospel of John," *Dialog* 19, no. 3 (1980): 219.

31. Raymond E. Brown, *The Death of the Messiah: From Gethsemane to the Grave: A Commentary on the Passion Narratives in the Four Gospels* (New York: Doubleday, 1994), 1:759.

32. See, for example, Urban C. von Wahlde, "The Gospel of John and the Presentation of Jews and Judaism," in *Within Context: Essays on Jews and Judaism in the New Testament*, ed. Mary C. Boys et al. (Collegeville: Liturgical Press, 1993), 67–84.; Lowe, "Who Were the IOYΔAIOI?" 101–30.

33. David Rensberger, "The Politics of John: The Trial of Jesus in the Fourth Gospel," *Journal of Biblical Literature* 103 (1984): 395–96.

34. Wilson, *Related Strangers.* 72. R. Alan Culpepper, "The Gospel of John and the Jews," *Review & Expositor* 84, no. 2 (1987): 283 suggests that the Fourth Gospel was written at the onset of separation in one locality and probably contributed to the ultimate separation between the two. Martin Hengel, *The Johannine Question* (London: SCM Press, 1989), 114–15, offers a contrary view, arguing that "the 'expulsion' of the Christians from the synagogue took place, rather, in a lengthy and painful process which began even before Paul with the martyrdom of Stephen." It was the "ultimate consequence" rather than the starting point of "a development full of combat and suffering." For detailed analysis of the place of John 9 in the process of separation between Judaism and Christianity, see John Painter, "John 9 and the Interpretation of the Fourth Gospel," *Journal for the Study of the New Testament* 28 (1986): 31–61.

35. The most developed theory is that of Brown, *The Community of the Beloved Disciple*.

36. See, for example, Bassler, "Mixed Signals: Nicodemus in the Fourth Gospel," 635–46; Sarah J. Tanzer, "Salvation Is for the Jews: Secret Christians in the Gospel of John," in *The Future of Early Christianity: Essays in Honour of Helmut Koester*, ed. Birger A. Pearson et al. (Minneapolis: Fortress Press, 1991), 285–300.

37. Culpepper, "The Gospel of John and the Jews," 273–88. In his later writings Kysar critiqued his own earlier interpretation and viewed the expulsion hypothesis,

and its homiletical utility, as incorrect and highly problematic. See Robert Kysar, "The Expulsion from the Synagogue: The Tale of a Theory," in *Voyages with John Charting the Fourth Gospel.* (Waco: Baylor University Press, 2006), 237–45, http://search.ebscohost.com/login.aspx?direct=true&scope=site&db=nlebk&db=nlab k&AN=147100.

38. Kysar, "The Promises and Perils of Preaching on the Gospel of John," 219–20.

39. Samuel Sandmel, *Anti-Semitism in the New Testament?* (Philadelphia: Fortress Press, 1978), 119.

40. The reference is to Townsend, "The Gospel of John and the Jews," 60.

41. Janis E. Leibig, "John and 'the Jews': Theological Anti-Semitism in the Fourth Gospel," *Journal of Ecumenical Studies* 20, no. 2 (1983): 224.

42. Robert Kysar, *Voyages with John: Charting the Fourth Gospel* (Waco: Baylor University Press, 2006), 156.

43. Kysar, 156.

44. Reuven Kimelman, "*Birkat Ha-Minim* and the Lack of Evidence for an Anti-Christian Jewish Prayer in Late Antiquity," in *Jewish and Christian Self-Definition, 2* (Philadelphia: Fortress, 1981), 244.

45. Ruth Langer, *Cursing the Christians? A History of the Birkat Haminim* (New York: Oxford University Press, 2011).

46. Steven T. Katz, "Issues in the Separation of Judaism and Christianity after 70 CE: A Reconsideration," *Journal of Biblical Literature* 103, no. 1 (1984): 74.

47. See, for example, Michael S. Berger, *Rabbinic Authority* (New York: Oxford University Press, 1998), 42.

48. See, for example, Shaye J. D. Cohen, "The Significance of Yavneh: Pharisees, Rabbis, and the End of Jewish Sectarianism," *Hebrew Union College Annual* 55 (1984): 27–53. Daniel Boyarin, "A Tale of Two Synods: Nicaea, Yavneh, and Rabbinic Ecclesiology," *Exemplaria* 12, no. 1 (2000): 21–62.

49. Martyn's presentation seems to view "orthodox" or "mainstream" Judaism (Jamnia) as analogous to Roman Catholicism, complete with a centralized authority analogous to the Vatican.

50. Wayne A. Meeks, "Breaking Away: Three New Testament Pictures of Christianity's Separation from the Jewish Communities," in *"To See Ourselves as Others See Us": Christians, Jews, "Others" in Late Antiquity*, ed. Jacob Neusner, Ernest S. Frerichs, and Caroline McCracken-Flesher (Chico: Scholars Press, 1985), 102.

51. Painter, "John 9 and the Interpretation of the Fourth Gospel," 38. See also Culpepper, "The Gospel of John and the Jews," 281, who suggests that the exclusion was carried out by a process similar to the use of the Twelfth Benediction but prior to its adoption at Jamnia.

52. Culpepper, "The Gospel of John and the Jews," 283. See Claudia Setzer, *Jewish Responses to Early Christians: History and Polemics, 30–150 C.E.* (Minneapolis: Fortress Press, 1994). See also David K. Rensberger, *Johannine Faith and Liberating Community* (Philadelphia: Westminster Press, 1988), 24.

53. J. Louis Martyn, "The Johannine Community among Jewish and Other Early Christian Communities," in *What We Have Heard from the Beginning: The Past, Present, and Future of Johannine Studies*, ed. Tom Thatcher (Waco: Baylor Uni-

versity Press, 2007), 183–90. See also the vigorous defense by Joel Marcus, "Birkat Ha-Minim Revisited," *New Testament Studies* 55, no. 4 (2009): 523–51.

54. Josephus, *Ant.* 20.97–99.

55. Palestinian Talmud Ta'anit 68d.

56. On the pervasive role of messianism in Jewish history, see R. J. Zwi Werblowsky, "Messianism in Jewish History," *Cahiers d'histoire mondiale. Journal of World History. Cuadernos de Historia Mundial* 11, no. 1 (1968): 30–46. https://search.proquest.com/docview/1298902935?accountid=14701.

57. On the synagogue in the first century, see Lee I. Levine, *The Ancient Synagogue: The First Thousand Years* (New Haven: Yale University Press, 2000); Anders Runesson, Donald D. Binder, and Birger Olsson, *The Ancient Synagogue from Its Origins to 200 C.E.: A Source Book* (Leiden: Brill, 2008).

58. Bernier, *Aposynagōgos and the Historical Jesus in John*. The argument is unconvincing, however. I agree with Ruth Edwards's assessment that "Bernier's arguments are weakened by too heavy a reliance on the historical trustworthiness of NT writers without adequate consideration of conventions in ancient historiography and problems in identifying authorial 'intent'." Ruth B. Edwards, "Aposynagōgos and the Historical Jesus in John: Rethinking the Historicity of the Johannine Expulsion Passages," *Journal for the Study of the New Testament* 37, no. 5 (August 2015): 53–53.

59. Edward W. Klink III, "Expulsion from the Synagogue? Rethinking a Johannine Anachronism," *Tyndale Bulletin* 59, no. 1 (2008): 99–118. See Daniel Boyarin, "Justin Martyr Invents Judaism," *Church History* 70, no. 3 (2001): 428–29.

60. John S. Kloppenborg, "Disaffiliation in Associations and the Ἀποσυναγωγός of John," *HTS Teologiese Studies Theological Studies* 67 (2011), https://doi.org/10.4102/hts.v67i1.962.

61. Smith, *Johannine Christianity,* 209. The link between *Birkat ha-minim* and the Gospel is also questioned by Setzer, *Jewish Responses to Early Christians*, 91.

62. For detailed argumentation and consideration of alternate interpretations, see Reinhartz, "The Johannine Community and Its Jewish Neighbors," 111–38.

63. Note that the fulfillment formula (e.g., *hina hē graphē plērōthē,* 19:24) used to identify prophetic speech is also used with respect to Jesus's words (*hina ho logos tou iēsou plērōthē,* 18:34). Other examples include Jesus's prophecies of his betrayal at the hands of Judas (6:70, 13:21), fulfilled in 18:3–5, and of Peter's denial (13:38), fulfilled in 18:17, 25, 27. See Reinhartz, "Jesus as Prophet," 3–16.

64. My comments concern the Gospel's rhetorical use of these prophetic sayings; though the Gospel implies the facticity of the events that fulfil these sayings, New Testament historians are not obligated to do the same. The question of whether and to what degree the Fourth Gospel can be used as a source for the historical Jesus remains open, despite the abundance of recent work intended to support the Gospel's value for historical Jesus research. See the discussions in the contributions to Paul N. Anderson, Felix Just, and Tom Thatcher, *John, Jesus, and History* (Atlanta: Society of Biblical Lit, 2007).

65. The fact that a compliant reader like Alexandra would likely have viewed John's story as historical does not mean that we should. Some scholars argue for the

use of the Fourth Gospel in historical Jesus research. See, for example, the essays in Anderson, Just, and Thatcher. I remain unpersuaded.

66. This is not at all to say, *pace* Bernier, that an exclusion from the synagogue did historically occur in the time of Jesus. It is highly unlikely that 1) the early first-century synagogue was used to refer to Jews writ large, or that 2) there would have been enough Christ-confessors to constitute a threat, even if it could be shown that exclusion would take place on the basis of confession of a human being as Messiah.

67. See Adele Reinhartz, "On Travel, Translation, and Ethnography: The Gospel of John at the Turn of the Century," in *What Is John? Literary and Social Readings of the Fourth Gospel*, ed. Fernando F. Segovia, vol. 2 (Atlanta: Scholars Press, 1998), 249–56. For a detailed analysis and critique of the "Johannine community" hypothesis, see Lamb, *Text, Context and the Johannine Community*. Lamb too proposes that a "textual community" in Stock's sense formed around the Gospel of John, and that the Gospel as such does not presuppose or indirectly refer to a "Johannine community" that existed prior to its writing. Lamb, 202. Lamb does not claim to have "killed off" the Johannine community entirely, but he has marshalled convincing arguments for limiting it, as I do, to those who responded positively to the Gospel after it had reached something like its current form. Lamb, 204–5.

68. Werner Georg Kümmel, *Introduction to the New Testament*, trans. Paul Feine (Nashville: Abingdon Press, 1975), 232.

69. Martyn, *History and Theology in the Fourth Gospel*, 30.

70. R. G. Collingwood, *The Idea of History*, (Oxford: Clarendon Press, 1946), 233.

71. Collingwood, 247.

72. Collingwood, 218.

73. Collingwood, 288. See also William H. Dray, *History as Re-Enactment: R.G. Collingwood's Idea of History* (Oxford: Clarendon Press, 1995).

74. My own detailed study comparing life of Jesus research and Jesus novels provided ample support for Collingwood's position. See Reinhartz, *Caiaphas the High Priest*.

Chapter Seven

"We Wish to See Jesus"

John, Alexandra, and the Propulsion Theory

J. L. Martyn's attempt to see with the eyes of the Gospel's audience led him to construct a Jewish community that has been expelled from the synagogue on account of their confession of Jesus as the Messiah. According to the expulsion hypothesis, Alexandra, our compliant listener, was a Jewish believer in Jesus recently disoriented and traumatized by her experience of expulsion. She heard the Gospel in a church or housechurch, during worship or a meal with her fellow community members. Hearing the Gospel inspired her to persevere, and reminded her of the promise of eternal life to those who believe. She was comforted by the Gospel's message of perseverance, but also confirmed in a suspicion of Jews, or, at least, of Jewish authorities, who had expelled her and her community from their midst.

THE NARRATIVE

My own effort to see with the eyes of the Gospel's audience has led me in a different direction. My narrative begins not in a church filled with members of an already-existing Johannine community, but in a crowded agora in an urban Greek-speaking center such as Ephesus. The market is bustling with merchants, craftspeople, and customers who exchange goods and gossip, and with passersby on their way to or from home, work, or school.[1] At one end of the agora stands a podium or rostra, on which a number of orators are holding forth.[2]

One of these orators is our friend John. He is proclaiming a familiar text: "In the beginning was the word . . ." As he recites, a small crowd gathers,

Alexandra among them. Some stay for a short while; Alexandra and some others, however, linger to hear John out to the end. This may be the first time they have heard John speak, or perhaps they have heard him several times before.[3] In any case, for reasons known only to them, they find his message both appealing and persuasive. They begin attending meals and other gatherings of John's fledgling but growing group, and become Christ-confessors. Like Peter, Philip, and Nathanael, they are eager to be reborn as the children of God, Jews as God's family. What the Gospel recounts, I suggest, is not the expulsion of the Johannine Jewish Christ-believers from the synagogue, but the propulsion of those Christ-believers into the coveted role of God's covenant people. As a result, they not only have access to the treasured tokens of covenantal relationship, but they must also separate themselves from the non-Christ-confession Jews (*Ioudaioi*) whom they have ousted. If, as John warns them, Christ-believers are in danger of persecution in the earthly realm, they can be assured that on the cosmological plane, those who reject Jesus have already been cast forth from their life-giving relationship to God.

Whereas Martyn's narrative is ecclesiological—centered on the conflict between a Johannine community and the synagogue in the late first century—mine is cosmological—centered on the conflict between God and Satan. If Martyn's Johannine community and synagogue are reflected in the characters within John's story of Jesus, so too the players in my narrative mirror the cosmic combatants I am positing. And if Martyn's narrative has implications for a parting of the ways instigated by the Jews' expulsion of Johannine believers from the synagogue, mine suggests that from the perspective that this Gospel encourages, a cosmic and profound parting of the ways has been instigated by the propulsion of Christ-confessors into the coveted covenantal relationship with God that the Jews forfeited by rejecting God's son.

The group that I imagine therefore does not view the Gospel as a window to their past experience but as a dynamic force that propels them towards a radically new identity and reframes their relationship with others, notably, the Jews. That disaffiliation or separation from others often accompanies the formation of new social identities is a commonplace of social identity theory.[4] Social scientists emphasize the importance of boundary formation, and the push/pull of internal and external factors that propel people to distance themselves from one group even as they enthusiasticalliy embrace another.[5] The question then becomes: how might my narrative lead us to imagine the social circumstances that could have stimulated such a thoroughgoing attempt at boundary creation?

ASSUMPTIONS

Audience and Aim

Whether the Gospel's first real readers constituted a group that was loosely or tightly organized, small or large, long- or short-lived, part of a larger network or isolated: these are questions that a rhetorical analysis cannot answer.[6]

These audiences may remain literary constructs akin to the implied or ideal readers that we infer from the texts that we hear or read. One cannot, however, rule out the possibility that the Gospel of John created a "textual community" that was not only an interpretive community centered on this version of Jesus's story, but also a social entity.[7] It can safely be assumed that some people, somewhere, responded to the Gospel's rhetoric. This response was enough to ensure that it was copied and recopied, distributed widely, and eventually incorporated into the New Testament canon, thereby ensuring that its persuasive message would circulate far beyond the time and place of its writing.[8] In this sense, the Gospel is like all successful stories: it makes its audience, causing them to see, understand, and experience what they had not done before.[9] "In just such a way," notes Averil Cameron, "did Christian literature and Christian discourse make Christians."[10] One has only to watch the crowds at sporting events waving placards with "John 3:16" written on them to know that the rhetorical use of the Fourth Gospel continues to this day.

The Ethnic Identity or Identities of the Implied Audience

All we can say for certain about John's intended audience is that they were capable of understanding Koine Greek. Any other thoughts about their response to the Gospel, or their ethnic, cultural, or other identities, their geographical location, or other demographic features can only be extrapolated from the Gospel itself and, more importantly, from the particular lens through which we view the Gospel.

"Jewish-Christian" implied audience. The expulsion theory requires that the Gospel's audience be ethnically Jewish Christ-believers; otherwise they would not have been affected, let alone traumatized, by a putative expulsion decree. This identification accounts for the Gospel's references to exclusion from the synagogue, its sophisticated use of the Jewish scriptures, and its portrayal of Jesus as a participant in Jewish festivals.

A number of important points, however, are not explained by this hypothesis. These include references to festivals "of the *Ioudaioi*" (2:13, 5:1; 6:4; 7:2; 11:55), which suggest that these feasts were not familiar to the implied audience. The same is true of the reference to Jewish handwashing and burial practices (2:6; 19:40), and the narrator's translation of the "Hebrew" term *rabbouni* as "teacher" (20:16).[11] Furthermore, Jesus, who throughout most of the Gospel seems at home with Jewish ideas and values, twice refers to "your law" when speaking to his fellow Jews. In John 8, Jesus says to the *Ioudaioi:* "In your law it is written that the testimony of two witnesses is valid" (8:17); and later asks: "Is it not written in your law, 'I said, you are gods'?" (10:34).

Samaritan implied audience. Some argue for a Samaritan audience in addition to the Jewish-Christ-confessing core of the Johannine community. This argument has been made most directly by Raymond Brown. Using Martyn's expulsion hypothesis as a foundation, Brown developed a theory of multiple redactions. According to this theory, the first edition of the Gospel was addressed to a "Jewish-Christian" Johannine community—a pre-Gospel group founded by the Beloved Disciple—who had formerly been followers of John the Baptist.[12] Subsequent redactions, however, were geared towards new members from other ethnic backgrounds. The second redaction, in his view, took into account a large number of Samaritan participants, whose entry is worked into the narrative in John 4:4–42.[13]

Brown finds evidence for a Samaritan component to the community not only in John 4 but also in John 8:48, in which "the Jews answered him, 'Are we not right in saying that you are a Samaritan and have a demon?'" (8:48). To Brown, this verse suggests "that the Johannine community was regarded by Jews as having Samaritan elements."[14] This is not to say that the second group was entirely Samaritan. Rather, on the basis of the Temple discussion in 4:20–23, he suggests that they may have consisted of "Jews of peculiar anti-Temple views who converted Samaritans and picked up some elements of Samaritan thought, including a christology that was not centered on a Davidic Messiah."[15]

Certainly this hypothesis explains the attention paid to the encounter between Jesus and the Samaritan woman and the salutary outcome to that meeting: the faith confession of "many Samaritans" (4:39–42). The Samaritans disappear from the narrative, however, after 4:42. To be sure, some of the Christological language in the Gospel would have resonated with Samaritan theology. John Bowman notes the Samaritan expectation of a Prophet like Moses as outlined in Deuteronomy 18:18. He argues that the division among the people in John 7:40–43, between those who viewed Jesus as the prophet and those who saw him as the Messiah, reflects the presence of Samaritans among the Jewish crowds in the Temple area during the Feast of Tabernacles.[16] Similarly, Edwin Freed argues that some of the locations mentioned by John, (Aenon, Salim, Sychar, and Ephraim); the Samaritan connotations of τόπος as it is used in 4:20; 11:48; the denigration of both Moses and Abraham; the use of Samaritan terminology such as "our father" and "our fathers" (4:12, 20; 6:31: 8:39, 53, RSV); and Jesus's declared independence "from both the fathers and the law" (6:49; 8:38, 31, 56; 8:17; 10:34) imply that the Gospel addresses Samaritans, at least in part.[17]

The problem with this evidence, as Freed himself understood, is that this terminology resonates not only with Samaritan ideas but also with Jewish ones. For example, it was common for Jews to refer to the biblical patriarchs as "our fathers."[18] Many other affinities with Samaritan thought can be explained on the basis of the scriptures they shared with Jews.[19]

Gentile members of the "Johannine community." Brown sees "clear signs of a Gentile component among the recipients of the Gospel." Gentiles constitute the third group that entered the community, after an initial group of Jewish Christians that include the Baptist's disciples and a second group of anti-Temple Jewish-Christians and their Samaritan converts. Brown cites 12:20–23 and 37–40, in which "the arrival of 'some Greeks' serves Jesus as a sign that his ministry has come to an end" and John describes the Jews' blindness as a fulfillment of Isaiah 6:10.[20]

Brown's entire reconstruction, detailed and imaginative as it is, has not taken hold in the same way as the expulsion hypothesis which it incorporates. For one thing, Brown's argument seems to be based on the assumption that the Gospel's chronology, which introduces the Jews in chapter 1, the Samaritans in chapter 4, and the Gentiles ("Greeks") in chapters 7 and 12, reflects the order in which people from particular ethnic groups joined the Johannine community. This is possible, but it seems too neat a schema to be convincing. Another problem is that there are other ways to interpret the same evidence. In the third edition of *History and Theology in the Fourth Gospel*, Martyn offered a detailed critique of Brown's chronology, in which he followed Hans Joachim Schoeps in seeing the "hellenes" of John 12 not as Gentiles but as Greek-speaking Jews.[21] Contra Brown, Martyn remained convinced that "the history of the Johannine community from its origin through the period of its life in which the Fourth Gospel was composed forms to no small extent a chapter in the history of *Jewish* Christianity" (emphasis in the original).[22]

The current consensus remains with Martyn's view that John's actual late first-century audience consisted of Jewish Christ-believers. One wonders, however, whether such a group, no matter how angry about their expulsion from the synagogue, would have resonated with the stark dissociation from the label *Ioudaioi* that is so central to Johannine rhetoric.

THE GOSPEL'S AUDIENCE AS GENTILE OUTSIDERS

My own theory—that the Gospel serves as a vehicle for persuading an audience to undergo rebirth as the children of God who have usurped the Jews as God's covenantal partners—implies an audience that is neither part of an existing Johannine community nor Jewish.

Internal Evidence

Like Martyn, I draw on internal evidence to support my construction of the Gospel's audience as primarily pagan.[23] I turn first, however, to the difficult question of whether we should see the Gospel as addressed to those who already believe, or to those who do not yet believe. Readers of the NRSV may think that this is a simple question; after all, in the NRSV translation, 20:31 states that the Gospel was written "so that you may come to believe that Jesus is the Messiah, the Son of God, and that through believing you may have life in his name." The problem, as all commentators note, is that the Greek of this verse has a textual variant. Some manuscripts do indeed have the aorist subjunctive πιστεύσητε, which has a future sense, as indicated by the NRSV translation. This variant suggests that the Gospel's intended hearers are not yet believers. But there is also strong textual evidence for the present subjunctive πιστεύητε, which implies "that you may continue to believe," suggesting that the hearers are already believers.[24]

It would seem in theory that answering the text-critical question, that is, determining which reading is more likely to be original, would resolve the matter.[25] Many recent commentators prefer the present.[26] Harald Riesenfeld, for example, argues in favor of the present subjunctive, on the grounds that in Johannine literature, especially 1 John, this is the verb form that almost always follows "in order that" (*hina*; ἵνα).[27]

The situation, however, is ambiguous. The textual evidence is more or less evenly divided. This point is evident simply by comparing the Revised Standard Version, which preferred the present subjunctive reading, and the NRSV, which prefers the aorist. Further, the aorist is not always used in a future sense; for that reason, either reading could be used to defend the view that the Gospel is here addressing those who are not yet believers.[28] These points indicate that the Gospel's purpose—to evangelize or to confirm faith—cannot be decided on the basis of the variant or grammar. Complicating the issue even further is the likelihood that the Gospel was meant to be heard more than once—perhaps many times—and therefore had to be meaningful for both insiders and outsiders.[29]

The internal evidence that may (or may not) point to ethnic identity is also open to multiple interpretations. As we have seen, the expulsion theory can draw on numerous passages that seem to affirm an ethnic Jewish identity for the implied audience. My rhetorical analysis interprets those same passages as evidence for Johannine appropriation and expropriation of Jewish institutions; scholars committed to the expulsion theory, however, may not be easily convinced. In full awareness of the inevitably imaginative, speculative, and unverifiable nature of all attempts to identify the Gospel's audience and aim, I now turn to the passages that lead me imagine Alexandra and other members of John's implied audience as having pagan origins.

John 7:32–35:

> The Pharisees heard the crowd muttering such things about him, and the chief priests and Pharisees sent temple police to arrest him. Jesus then said, "I will be with you a little while longer, and then I am going to him who sent me. You will search for me, but you will not find me; and where I am, you cannot come." The Jews said to one another, "Where does this man intend to go that we will not find him? Does he intend to go to the Dispersion among [literally, of] the Greeks [τῶν Ἑλλήνων] and teach the Greeks [τοὺς Ἕλληνας]?

While some, following J. A. T. Robinson, have argued that the "Greeks" in 7:35 are Greek-speaking, Diaspora Jews, the formulation itself does not at all rule out that the reference here is to pagans.[30] Brown, for example, understands the verse "to refer to the pagan Gentiles of the Roman Empire who were influenced by Greek culture, and thus to be broader than Greek nationality."[31] Brown takes the genitive as one of direction: "they are suggesting that Jesus may go off and become one of the Jews of the Diaspora, living among the Gentiles and teaching them."[32]

John 10:16. At the end of the extended shepherd and sheep analogy, Jesus says: "I have other sheep that do not belong to this fold. I must bring them also, and they will listen to my voice. So there will be one flock, one shepherd." These other sheep will unite with those that are of "this" fold but who, strikingly, have followed the voice of the shepherd out of the sheepfold into the pastures beyond (10:3).[33]

For Martyn, the "sheep not of this fold" are Jewish-Christians from other groups.[34] He acknowledges, however, that most other commentators see this phrase as a reference to Gentiles.[35] This is yet another issue where the interpretation of a specific point depends upon the overall hypothesis that one wishes to argue. Here, as elsewhere, there are not enough direct clues to pinpoint the meaning precisely. But the interpretation of the "sheep not of this fold" as Gentiles makes sense if one keeps in mind the biblical and post-biblical use of sheep imagery as a metaphor for God's people Israel.

In the Torah and prophetic literature, shepherd is a metaphor for leader, and used variously of the leaders (Jer 23:1; Ezek 34:1–6), Moses (Exod 3:1–6), and, especially, David (1 Sam 17:34–35) and the future Davidic Messiah (Jer 23:4–6; Ezek 34:23). These motifs retain their importance in Second Temple Jewish literature, where "shepherd" may refer to a teacher of the "law" (2 Bar

77.13–17) or to Moses (Bib Ant 19:3; Philo, *Life of Moses* 1.60–62). Psalms of Solomon 17 describes David as the shepherd who, on the one hand, will bring the Gentile nations under his yoke (17:30) but, on the other hand, will attract "all nations" who "will come from the ends of the earth to see his glory, bringing as gifts her children who had become quite weak, and to see the glory of the Lord with which God has glorified her" (17:31). First Enoch 89 focuses on the "Lord of the sheep" (1 Enoch 89:21, 23, and throughout).[36]

In these and other passages, the sheep are Israel, that is, the nation or people that is in covenantal relationship with God. If the Gospel, as we have argued, has propelled Christ-believers into the covenantal position of Israel, it is they who are Jesus's sheep in John 10. And if so, the "other sheep that do not belong to this fold" (10:16) looks ahead to a time when others—the Gentiles, I argue—will join those who became members of God's flock during the time of Jesus.

John 11:49–52. In this passage, the high priest Caiaphas counsels the other Jewish authorities that "it is better for you to have one man die for the people than to have the whole nation destroyed" (11:50). The narrator then explains that Caiaphas "did not say this on his own, but being high priest that year he prophesied that Jesus was about to die for the nation, and not for the nation only, but to gather into one the dispersed children of God" (10:51–52).

Caiaphas's words express concern for "the people" [λαός] and "the nation" (ὑπὲρ τοῦ λαοῦ καὶ μὴ ὅλον τὸ ἔθνος ἀπόληται) which, according to the context, implies the Jewish people or the Jewish nation. When he explicates Caiaphas's so-called prophecy, however, the narrator enlarges this meaning: Jesus was about to die "not for the nation only" (καὶ οὐχ ὑπὲρ τοῦ ἔθνους) but for the ingathering of the "dispersed children of God" (τὰ τέκνα τοῦ θεοῦ τὰ διεσκορπισμένα συναγάγῃ εἰς ἕν.).

This reformulation is pertinent for two reasons. First, it uses the verb συναγάγῃ (συνάγω) [third person singular aorist active subjunctive], to which the noun synagogue is related. This usage may imply a contrast between the future ingathering that is fulfilled in Jesus and the present exclusion of which the Jews are accused. Second, and more important, it broadens the prophecy to refer not only to the Jews, or to Diaspora Jews, but to the children of God whom the Prologue has already defined as those "who received him [the *Logos*], who believed in his name" (1:12). In other words, these are believers who are not Jews, therefore Gentiles. Here the Johannine narrator broadens out the prophecy of the ingathering of the exiles to refer not only to Israelites or Jews, as per the prophetic literature and its later Jewish interpreters, but also to believers in Jesus, arguably, Gentiles.[37]

The Hebrew phrase for "ingathering of exiles," *kibbutz galuyyot* (קִבּוּץ גָּלֻיּוֹת), does not appear until rabbinic literature but the idea is much older. The expectation of eschatological return to the land is first mentioned in Deuteronomy

Ingathering of exiles . . .

30:3–4, in which God promises that in the future "the LORD your God will re-store your fortunes and have compassion on you, gathering you again from all the peoples among whom the LORD your God has scattered you. Even if you are exiled to the ends of the world, from there the LORD your God will gather you, and from there he will bring you back."[38] ⊙

The conviction that the Gentiles are included in this ingathering may be hinted at in Isaiah 11:12: "He will raise a signal for the nations, and will as-semble the outcasts of Israel, and gather the dispersed of Judah from the four corners of the earth." But if one accepts the Johannine view that 1) Christ-believers have replaced the *Ioudaioi* as the covenant people, and 2) Gentiles are now welcomed into the believing group, then the ingathering of exiles would refer to Gentiles as well.

John 12:20–24. John 12 describes an event that took place just prior to Jesus's final meal.

> Now among those who went up to worship at the festival were some Greeks. They came to Philip, who was from Bethsaida in Galilee, and said to him, "Sir, we wish to see Jesus." Philip went and told Andrew; then Andrew and Philip went and told Jesus. Jesus answered them, "The hour has come for the Son of Man to be glorified. Very truly, I tell you, unless a grain of wheat falls into the earth and dies, it remains just a single grain; but if it dies, it bears much fruit."

Several points stand out. First, as in John 7, the Greeks are likely to be Gen-tiles rather than Greek-speaking Jews. This point has been demonstrated per-suasively by Mary Coloe, who looks carefully at the prophetic quotations and allusions in John 12 to situate this brief narrative in an eschatological context in which all nations will acknowledge the sovereignty of Israel's God.[39]

Second, the Greeks do not approach Jesus directly but through his dis-ciples: they come to Philip who in turn finds Andrew, and the two of them together go to ask Jesus. This process evokes the pattern of recruitment de-scribed in the call of the first disciples (1:29–51) and in the coming of the Samaritans (4:39–42). As we have seen, this pattern is associated with true discipleship, in contrast to the dimished faith of those who believe only when they see signs (2:23–25; 6:15).

Third, Jesus's response does not address directly the Greeks' request. He does not send Philip and Andrew back with a yes or no answer. Rather, he declares that the time has come for him to be glorified. As Brown noted, this declaration marks a turning point. Until now, Jesus has insisted that his hour has not yet come (2:4; 7:30; 8:20) but, with the coming of the first Gentiles, the hour has finally arrived.[40] The hour of glorification is also the hour of his death, a death that is necessary in order for his mission truly to bear fruit. This complex of ideas suggests that the Greeks who wish to see Jesus are

⊙ *i.e. corporate identity of Abraham's descendants* ⟍ *Replacement theory [the Judeans, an ethnic group primarily] (Jesus accepts corporate identity of Israel—with a difference*

themselves the fruit that will flourish on account of his (impending) death. This latter point is reinforced by 12:32, in which Jesus declares: "And I, when I am lifted up from the earth, will draw all people to myself."

Fourth, it is significant that what the Greeks request is to *see* Jesus. In this regard, the Greeks are anxious to do what the Jews refuse to do: truly see Jesus for who he is. This contrast—between the Greeks who ask to see and the Jews who refuse to see—is key to this passage, to the rhetorical message of the Gospel as a whole, and to its aim and audience.

Throughout the Gospel narrative to this point, the Jews' adamant blindness has been firmly established. This point is made most explicitly in 9:39–41:

> Jesus said, "I came into this world for judgment so that those who do not see may see, and those who do see may become blind." Some of the Pharisees near him heard this and said to him, "Surely we are not blind, are we?" Jesus said to them, "If you were blind, you would not have sin. But now that you say, 'We see,' your sin remains."

The narrator reminds us of this theme in 12:37–40, just a few verses after the Greeks make their request. In 12:37, the narrator summarizes the first twelve chapters of the Gospel: "Although he had performed so many signs in their presence, they [the Jews] did not believe in him." The choice had been put before them so many times, and as recently as 12:36: "While you have the light, believe in the light, so that you may become children of light." Their refusal of the light was not a failure of God, Jesus, or the proclamation, but rather a fulfillment of Isaiah's prophetic words: God "has blinded their eyes and hardened their heart, so that they might not look with their eyes, and understand with their heart and turn" (12:39–40; cf. Isaiah 6:10). The Jews' blindness prevents them from seeing and consigns them to the realm of darkness. The Greeks' desire to see Jesus, by contrast, presages their entry into the light of faith and eternal life. As Jesus cries out at the end of the chapter: "Whoever sees me sees him who sent me. I have come as light into the world, so that everyone who believes in me should not remain in the darkness" (12:45–46).

John 12 therefore implies a narrative chronology: Jesus first came to the Jews, was rejected by them, and subsequent to his death, was embraced by the Greeks or Gentiles, who became children of light and thereby also children of God. This chronology is adumbrated in the Prologue which introduces the Gospel narrative.

> He was in the world, and the world came into being through him; yet the world did not know him. He came to what was his own, and his own people did not accept him. But to all who received him, who believed in his name, he gave

power to become children of God, who were born, not of blood or of the will of the flesh or of the will of man, but of God. (1:10–13)

Indeed, the entire signs sequence, from the wedding at Cana in John 2 to the raising of Lazarus in John 11, illustrates the opportunities to see, accept, and believe that the Jews have squandered, in fulfillment of the divine plan as articulated in Isaiah's prophecy.°

Israel's loss is the Gentiles' gain. The Greeks' desire to see Jesus will be satisfied imminently, with Jesus's death. John 12:24 indicates that it is only by dying that Jesus, and his followers, can bear fruit, that is, spread the message and bring others to "see Jesus." As Coloe notes, "The coming of the Greeks, representative of 'the world' in the words of the Pharisees, sets into motion the ultimate cosmic victory of God."[41] Only when he is lifted up from the earth will he draw all (πάντας) to himself (12:32). With the coming of the Greeks, the focus of the Gospel moves away from the signs stories and their accompanying discourses, to a future, eschatologically oriented mode that addresses the disciples, and, through them, the Gospel's audience outside the narrative. This is seen most directly in Jesus's words to Doubting Thomas in 20:29: "Have you believed because you have seen me? Blessed are those who have not seen and yet have come to believe."

The Gospel's audience is already living in the time after Jesus's death, when all is known, when the Paraclete, the Spirit of Truth, has come to reveal all things, and when the eschatological promises can be fulfilled. I would therefore argue that the Gospel presents itself rhetorically as the vehicle through which the Gentiles *see* Jesus after his death has completed the divinely prescribed narrative arc that began when the *Logos* became flesh (1:14).

External Evidence: Gentile Mission

These passages provide ample basis for imagining a Gentile audience for the Gospel's persuasive rhetoric. More speculative is the question of missionary purpose, which this hypothesis suggests. As we have seen, John's statement of purpose in 20:30–31 is ambiguous; the very existence of strongly-attested textual variants suggests that scribes themselves could not decide whether the Gospel was intended for the not-yet-Christian or the already-Christian.

The missionary position has been promoted most forcefully by D. A. Carson, who, in two articles from 1985 and 2005, argued that the Gospel participates in a mission to Jews.[42] Carson pointed out, as we have already noted, that the textual evidence is not determinative; both major variants in 20:31 can be interpreted to support either position. Carson argued that in order to view the Gospel as intended for Christians, one must interpret the phrase

° However, the Gospel acknowledges that many Ἰουδαῖοι come to believe in Jesus — replacement is only partial

"Jesus is the Messiah, the Son of God" (20:31) as an answer to the question: "Who is Jesus?"

On the basis of exhaustive linguistic analysis, however, Carson suggested that, on the contrary, the question underlying 20:31 is not "Who is Jesus?," the answer being "Messiah, Son of God," but "Who is the Messiah?," the answer being "Jesus." The only ones who would be interested in this question, he argued, are non-Christian Jews, who expect a coming Messiah but do not yet know that this is Jesus.[43] Carson therefore agrees with others such as W. C. van Unnik, J. A. T. Robinson, and K. Bornhäuser that John's primary audience may have been Hellenistic (Greek-speaking) Jews, to which Carson would add also God-fearers and Gentile proselytes to Judaism, as they "would also have considerable exposure to the OT and . . . would ask the question in the same way as the Jews with whom they had come to worship."[44]

Is it plausible that a Gospel that engages in an anti-Jewish rhetoric of vituperation would be a viable vehicle for bringing non-Christ-confessing Jews around to the belief that Jesus is indeed the promised Messiah? Carson insisted that the evangelistic purpose he is suggesting is not contradicted by the Gospel's negative construction of the Jews because "the Fourth Gospel is not as anti-Jewish as many have argued. Salvation is still 'from the Jews'" (4:22). But, he continues, "insofar as those strong confrontations occur, they are not inimical to evangelistic purposes. It may even have been part of John's strategy to drive a wedge between ordinary Jews and their leaders among his readership, while still in the example of Nicodemus, leaving hope even for the leaders themselves."[45] From Carson's perspective, the Gospel does not posit an opposition between the *Ioudaioi* and Jewish-Christ-confessing members of a Johannine community, but between two groups of Jews: those who believe in Jesus and those who do not (yet) do so.

As Terence Donaldson notes, the idea that the Gospel intends to missionize among Jews could make sense in a post-70 context once the Temple and the traditional structures of Jewish life were no longer viable:

> In such a context, John's community declared Jesus to be the Messiah of Israel and the replacement for the destroyed Temple, presented itself as the representatives of "the nation" for whom the Messiah had died (11.51), and invited other Israelites—perhaps especially those of the diaspora (cf. 11.52)—to join them. In order to bring those Israelites to belief in Jesus, John's community had to dissuade them from giving their allegiance to those others, found especially among the synagogue leadership in Judea (i.e., "the Jews"), who were also attempting to rebuild the house of Israel after the war with Rome. In such a situation, John's treatment of "the Jews" and Judaism would have functioned as an instrument of persuasion in an inner-Jewish debate.[46]

This is mere conjecture, and, to be clear, Donaldson is not advocating this interpretation but merely describing it. There is no real evidence for Jewish movement towards Christ-confessing groups after the Temple's destruction, though it is of course not impossible that some Jews may have done so.

Although it seems unlikely that the Gospel was directed towards non-Christ-confessing Jews, the possibility of a missionary aim should not be discarded. Indeed, the idea that John participates in the Gentile mission is plausible in the context of what we know about the late first century. The fact that the Gospel is written in Greek rendered it accessible to Gentiles, though of course also to Diaspora Jews. That there was a Gentile mission is evident from the undisputed letters of Paul as well as the Book of Acts. The rapid growth of this mission strongly suggests that Paul was not the only apostle to the Gentiles; other figures and other texts must have participated in outreach to interested Gentiles.

Furthermore, an author like John, who is deeply immersed in Jewishness even as he repudiates Jews, may well have seen the incoming of Gentiles to the covenant community as a necessary element of the divine cosmological victory over the ruler of this world that was inaugurated by the Son's sojourn in the world. Biblical and Second Temple Jewish texts provide ample testimony to the belief that the Gentiles would enter the covenant in the eschaton, though whether they had to first become Jews is a matter of dispute.[47] 1 Enoch describes the eschaton as a time "after the reestablishment of righteousness within Israel and the defeat of Israel's enemies, Jerusalem is gloriously refurbished, the exiles are delivered and reunited with their compatriots, and the Gentiles who have survived the judgment come to Jerusalem to join the grand gathering, where they are transformed into the purity of the primordial era (1 En 90:30–38)."[48] While Psalms of Solomon 17 makes a clear distinction between Israel and the nations, (e.g., in v. 28), most other Second Temple texts are ambiguous as to whether Gentiles join in the eschaton as Gentiles or as proselytes to Judaism.[49] In either case, as Donaldson notes, "the inclusion of the Gentiles in the final consummation was an essential part of Israel's expectations and self-understanding."[50]

WHAT SORT OF GENTILES WOULD
BE ATTRACTED TO THE GOSPEL?

Gentiles in urban centers in Asia Minor or elsewhere in the Roman world would have had exposure to Jewish tradition and some would have participated in Jewish activities with or without formal conversion.[51] Familiarity with and attraction to Judaism would have occurred through the sorts of social contact that take place when Jews and Gentiles live in proximity to one another. As Michele Murray notes, "The dispersion of many Jewish communities throughout the Roman Empire meant that Gentiles and Jews often shared the same city. Gentiles had Jewish friends and maybe relatives, and they would have had opportunities to participate in Jewish festivals and to attend synagogue services."[52]

Attributing to Alexandra and other members of a Gentile audience some prior knowledge of and/or interest in Jewish scriptures, practices, and beliefs brings us into the God-fearers debate. The term refers to pagans who affiliated themselves in some way with Jews and Judaism without undergoing the rites of conversion. The existence of God-fearers is clear from inscriptions and other sources. But who and how many they were, and, especially, what role they played in the growth of the early Jesus movement is very difficult to determine. Sibylline Oracles 4:24–55 expresses confidence that God-fearers are joined to Jews in God's providential plan.[53] Juvenal's Satire 14.96–99 describes God-fearing as a common phenomenon.[54] Also important is Acts 9:36–10:6, as well as the Aphrodisias inscription, which contains a list of donors, many of whom are described as God-fearers or God-worshippers.[55]

Bernd Wander concludes his exhaustive study of the term God-fearers by pointing to its fuzziness, and suggests that it would be more accurate to use the term sympathizers or even proselytes.[56] Bruce Chilton cites evidence that implies the existence of a substantial and well-known group of "non-Jews who, despite their identity as gentiles, sympathized with the religion of Israel."[57] Judith Lieu, however, cautions against relying too much on the category in order to explain the rapid growth of the Jesus movement among Gentiles. She questions the assumptions that 1) there were a significant number of God-fearers—Gentiles who frequented synagogues and Jewish activities without becoming circumcised—and 2) this group constituted the "vital bridge for the spread of early Christianity into the non-Jewish world."[58] While she does not deny that God-fearers existed, she suggests that their participation was more social than religious.[59]

It remains possible, however, that even Gentiles who did not enter synagogues may have been aware of some of the most important stories in the Jewish scriptures, especially the Abraham and Moses sagas on which John draws so extensively. John Cook suggests that Celsus and others knew important sections of the Jewish scriptures, though this does not mean that ordinary people would have.[60]

Finally, we might entertain the possibility that not all members of the Gospel's intended audience would have been expected to recognize John's biblical references and allusions. David Beck argues that lack of biblical knowledge would not have prevented an audience from understanding and entering into the Gospel or from using it as a vehicle for a genuine encounter with Jesus.[61] One may draw an analogy to modern movie-goers, who are capable of responding to a film without necessarily understanding all of its visual, aural, or narrative allusions or influences.

Gentiles who were attracted to Judaism had a range of options. They could become Jewish, they could participate in some Jewish activities without becoming Jewish, or they could join a Jewish community of Christ-confessors. They could also, however, gain the spiritual and eschatological benefits of Jewishness by joining a Christ-confessing group, even without taking on Jewish ethnic or identity markers.[62]

The Gospel's rhetoric of fear, expressed in the phrase "for fear of the Jews" and by the *aposynagōgos* passages, would be appropriate if the Gospel's implied author(s) saw themselves as competing with the synagogue or with Judaizing Christ-confessing leaders for Gentile adherents. Like the existence of God-fearers, the question of whether the late first century was characterized by a "competition for souls" is very much debated.[63] While there is little direct evidence, competitive evangelizing may nevertheless have taken place. As Judith Lieu notes, "The Christians lived in two worlds: the world which they shared with their neighbours, the world of competing cults, a world that is so often hidden from our direct gaze; and the world that they constructed through their texts, a world in which the Christian worship of God brooked no competition."[64]

Summary

Neither the historical identity of the Gospel's intended audience nor the Gospel's precise aim can be determined with any certainty. Both the internal and external evidence can be interpreted to support several competing hypotheses. To Martin Hengel, for example, it was obvious that John participated in the Gentile mission, pointing to the absence of Jewish particularism. Hengel views the Samaritans as "semi-Gentiles" and, for that reason, the depiction of Jesus as the "savior of the world," and the prophecy that future worship would take place neither on Gerizim nor in Jerusalem, represents an appeal beyond the Samaritans to the broader Gentile world.[65] Martyn, on the other hand, strongly disagreed,[66] citing the explanations of Jewish holy times, the references to teaching Greeks in John 7, other sheep, Caiaphas in John 11, Greeks in John 12, and failure to believe despite many signs."[67]

Pace Martyn, a case can be made for the hypothesis that the Gospel participated in the early church's mission to the Gentiles. The references to the Greeks' interest in Jesus and the eschatological incoming of the Gentiles hints at a schematic view of history: initially God's covenant was with the

Judaizing Christians (with low christology and Synoptic sympathies?)

Jews, and the renewed covenant through Jesus was also offered to the Jews. The Jews rejected that offer, with the result that God turned against the Jews, removed them from the covenant community, and instead offered the gift of eternal life to the Gentiles, who themselves were searching and therefore eager to accept the offer. In situating God's turning away from the Jews and towards the Gentiles in Jesus's own lifetime, the Gospel is making a rhetorically powerful claim. Although historically implausible, this claim is consistent with the Gentile mission of Paul and other post-Easter apostles.[68] It also makes sense of both the Jewishness—the appropriation of Jewish symbols and institutions—and the anti-Jewishness—the insistence that the Jews have forfeited their covenantal relationship with God—that mark this Gospel from beginning to end.

THE "PARTING OF THE WAYS"

What are the implications of this propulsion theory for the historical "parting of the ways" or, to be more precise, for the process by which the Jesus movement of Christ-confessors developed institutions, practices, and, most important, a self-identification that explicitly placed itself outside the Jewish realm?[69]

The analysis in chapters 1–4 has shown that the Gospel at the very least is constructing a profound rhetorical chasm between Christ-confessors and *Ioudaioi*. Christ-confessors are children of God, who experience eternal life in the present and future. Christ-confessors are not *Ioudaioi*, nor can *Ioudaioi* be Christ-confessors. This is not to say that Christ-confessors could not have been ethnically or genealogically Jewish, as were Jesus and the disciples. In undergoing the transformative process proposed and facilitated by the Gospel, however, the Jewish Christ-confessors become children of God and thereby cease being *Ioudaioi* who, having rejected Christ, have the devil as their father.

Whether or not we view the Gospel as reflecting a process that was already happening in the vicinity of its author and/or audience will depend on our understanding of the historical processes that governed how, when, and why the "ways parted."

When Did the Ways Part?

Until the late twentieth century, the "parting of the ways" was most often seen as a more or less one-time event that took place between the first and second revolts. Parting did not preclude social contacts, which always existed, but focused on the crystallizing differences between Jews and Christians—Jewishness and Christianity—with regard to their sense of identity and "groupness."[70] By the early twenty-first century, however, the consensus was beginning to shift. Far from parting in the late first or early second century, it was now thought that the ways did not part until the fourth century with the Christianization of the Roman Empire under Constantine, or even later.[71] The proponents of this view pointed to the evidence of ongoing and extensive social contact between Jews and Christians as an argument against the view that the ways had already parted in the late first or early second century.[72] Anders Klostergaard Petersen argues that some of the evidence that was earlier taken to refer to separation, such as patristic warnings against intermarriage, Sabbath and festival observance, and attendance at the synagogue, in fact testify to ongoing participation of Christians in Jewish behaviors, and the idea that such participation was not seen as incompatible with Christian beliefs.[73]

This view has gained many adherents. Nevertheless, it makes at least two assumptions that do not stand up to scrutiny. One is that social contact is a criterion for separation. There is in fact no reason that differentiation should preclude social contact; indeed, social contact between Jews and Christians has existed throughout history to the present day, long after the "ways" had clearly parted. Second, the fact that some, or many, were traversing porous boundaries does not in itself demonstrate that the boundaries did not exist, but simply that it was possible to cross them. Some Christians may not have seen participation in Jewish activities as taboo, but this does not mean they did not understand these activities as not-Christian.

A number of scholars are pushing back against the position that there was no parting, anywhere, prior to the fourth century. Leonard Rutgers calls "the ways that never parted" a "poorly elaborated concept" and an exercise in self-referentiality that "fails to take seriously into account the massive amounts of pertinent evidence generated by archaeologists and runs counter to a wealth of empirically-based evidence on 'typical' inter-group behavior as generated by cultural anthropologists, sociologists, and social psychologists."[74] Shaye Cohen argues that Christ-confessors not only began to see themselves as differentiated from Jews by the late first and early second centuries, but also that they were seen that way by Romans. To support this point, Cohen points to Roman persecutions of Christians, which, throughout second and third centuries, did not target Jews. He concludes that "in the eyes of the Romans, Christians were not Jews, and Jews were not Christians. The two communities were separate."[75]

That Romans were aware that Christians were not Jews is also implied by the changing terms of the *Fiscus Judaicus* (the Jewish tax). Originally imposed by the emperor Vespasian in the early 70s, the *Fiscus Judaicus* required Jews to contribute an annual half shekel, formerly sent to the Jeru-salem Temple, to support the temple of Jupiter Capitolinus in Rome.[76] The emperor Domitian (81–96) then applied the tax to anyone connected with Jewish practice, a move that potentially included Jewish participants in the Jesus movement. His successor Nerva, however, decreed that the tax should be applied only to those "who continued to observe their ancestral customs," thereby exempting Gentile and Jewish Christians alike. "Christianity," notes Cohen, "was now seen by the Romans as not-Judaism; the *fiscus Judaicus* applied to neither gentile Christians nor Jewish Christians."[77]

The controversy over when, how, and why the process of differentiation began depends at least in part on the choice and weighting of criteria. Cohen and Heemstra, for example, consider perceptions of difference, as demon-strated by Roman actions (persecutions) and law (*Fiscus Judaicus*), to be decisive. Reed, Becker, and the authors in their anthology look primarily to social interactions. Both perspectives, however, are reductionist; while scholars acknowledge that the process by which Christians began to see themselves as not-Jews was complex and by no means uniform throughout the Roman Empire, the very metaphor of "the parting of the ways"—its use of the definite article "the" and the singular "parting"—almost inevitably steers the discussion towards a linear, monolithic, and totalizing process.

A Rhetorical Parting

How exactly to situate the Gospel of John in the processes by which Christians developed a separate identity is difficult to say. At the very least, however, I would suggest that, as part of its rhetorical project, the Gospel ascribes differen-tiation between Christ-followers and Jews to the time of Jesus *in order to pro-mote a parting in its own time and place*. From John's perspective, this parting was not a consequence of broader social, political, or other external factors but a necessary, divinely mandated step in God's plan of salvation that was initi-ated when the "word became flesh," furthered by Jesus's death (3:16), and to be completed when believers would join Jesus in his Father's house (14:2). The Gospel is emphatically attempting to produce a separation of Christ-confessors from the *Ioudaioi* by exhorting its audience to see themselves as "not-Jews" even as they maintain or take on Jewish identity markers such as belief in the God of Israel and in the revelatory status of the Jewish scriptures.

Whether the Gospel was immediately successful in this objective cannot be determined. But it is interesting to note that it was used by church fathers for this very same purpose: to support the view that God had turned away from Jews towards Gentile Christians, and that a Christian separation from Jews and Judaism was essential for Christian identity. In Homily 1 of *Against the*

handwritten note: The Fourth Gospel has it both ways: many/most Judeans rejected Jesus and many/most Judeans believed in him—secretly. This: • "explains" synagogues that reject the new faith and synagogues that are neutral or even receptive • reobains Judean unwillingness to join the Christian community

Jews, Chrysostom uses kinship language—"children of God"—as John does, to describe this difference.

> But do not be surprised that I called the Jews pitiable. They really are pitiable and miserable. When so many blessings from heaven came into their hands, they thrust them aside and were at great pains to reject them. The morning Sun of Justice arose for them, but they thrust aside its rays and still sit in darkness. We, who were nurtured by darkness, drew the light to ourselves and were freed from the gloom of their error. . . . From their childhood they read the prophets, but they crucified him whom the prophets had foretold. We did not hear the divine prophecies but we did worship him of whom they prophesied. And so they are pitiful because they rejected the blessings which were sent to them, while others seized hold of these blessings and drew them to themselves. Although those Jews had been called to the adoption of sons, they fell to kinship with dogs; we who were dogs received the strength, through God's grace, to put aside the irrational nature which was ours and to rise to the honor of sons. . . . Do you wish to find out how we, who at first were dogs, became children? "But to as many as received him, he gave the power of becoming sons of God" (John 1:12).[78]

As in John 8, so too for Chrysostom, God has disowned the Jews and replaced them with believers—now definitively identified as Gentile Christians—who are now God's beloved children and covenant partners.

For his part, Augustine sees the incoming of the Gentiles as having been prophesied in Jesus's words to Thomas in John 20:29 (Augustine, Tractate 16 on John 20:29):

> Therefore, when the Lord was saying to Thomas, "Come, put in your hand; and be not faithless, but believing," and when he exclaimed, after touching the places of the wounds, and said, "My Lord and my God!" he is reproached and it is said to him, "Because you have seen, you have believed." Why, except that "a prophet has no honor in his own country"? But because this prophet has honor among foreigners, what follows? "Blessed are they who do not see and believe." We have been foretold; and what that Lord praised before, he has designed to fulfill even in us. They who crucified him saw him, touched him, and so a few believed. We have not seen him, have not handled him; we have heard, we have believed. Let the happiness which he promised come to be in us, let it be accomplished in us, both here because we have been preferred to his own country, and in the world to come because we have been grafted in place of the broken branches.[79]

In his comments on John 2:13–22, Augustine picks up on John 12:40, which describes the Jews' refusal to "see" the truth as a fulfillment of Isaiah 6:10:

> The Jews said to him, "What sign do you show to us, seeing that you do these things?" And the Lord said "Destroy this temple, and in three days I will raise it up." The Jews then said, "Forty-six years has this temple been in building, and do

ss than outright rejection of "their own Messiah" — difficult to explain for Christians (full 135 &)

you say, 'in three days I will raise it up?'" They were flesh; they knew the things
of flesh. But he was speaking spiritually. And who could understand what temple
he was speaking about? But we have not far to seek. Through the Evangelist he
made it clear to us; he mentioned what temple he was speaking about. . . . "But,"
says the Evangelist, "He was speaking about the temple of his body."

(2) And it is clear that the Lord was killed and rose again after three days.
This is now known to all of us; even if it was concealed from the Jews because
they stand outside, still it has been opened to us because we know in whom we
believe.[80]

As John 12:40 implies, it was divine will, prophesied by Isaiah, that the
Jews—from whom the truth was concealed—refuse to see while the Gentiles
know the truth because it was communicated to them in the Gospel.

As this brief selection shows, many of the same passages that have been
brought in support of the hypothesis that the Gospel had Gentiles in mind
as being among his intended audience are used by the Church Fathers for a
supersessionist purpose: to proclaim that God's covenant has been removed
from the Jews and extended to the Gentile Church.

That some of the Fathers read John as a history of God's turning from the
synagogue to the church, from the Jews to the Gentiles, has no historical bearing on the real audience of the Fourth Gospel. Cyril, Augustine, and the other
Fathers were writing centuries later than John, after the church had become
a primarily gentile enterprise. Nevertheless, their reading of John suggests
that the Gospel too may be advocating this same view of history as part of its
rhetorical agenda.

CONCLUSION: THE PROPULSION THEORY

The historical circumstances—if any—that prompted John to write his Gospel, and the concrete rhetorical situation that he aimed to address, are ultimately unrecoverable. This fact frustrates our desire for detailed knowledge
of the past, but it also frees us up to piece together a back story in different
ways. Martyn imagined himself in the pews of the Johannine church, listening to the preacher provide consolation and encouragement to maintain their
faith in the face of adversity. I imagine myself in ancient Ephesus,[81] looking
on as a pagan woman named Alexandra listens in rapt attention to a Christian preacher named John. I imagine Alexandra as being buoyed by her new
identity as a child of God, a branch on God's vine, a sheep in God's flock.
At the same time, whether she realizes it or not, her relationships with others—her family of origin, her friends, her neighbors—have shifted. Now that
she has seen the light, and has accepted Jesus as the only way to the Father,

she feels an affinity for those like her, even if they worship at other churches with different leaders. But she distances herself from those who continue in their pagan ways, and, especially, from the Jews who do not share her beliefs, or who may not even have heard of this Messiah, Son of God, about whom John preaches so passionately. Does she hate and despise them? Does she truly believe they have the devil as their father? I hope not, but, yes, it is quite possible that she does.

NOTES

1. In my earliest work, I too presumed the existence of a prior Johannine community See, for example, Reinhartz, "The Johannine Community and Its Jewish Neighbors," 137. I have since reconsidered this position, as this book attests.

2. I picture this scenario along the lines of the famous "gourd" scene in *Monty Python's Life of Brian*, in which Brian, escaping from his pursuers, finds himself in a lineup of orators, each exhorting their listeners to follow them. To avoid detection, Brian too begins to orate, and, to his surprise, gathers a large and responsive crowd who then follow him out into the wilderness. I have no doubt that the Python troupe modeled their scene on the known practices of mass oratory in ancient Rome, and, I suspect, also on the ongoing practice of public oratory at Speakers' Corner in Hyde Park in London.

3. John 3:24, which refers to the imprisonment of John the Baptist, seems to presume prior knowledge of this key event, which is not narrated in the Fourth Gospel. John 11:2, on the other hand, presumes prior familiarity with John's narrative as such: it refers to Mary of Bethany as "the one who anointed the Lord with perfume and wiped his feet with her hair," an event that is not recounted until the following chapter (12:3).

4. Hakola, *Identity Matters*; Hakola, *Reconsidering Johannine Christianity*.

5. Richard Jenkins, *Social Identity* (London: Routledge, 2008). Joane Nagel, "Constructing Ethnicity: Creating and Recreating Ethnic Identity and Culture," *Social Problems* 41, no. 1 (1994): 152–76.

6. My agnosticism about a historical Johannine community does not put me in the camp that holds that this Gospel was written for "all Christians." Richard Bauckham, *The Gospels for All Christians: Rethinking the Gospel Audiences* (Grand Rapids: W.B. Eerdmans, 1998). For my critique of Bauckham's position, see Adele Reinhartz, "Gospel Audiences: Variations on a Theme," in *The Audience of the Gospels: The Origin and Function of the Gospels in Early Christianity*, ed. Edward W. Klink (London: T & T Clark, 2009), 134–52. It may well be that John—an evangelist who himself is a scholarly construct extrapolated from the Gospel—hoped for a broad audience, much as academics do when writing for colleagues in their specialized fields. But just as I have my Johannine colleagues in mind as I write these words, so do I imagine John directing his rhetoric in the first instance towards a specific audience. Whether this audience already constituted a group, or community, however, at the time they encountered the Gospel, we cannot know.

7. Brian Stock, *Listening for the Text: On the Uses of the Past* (Baltimore: Johns Hopkins University Press, 1990), 151. Stock argues that in the Middle Ages, texts could start up communities, but in antiquity, communities preceded texts. He turns to the Mishnah, the third-century codification of rabbinic law as an example of a text that codified existing laws and traditions, and thereby shaped community practice of the future. *Pace* Stock, however, there is no basis for assuming that in antiquity, communities always preceded texts. Of course, the letters of Paul, for example, were directed towards existing groups or churches; scholars like Martyn generally assume that the Gospels were written for specific groups who already held the views described in particular Gospels, or, as the prologue to Luke's Gospel suggests, to individual patrons, or both. While this assumption adds concreteness to our efforts to situate the Gospels in their historical contexts, it can neither be verified nor disproven. The possibility that the New Testament texts, which originated within Jewish circles, could themselves create new groups is implied by Judith Lieu, who argues "the experience of Judaism from the mid-second century BCE demonstrates how the extension of the ability to interpret, or the emergence of different claimants to the right to interpret, could generate new groupings and self-identities." Lieu, *Christian Identity in the Jewish and Graeco-Roman World*, 60. Lieu is speaking most immediately of the groups that developed in conjunction with different readings of the Hebrew Bible, which included the Qumran community as well as the Jesus movement, which introduced its own Christological interpretations of the Torah, Prophets, and Writings. The same could be true for one or more of the New Testament texts. If John's Gospel proclaims itself as an authoritative interpreter of Jesus as divine revelation, then it too may be among those new groups with a self-identity that was generated out of a specific interpretation as enshrined in the Gospel as divine revelation.

8. For a recent survey and discussion of the relationship between John and 1 John, see R. Alan Culpepper, "The Relationship between John and 1 John," in *Communities in Dispute: Current Scholarship on the Johannine Epistles*, ed. R. Alan Culpepper and Paul N. Anderson (Society of Biblical Literature, 2014), 95–120, http://www.jstor.org.proxy.bc.edu/stable/j.ctt9qh1w6; R. Alan Culpepper, *The Gospel and Letters of John* (Nashville: Abingdon Press, 1998).

9. Booth, *The Rhetoric of Fiction*, 397–98.

10. Averil Cameron, *Christianity and the Rhetoric of Empire: The Development of Christian Discourse* (Berkeley: University of California Press, 1991), 46.

11. Brown, *The Gospel According to John*, 2.991–92.

12. Brown, *The Community of the Beloved Disciple*, 37.

13. Brown, 37.

14. Brown, 37.

15. Brown, 38. The Samaritan hypothesis, with variations, is also argued by George Wesley Buchanan, "Samaritan Origin of the Gospel of John," in *Religions in Antiquity; Essays in Memory of Erwin Ramsdell Goodenough* (Leiden: Brill, 1968), 149–75; Freed, "Did John Write His Gospel Partly to Win Samaritan Converts?" 241–56; Edwin D. Freed, "Samaritan Influence in the Gospel of John," *The Catholic Biblical Quarterly* 30, no. 4 (1968): 580–87.

16. John Bowman, "The Fourth Gospel and the Samaritans," *Bulletin of the John Rylands Library* 40 (1958): 300.

17. Freed, "Did John Write His Gospel Partly to Win Samaritan Converts?" 242. He spells these arguments out in detail in his earlier essay, Freed, "Samaritan Influence in the Gospel of John." and adds several more.

18. Margaret Pamment, "Is There Convincing Evidence of Samaritan Influence on the Fourth Gospel?" *Zeitschrift Für die Neutestamentliche Wissenschaft und die Kunde der älteren Kirche* 73, no. 3–4 (1982): 223.

19. Pamment, 229–30.

20. Brown, *The Community of the Beloved Disciple*, 55.

21. Hans-Joachim Schoeps, *Jewish Christianity: Factional Disputes in the Early Church* (Philadelphia: Fortress Press, 1969), 131. Martyn, *History and Theology in the Fourth Gospel*, 164.

22. Martyn, 167.

23. This proposal has some proponents internationally but (so far) relatively little currency in North America. This may be due to the general consensus around the expulsion hypothesis, which, as we have seen, meshes well with the view that the Gospel is directed towards a pre-Gospel Johannine community that was predominantly Jewish. See Hengel, *The Johannine Question*, 121. Others who have argued this point include Jörg Frey and Mary Coloe. Jörg Frey, "Heiden—Griechen—Gotteskinder: Zu Gestalt und Funktion der Rede von den Heiden in vierten Evangelium," in *Die Herrlichkeit des Gekreuzigten: Studien zu den Johanneischen Schriften I* (Tübingen: Mohr Siebeck, 2013), 297–338, http://www.zora.uzh.ch/85152. Mary L. Coloe, "Gentiles in the Gospel of John: Narrative Possibilities—John 12:12–43," in *Attitudes to Gentiles in Ancient Judaism and Early Christianity*, ed. David C. Sim and James S. McLaren (London: Bloomsbury T & T Clark, 2013), 209–23.

24. On the text-critical issues, see Porter, *John, His Gospel, and Jesus in Pursuit of the Johannine Voice*, 240.

25. Some may (Ì66vid ℵ* B Θ 0250 *pc*) read the present subjunctive πιστεύητε after ἵνα ("that you may continue to believe) while others (ℵ2 A C D L W Ψ Ë1,13 33 Ï) read the aorist subjunctive πιστεύσητε after ἵνα ("that you may come to believe"). The present tense therefore implies that the Gospel was addressed to believers and encouraged them to maintain their faith; the aorist suggests that the Gospel was speaking to potential believers and encouraged them to adopt this faith. The present subjunctive has slightly greater textual support, and is considered by many scholars to be more consistent with the overall tone of the Gospel. For detailed discussion, see Brown, *The Gospel According to John*, 2.1056–61.

26. Brown, *The Gospel According to John*, 2.1056. See also D. A. Carson, "The Purpose of the Fourth Gospel: John 20:31 Reconsidered," *Journal of Biblical Literature* 106, no. 4 (1987): 640, https://doi.org/10.2307/3260824.

27. Harald Riesenfeld, "Zu Den Johanneischen Hina-Sätzen," *Studia Theologica* 19, no. 1–2 (1965): 213–20.

28. Carson, "The Purpose of the Fourth Gospel," 640.

29. On the possible (and hypothetical) liturgical use of the Gospel, see Adele Reinhartz, "Torah Reading in the Johannine Community," *Journal of Early Christian History* 5, no. 2 (2016): 111–16.

30. John A. T. Robinson, "The Destination and Purpose of St John's Gospel," in *New Testament Issues* (New York: Harper and Row, 1970), 191–209.

31. Brown, *The Gospel According to John*, 1.314.

32. Brown, 1.314.

33. In an earlier work, I have analysed this passage also as a reference to the "harrowing of hell." See Reinhartz, *The Word in the World*.

34. Martyn, *History and Theology in the Fourth Gospel*, 167.

35. Martyn, 164. See also Koester, *Symbolism in the Fourth Gospel*, 112.

36. A review of the sources can be found in Young S. Chae, *Jesus as the Eschatological Davidic Shepherd: Studies in the Old Testament, Second Temple Judaism, and in the Gospel of Matthew* (Tübingen: Mohr Siebeck, 2006).

37. For detailed discussion of the ingathering motif as it pertains to John 11:49–52, see John A. Dennis, "Jesus's Death and the Gathering of True Israel: The Johannine Appropriation of Restoration Theology in the Light of John 11.47–52" (Tübingen: Mohr Siebeck, 2006).

38. The idea is prominent in prophetic literature, especially the books of Isaiah (11:12; 27:13; 56:8; 66:20), Jeremiah (16:15; 23:3, 8; 29:14; 31:8; 33:7), and Ezekiel (20:34, 41; 37:21).

39. Coloe, "Gentiles in the Gospel of John: Narrative Possibilities—John 12:12–43," 218–19 and throughout.

40. Brown, *The Gospel According to John*, 1.466.

41. Coloe, "Gentiles in the Gospel of John: Narrative Possibilities—John 12:12–43," 216.

42. Carson, "The Purpose of the Fourth Gospel"; D. A. Carson, "Syntactical and Text-Critical Observations on John 20:30–31: One More Round on the Purpose of the Fourth Gospel," *Journal of Biblical Literature* 124, no. 4 (2005): 693–714, https://doi.org/10.2307/30041065.

43. Carson, "The Purpose of the Fourth Gospel," 645.

44. Carson, 646. See Karl Bornhäuser, *Das Johannesevangelium, eine Missionsschrift für Israel* (Gütersloh: C. Bertelsmann, 1928); W. C. van Unnik, "The Purpose of St. John's Gospel," *Studia Evangelica*, 1959, 382–411; Robinson, "The Destination and Purpose of St John's Gospel." Carson's linguistic arguments were analysed by Gordon D. Fee, "On the Text and Meaning of John 20, 30–31," in *The Four Gospels: Festschrift Frans Neirynck. Vol. 3*, ed. Frans van Segbroeck (Leuven: Leuven University Press, 1992), 2193–2205. Fee argued that, based on John's general pattern, the present subjunctive is most likely correct in 20:31. Carson's 2005 article is largely a response to Fee's argument. Carson agrees with Fee that the present is more likely in 20:31. He disputes, however, the conclusion that the use of a tense that implies ongoing activity e.g. "continuing to believe," means that the Gospel was aimed at those who are already "Christian." Rather, his own analysis, not only of the present subjunctive but also of John's references to "Jesus," "the Christ," and "the Son of God" continues to support his earlier analysis that 20:30–31 is meant to answer the question

"Who is the Messiah?" and not "Who is Jesus?" Nevertheless, he acknowledges now that the opposite viewpoint can be defended, and asks only that scholars keep an open mind to other possibilities. Carson, "Syntactical and Text-Critical Observations on John 20:30–31" 703, 714 and passim.

45. Carson, "Syntactical and Text-Critical Observations on John 20:30–31," 648.

46. Donaldson, *Jews and Anti-Judaism*, 107.

47. Terence L. Donaldson, *Judaism and the Gentiles: Jewish Patterns of Universalism (to 135 C.E.)* (Waco: Baylor University Press, 2007), 501.

48. Donaldson, 502. Also relevant are Sib Or 3:719, 772. Ps of Sol 17; also 4 Ezra 13:35 and 2 Baruch 71:1 and ch 72.

49. Donaldson, 504.

50. Donaldson, 505. The possibility of Gentile attraction to John is suggested also by the fact that in some of its materials, at least, it seems to be making use of pagan practices. For an exploration of this idea especially in the Bread of Life discourse, see Kobel, *Dining with John*, 251–70.

51. Shaye J. D. Cohen, "Crossing the Boundary and Becoming a Jew," *Harvard Theological Review* 82, no. 1 (1989): 13–33; Shaye J. D. Cohen, "Respect for Judaism by Gentiles According to Josephus," *Harvard Theological Review* 80, no. 4 (1987): 409–30.

52. Michele Murray, *Playing a Jewish Game: Gentile Christian Judaizing in the First and Second Centuries CE* (Waterloo: Published for the Canadian Corp. for Studies in Religion = Corp. canadienne des Sciences religeuses by Wilfrid Laurier University Press, 2004), 26–27. Murray uses this point as a basis for arguing that Christian anti-Jewish polemic is not directed at Jews per se but at judaizing Christians, that is, Christians who participated in Jewish practice; such Christians were dangerous because they blurred the boundaries between Jews and Christians. Murray, 117. Nevertheless, this interpretation does not explain the anti-Jewish statements in the Gospel of John, which focus precisely on the Jews' lack of belief.

53. Bruce Chilton, "The Godfearers: From the Gospels to Aphrodisias," in *Partings: How Judaism and Christianity Became Two,* ed. Hershel Shanks, 55–71 (Washinton, D.C.: Biblical Archaeology Society, 2013), 59.

54. Chilton, 60. The relevant section of the Satire is translated as follows: "Some who have had a father who reveres the Sabbath, worship nothing but the clouds, and the divinity of the heavens, and see no difference between eating swine's flesh, from which their father abstained, and that of man; and in time they take to circumcision. Having been wont to flout the laws of Rome, they learn and practise and revere the Jewish law, and all that Moses committed to his secret tome, forbidding to point out the way to any not worshipping the same rites, and conducting none but the circumcised to the desired fountain. For all which the father was to blame, who gave up every seventh day to idleness, keeping it apart from all the concerns of life." "Juvenal, Satires," n.d., http://www.tertullian.org/fathers/juvenal_satires_14.htm#6.

55. Chilton, "The Godfearers: From the Gospels to Aphrodisias," 66. See Joyce Marie Reynolds and Robert Tannenbaum, *Jews and God-Fearers at Aphrodisias: Greek Inscriptions with Commentary: Texts from the Excavations at Aphrodisias Conducted by Kenan T. Erim* (Cambridge: Cambridge Philological Society, 1987).

56. Bernd Wander, *Gottesfürchtige Und Sympathisanten: Studien Zum Heidnischen Umfeld von Diasporasynagogen* (Tübingen: Mohr Siebeck, 1998), 231.

57. Chilton, "The Godfearers: From the Gospels to Aphrodisias," 55.

58. Judith Lieu, *Neither Jew nor Greek? Constructing Early Christianity* (Edinburgh: T & T Clark, 2002), 31.

59. This is a summary of Lieu's argument in Lieu, 31–45. But the assumption that one can distinguish clearly between social and religious Jewish practice is incorrect. Many Jewish practices that one might call religious, such as participation in the Sabbath and festivals as well as communal prayer, have a strong social component and satisfy both social and religious needs. Today, of course, there are secular Jews who fulfill their social needs in ways other than Jewish communal practice, but among first-century Jews such secular practice is not attested. Therefore Gentiles who engaged socially with Jews would also likely have participated in Jewish religious life to some extent.

60. This is evident in e.g. Celsus on Abraham; Celsus on Exodus; Porphyry on Moses; Julian on Abraham and the Exodus. John Granger Cook, *The Interpretation of the Old Testament in Greco-Roman Paganism* (Tübingen: Mohr Siebeck, 2004), 106, 116–25; 177; 276–88.

61. David R. Beck, *The Discipleship Paradigm: Readers and Anonymous Characters in the Fourth Gospel* (Leiden: Brill, 1997), 48.

62. The number of writings, and perspectives, on this topic is legion. See, for example, Paula Fredriksen, *Paul, The Pagan's Apostle* (New Haven: Yale University Press, 2017), 69–73. Murray, *Playing a Jewish Game*, 29–41.

63. Lieu, *Neither Jew nor Greek?*, 78–79.

64. Lieu, 78–79.

65. Hengel, *The Johannine Question*, 121–22.

66. J. Louis Martyn, "A Gentile Mission That Replaced an Earlier Jewish Mission?" in *Exploring the Gospel of John: In Honor of D. Moody Smith*, ed. R. Alan Culpepper and C. Clifton Black (Louisville: Westminster John Knox Press, 1996), 134.

67. Martyn, 135.

68. This is true also in patristic use of the Gospel of John to contrast Jews and Gentiles, and portray the Gentile church as the true followers of Christ. The Fathers further develop the absolute opposition between Jews and Christians, often using Johannine language. Robert Louis Wilken, *John Chrysostom and the Jews: Rhetoric and Reality in the Late 4th Century* (Berkeley: University of California Press, 1983); David P. Efroymson, "Jews and Judaism in Chrysostom on John," in *Proceedings of the Fifth Biennial Conference on Christianity and the Holocaust: "Christianity and Judaism: History, the Holocuast [Sic] and Reconciliation in the Third Millennium": Held at Princeton Marriott Forrestal Village, Princeton, New Jersey, October 18–19, 1998* (Lawrenceville: Rider University, 1998), 177–90. Paula Fredriksen, *Augustine and the Jews: A Christian Defense of Jews and Judaism* (New York: Doubleday, 2008).

69. The "Parting of the Ways" is currently the metaphor most often used to describe the process of Christian self-definition. It is hardly satisfactory, however

for at least two reasons. First, and contrary to the evidence, it implies a singular and well-defined process. Second, the metaphor implies that the process by which Christ-followers developed an identity separate from and over against Jews was as significant for Jews as it was for Christ-confessors. Nevertheless, in the absence of a better alternative, I shall continue to use it—for now. On this and other metaphors, see Adele Reinhartz, "A Fork in the Road or a Multi-Lane Highway? New Perspectives on the 'Parting of the Ways' between Judaism and Christianity," in *Changing Face of Judaism, Christianity, and Other Greco-Roman Religions in Antiquity* (Gütersloh: Gütersloher, 2006), 280–95.

70. James D. G. Dunn, *Jews and Christians: The Parting of the Ways AD 70 to 135*, Wissenschaftliche Untersuchungen zum Neuen Testament (Tübingen: Mohr, 1992); Wilson, *Related Strangers*.

71. For the arguments in favor of this position, see the introduction and articles in Adam H. Becker and Annette Yoshiko Reed, *The Ways That Never Parted: Jews and Christians in Late Antiquity and the Early Middle Ages* (Minneapolis: Fortress Press, 2007).

72. Adam H. Becker and Annette Yoshiko Reed, eds., "What 'Parting of the Ways'? Jews, Gentiles, and the Ancient Mediterranean City," in *The Ways That Never Parted: Jews and Christians in Late Antiquity and the Early Middle Ages* (Minneapolis: Fortress Press, 2007), 35–63.

73. Anders Klostergaard Petersen, "At the End of the Road: Reflections on a Popular Scholarly Metaphor," in *The Formation of the Church: Papers from the Seventh Nordic New Testament Conference in Stavanger 2003*, ed. Jostein Ådna (Tübingen: Mohr Siebeck, 2005), 68.

74. Leonard Victor Rutgers, *Making Myths: Jews in Early Christian Identity Formation* (Leuven: Peeters, 2009), 12–13.

75. Shaye J. D. Cohen, *From the Maccabees to the Mishnah*, 3rd ed. (Louisville: Westminster John Knox Press, 2014), 234.

76. The most detailed study is by Marius Heemstra, *The Fiscus Judaicus and the Parting of the Ways* (Tübingen: Mohr Siebeck, 2010).

77. Cohen, *From the Maccabees to the Mishnah*, 235–36.

78. "Chrysostom. Adversus Iudaeos," n.d., http://www.tertullian.org/fathers/chrysostom_adversus_judaeos_01_homily1.htm.

79. Augustine, *Tractates on the Gospel of John 11–27*, trans. John W. Rettig, vol. 79, The Fathers of the Church (Washington, D.C: Catholic University of America Press, 2010), 104.

80. Augustine and John W. Rettig, *Tractates on the Gospel of John, 1–10*, vol. 78, The Fathers of the Church (Baltimore: Catholic University of America Press, 2010), 221.

81. The Basilica of St. John the Evangelist was built in the 6th century by Justinian I. For a detailed discussion of ancient Ephesus, see Athanasios Sideris et al., *Ephesus: History, Archaeology, Architecture* (Cambridge, MA: Harvard Univeristy Center for Hellenic Studies, 2012); Trebilco, *The Early Christians in Ephesus from Paul to Ignatius*.

Conclusion

In 1998 I published a detailed critique of J. L. Martyn's theory that the Gospel was written for a Johannine community that had experienced a traumatic expulsion from the synagogue. Having deconstructed Martyn's methodology, results, and homiletical implications, it seemed incumbent upon me to propose an alternative. Developing such an alternative, however, was a much more difficult task than I had imagined. Only when I began to question the assumption that the Gospel was written for an already-existing Johannine community did I find a way forward. This way led me to a study of the Gospel's rhetorical program, and a new regard for the Gospel's potential to have a dynamic impact on the lives of people who are open to its message.

I am not one of those people. While I appreciate this Gospel, admire its complexity and rhetorical finesse, recognize its power, and respect those for whom it is sacred scripture, I remain personally unmoved by its call to faith and increasingly disturbed by its anti-Judaism. At a certain point in the writing process, I became aware that, although I had conceptualized this book as a lengthy response to Martyn, my real question was the one that so many before me had asked: How, or why, can a Gospel that is imbued with Jewish ideas, set in a Jewish religious, political and social context, and filled with Jewish characters also cast the Jews themselves as the enemies of Jesus, truth, and God? In other words, how can a Gospel that is so Jewish also be so anti-Jewish?

Along with many other scholars, I had a reasonable answer to this question before writing this book: No matter how thoroughly the Gospel writers may have shaped the received tradition to their own agendas, no matter how many of their own words they put in the mouths of Jesus and the other characters in their stories, they nevertheless could not ignore the fact that Jesus was a Jew, his friends were Jews, and they lived their lives in a predominantly

159

Jewish environment doing the things (keeping the Sabbath and festivals) that other Jews did and going to the places (synagogue, the Jerusalem Temple) that other Jews went to. The traditions the evangelists received were already imbued with Jewishness. The Jewishness of John's Gospel suggests that its (implied) author too was Jewish, or at least had considerable knowledge of Second Temple Jewish traditions and modes of biblical exegesis.

I was aware that, from this perspective, the anti-Jewishness of John stood in some tension with its Jewishness, but I thought it could be accounted for by the process of self-definition in which the Gospel is obviously engaged. This process required the creation of a boundary between the "self" and the "other."[1] For this Gospel, the "self" are the Christ-believers, and the "other" are the *Ioudaioi*, who claim to be God's children but reject faith in Jesus as the Messiah and Son of God, plot his death, and persecute his followers. The full force of this negative depiction, however, was seen to be mitigated by the Gospel's neutral or positive statements about the *Ioudaioi*, and, especially, by the Gospel's appreciation for the Jewish scriptures as a witness to Jesus, and its depiction of Jesus and the disciples as engaged in Jewish activities.

As I delved deeper, however, it became clear that the Gospel's Jewishness was itself mobilized to support the anti-Jewishness that is so deeply embedded in the Gospel's rhetorical project. Underlying this rhetoric is the following argument:

1) Mortality is universally dreaded; the desire for eternal life is the quintessential human desire.
2) This desire can be fulfilled only by believing that Jesus is the Christ, Son of God.
3) Accepting this belief causes ordinary human beings to be reborn as the children of God, a group that constitutes God's family and consequently lives in an intimacy with the divine that is mediated by his only son.
4) The children of God are in covenantal relationship with God.
5) This covenantal relationship is understood in Jewish terms as manifested textually in the scriptures (Torah and prophets) and spatially in the Temple.
6) This is an exclusive relationship: one can be with God only through Jesus. Jesus is the only way to God. All other paths lead away from God. Jews who do not believe may believe they retain the status of God's elect people but in reality they have forfeited that status. In effect, they have been cast out of the vine of Israel tended by the divine vinegrower, to wither and burn.
7) It is now the children of God who have access to and authority over the Jewish scriptures and their correct, divinely-mandated interpretation, and the Temple as God's house. The Sabbath and festivals become occasions

for John's Jesus to demonstrate his divine origins and authority, and to proclaim his message to large crowds. In doing so, Jesus displaces the Jewish authorities, the Pharisees and the priests, as the ones who control what happens on the Sabbath and in the Temple precincts. The Jews, on the other hand, are displaced from the covenant, fail to understand their own scriptures, and become as slaves rather than sons in the father's house. Their rejection of Jesus demonstrates that, far from being God's children, they have Satan as their father.

My initial intention was to set aside historical questions in order to focus solely on rhetoric. This seemed a solid approach, for the persuasive—rhetorical— intent of this story of Jesus is evident in virtually every chapter, and is founda- tional to virtually every study, whether or not the term "rhetoric" is used. While acknowledging that there are many different ways to read this Gospel, I was confident that my perspective could be defended exegetically.

Historical analysis, on the other hand, is uncertain terrain. Historical ques- tions depend upon external evidence. Such evidence, however, is largely unavailable for the late first century Mediterranean, which is the most likely setting for this Gospel. After so many years of critiquing hypotheses that rely on tautological reasoning in the absence of reliable external data, how could I in good conscience draw historical conclusions from what is fundamentally a literary-critical project?

I was prodded into rethinking this stance by the colleagues and students to whom I presented my ideas as they began to take shape. For most of them, the rhetorical analysis was valuable only insofar as it was helpful in addressing historical questions of aim, audience, and historical context. Their persistence urged me to venture out on the limb of historical speculation to propose an alternative to the expulsion theory that still holds sway among many New Testament scholars.

On the historical plane, my speculative efforts led to three suggestions. The first was that the Gospel was aimed in the first instance at Gentiles interested in Jewish matters and who therefore participated in the broader mission to the Gentiles that was already underway by the mid-first century CE. This does not preclude interested Jews but the thrust of the Gospel seems to presuppose an audience attracted to but not fully familiar with Jewish ideas and practices. °

The second was that the term *Ioudaios* had primarily rhetorical rather than denotative meaning. The Gospel's rhetorical purpose is to associate opposi- tion to its message with a specific known group even while the narrative provides evidence that not all members of that group were guilty of such opposition. The *Ioudaioi* are outside the circle of love promoted by the Gos- pel. The search for specific historical referents seems misplaced as well as

° *implied audience — but cf. pp. 144-6*

futile. From the Gospel's vantage point, believers by definition are outside the group of *Ioudaioi*, a point reinforced by the fact that the term is not used for Jews who are part of the in-group (Jesus and the disciples). The seventy-fold repetition of the term, along with its predominantly hostile usage, would also have driven home the message that Christ-following children of God must see themselves as separate from and opposed to the *Ioudaioi*, who have Satan as their father.

The third was that the Gospel, like all rhetorical documents, is a forward-rather than backward-looking document. It does not address a situation in the past but aims to shape the future. My analysis of the Gospel's rhetoric suggests that it envisions that future as including a firm boundary between its adherents and the *Ioudaioi*. In positioning the compliant audience over against the resistant *Ioudaioi* the Gospel posits the mutual exclusivity of these two identities.

Whether or not there were Christ-confessing groups in some locales that had begun to define themselves over against the *Ioudaioi* in the late first century, we cannot say on the basis of this Gospel alone. In my view, the evidence leans in that direction but it is not decisive. What we can say with some certainty, I argue, is that the Gospel's rhetoric pushes its audience to see such separation as essential to their own developing self-identification as children of God. In other words, we cannot know if the Gospel reflects a historical process of separation that was already underway, but we can say that part of its rhetorical agenda is to move such a process forward.

The Gospel's rhetoric prods its audience to discern and enter into the cosmological plane of the Gospel's narrative. This process is mediated by the Gospel itself, as a record of Jesus's words and deeds. Those who follow this path experience rebirth as the children of God and enter into covenantal relationship with God through their belief in God's son. The cosmological plane, including its understanding of truth, humankind, and the divine, as well as its tokens, symbols, and artifacts—Torah and Temple—are thoroughly Jewish. In situating its story of Jesus within the broader framework of the cosmological story, the Gospel is urging its audience to adopt this Jewish value system. To do so, however, they must follow the way set by Jesus and not the ways set by the *Ioudaioi*, who are blind to the identity of Jesus's identity as God's son, and refuse to accept the new covenantal terms that God has set out.

THE GOSPEL AND THE JEWS

Unlike modern scholars, the Gospel writer was unconcerned about whether the *Ioudaioi* constituted an ethnic group, a religious one, a political subgroup, or some other historically-verifiable entity. Nor was he interested in explaining why Jesus and the disciples, who by all objective criteria are Jews, are nevertheless never called *Ioudaioi*.

But rhetorical constructs can become enfleshed once a text is released into the world. This is true especially when these constructs share the label of an actual group of people. The animus that the Gospel displays towards the rhetorical *Ioudaioi* may serve a rhetorical purpose that can be detached from human history, but it can be too easily translated into hatred of flesh-and-blood *Ioudaioi*.

ETHICS AND EXEGESIS

In order to consider the Fourth Gospel's rhetorical program, and to construct a hypothesis concerning its historical target audience, I tried to see with the eyes—or rather, hear with the ears—of a compliant listener, that is, of a fictional someone who would be persuaded by its rhetoric, and undertake the transformation that it proclaims as essential to fulfilling the desire for eternal life. I also attempted to be both sympathetic and engaged, in order to give full weight to the potential of the Gospel's rhetoric to have a powerfully positive impact on its audience. In doing so I tried to resonate with those who understand Jesus as the divine word become flesh; who accept the claim that Jesus has the central role in the divine economy of salvation; who follow the way from the mundane world in which Jesus is persecuted and eventually killed by the Roman state, to the cosmological realm, in which Jesus's death marks his return to the Father in glory.

Imagining Alexandra as a younger, less Jewish, and more compliant version of myself made all of this easier to do. For me, however, this has been an intellectual rather than a spiritual journey. And having completed it, I return to my personal stance towards this Gospel and its message, which is marked not by compliance, sympathy, or engagement, but by resistance.[2] No doubt this resistance is grounded in my own Jewish identity and my knowledge of how this Gospel was used to justify anti-Semitism, as recently as in the Nazi era.[3] But it has been sharpened by concern about the polarizing discourse that seems to have taken increasing hold in the present century. Should we not resist any rhetorical program that vilifies the "other" in order to construct the "self"?

Some interpreters may value the expulsion hypothesis, according to which John's anti-Judaism is a natural, perhaps even conventional, response to rejection, because it lessens the tension between the canonical, and therefore authoritative, status of John's Gospel, and contemporary values that condemn both anti-Judaism and its close cousin, anti-Semitism.[4] Nevertheless, the expulsion hypothesis does not undo the Gospel's anti-Jewish rhetoric. Formative for my own thinking was Rosemary Radford Ruether's book, *Faith and Fratricide*, which was published in 1974 as I was completing my undergraduate degree in Jewish studies, and, even more important, Gregory Baum's thoughtful introduction to this book.[5]

Ruether's book holds the New Testament and early Christianity to account for promulgating the anti-Semitism that reached its most deadly expression in the Holocaust. She argues that anti-Semitism is not a veneer nor is it the product of later interpretation, but rather that it is inherent in New Testament christology as such. She is particularly critical of the Fourth Gospel, which, she argues, has given "the ultimate theological form to that diabolizing of 'the Jews' which is the root of anti-Semitism in the Christian tradition."[6] She emphasizes: "There is no way to rid Christianity of its anti-Judaism, without grappling finally with its christological hermeneutic itself."[7]

Gregory Baum's introduction picks up on this same point. He argues that "As long as the Christian Church regards itself as the successor of Israel, as the new people of God substituted in the place of the old, and as long as the Church proclaims Jesus as the one mediator without whom there is no salvation, no theological space is left for other religions, and, in particular, no theological validity is left for Jewish religion."[8]

Baum, a Jew who converted to Catholicism, was both an outsider and an insider, deeply committed to and yet profoundly concerned about the Church from the perspective of ethics and human rights. His blunt analysis still strikes me as an accurate reading of the Fourth Gospel, and, though published in 1974, as a moving articulation of the theological struggle in which I see many of my Christian colleagues engaged more than four decades later.

The works of both Baum and Ruether, which I encountered before I began my own engagement with the New Testament, support the approach that I have taken: to label anti-Judaism in John as such, and to resist efforts to explain away or other justify John's problematic statements.

In calling out the Gospel's anti-Judaism, I am hoping that others, including those for whom the Fourth Gospel is a canonical text, will also resist this aspect of its rhetoric, even as they may still be moved by other parts of its message. It occurs to me, however, that subjecting John to this type of ethical critique might also, inadvertently, risk inculcating the same anti-Jewish attitudes that I am trying to address. Are there those for whom this Gospel is authoritative who would also feel bound to uphold its anti-Jewish stance? I fear so. I have certainly encountered people who believe that being a faithful Christian also required them to see Jews as benighted Christ-killers destined for perdition; my experience is by no means unique. But I also know many who believe, as I do, that to be a faithful Christian or a faithful Jew does not require us to accept uncritically all of the views and attitudes that are present in our scriptures. Rather, we must continue to wrestle with our scriptures. Through such wrestling we may also come to recognize that certain positions which may have served a purpose when these texts were written are inimical to the values that are central to living a life of faith and integrity today.

In the end, exegesis cannot be separated from our identities and social locations; that I am a Jewish scholar born of Holocaust survivor postwar immigrants to Canada has helped to shape my interest in and approach to this Gospel. But other factors have also been important, including literary criticism and the many other intellectual currents that have entered our field, as well as the numerous encounters and conversations with colleagues and students that have been part of my intellectual formation and ongoing scholarly journey. In this context, I believe it is my responsibility to tell it like it is, or, at least, to tell it like I see it. The task of whether or how to integrate this view with Christian faith I must leave to others.

With these thoughts I descend the winding staircase from the sticky heart of the Gospel's web, having seen many curious things.[9] Whether I ascend again remains to be seen. I hope that my sojourn in the Gospel's "pretty parlor" is fruitful for my readers' own further thinking about the Gospel, its rhetoric, and its contribution to the process by which at least one group of believers in Christ began to construct a unique identity that in many ways continues to shape western society today.

NOTES

1. Jenkins, *Social Identity*. Joane Nagel, "Constructing Ethnicity." See also Raimo Hakola, *Reconsidering Johannine Christianity*.

2. On the range of possible readings and readers, see Reinhartz, *Befriending the Beloved Disciple*.

3. See the riveting discussion in Heschel, *The Aryan Jesus.*

4. It has become conventional to distinguish between anti-Judaism as a religious category and anti-Semitism as a racial category. Nevertheless, the lines are not always clearcut, and the ethical value of doing so is open to question. For a heated debate on the matter, see Robert Morgan, "Susannah Heschel's Aryan Grundmann," *Journal for the Study of the New Testament* 32, no. 4 (2010): 431–94, https://doi.org/10.1177/014206410366334; Susannah Heschel, "Historiography of Anti-Semitism versus Anti-Judaism: A Response to Robert Morgan," *Journal for the Study of the New Testament* 33 (2011): 257–279.

5. Gregory Baum's introduction was meaningful for several reasons. He had been one of my professors at the University of Toronto; he was a Jewish convert to Christianity who had never repudiated his Jewish identity, which included friendship with people in

my parents' survivor Bundist community, and he was an ex-priest who had challenged the Vatican on various human rights matters that were important to me. I subsequently learned that he had composed the first draft of the conciliar document *Nostra aetate*, the Declaration on the Relation of the Church with Non-Christian Religions.

6. Rosemary Radford Ruether, *Faith and Fratricide: The Theological Roots of Anti-Semitism* (New York: Seabury Press, 1974), 116.

7. Ruether, 116.

8. Gregory Baum, "Introduction," in *Faith and Fratricide: The Theological Roots of Anti-Semitism,* ed. Rosemary Radford Ruether (New York: Seabury Press, 1974), 5.

9. See Mary Howitt's poem, quoted as an epigraph to the Introduction of this book.

Bibliography

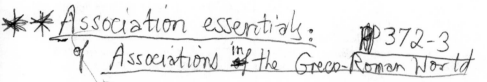

** Association essentials: PP372-3
of Associations in the Greco-Roman World

Abbott, H. Porter. *The Cambridge Introduction to Narrative*. Cambridge: Cambridge University Press, 2015.

Alikin, Valeriy A. *The Earliest History of the Christian Gathering: Origin, Development and Content of the Christian Gathering in the First to Third Centuries*. Supplements to Vigiliae Christianae v. 102. Leiden: Brill, 2010. http://www.jstor.org/stable/10.1163/j.ctt1w76wv6.

Anderson, Paul N., Felix Just, and Tom Thatcher, eds. *John, Jesus, and History*. Atlanta: Society of Biblical Literature, 2007.

Aristotle. *The Works of Aristotle*. Edited by W. D. Ross. Vol. 9. Franklin Center, PA: Franklin Library, 1978. http://books.google.com/books?id=8OskAQAAMAAJ.

Arnal, William. "The Collection and Synthesis of 'Tradition' and the Second-Century Invention of Christianity." *Method & Theory in the Study of Religion* 23, no. 3 (2011): 193–215. https://doi.org/10.1163/157006811X608359.

Arndt, William F., Frederick William Danker, and Walter Bauer. *A Greek-English Lexicon of the New Testament and Other Early Christian Literature*. 3rd ed. Chicago: The University of Chicago Press, 2000.

Ashton, John. "The Identity and Function of The Ἰουδαῖοι in the Fourth Gospel." *Novum Testamentum* 27, no. 1 (1985): 40–75.   **ON SENSE VS. REFERENT**

———. "The Transformation of Wisdom. A Study of the Prologue of John's Gospel." *New Testament Studies* 32, no. 2 (1986): 161–86. https://doi.org/10.1017/S0028688500013047.

Attridge, Harold W., and Wayne A. Meeks, eds. *The Harper-Collins Study Bible: New Revised Standard Version, with the Apocryphal/ Deuterocanonical Books*. San Francisco: HarperSanFrancisco, 2006.

Augustine. *On Christian Doctrine*. Edited by J. J. Shaw. Mineola: Dover Publications, 2009.

———. *Tractates on the Gospel of John 11–27*. Translated by John W. Rettig. Vol. 79. The Fathers of the Church. Washington, DC: Catholic University of America Press, 2010.

* ○ Andrée, A. "Peter Comester's [167] Lectures on the *glossa ordinaria* on the Gospel of John. . . ." *Traditio* 71 (2016): 203–34.
(provided a theol. framework for reading Scripture & doing theology— including writing sermons?)

Augustine, and John W. Rettig. *Tractates on the Gospel of John, 1–10.* Vol. 78. The Fathers of the Church. Baltimore: Catholic University of America Press, 2010.

Azar, Michael, "The Eastern Orthodox Tradition, Jews, and the Gospel of John," in *The Gospel of John and Jewish Christian Relations,* ed. Adele Reinhartz, (Lanham: Lexington, 2018)

Baker, Cynthia. "A 'Jew' by Any Other Name?" *Journal of Ancient Judaism* 2, no. 2 (2011): 153–80.

———. *Jew.* Key Words in Jewish Studies, 8. New Brunswick: Rutgers University Press, 2017.

Ball, David Mark. *"I Am" in John's Gospel: Literary Function, Background, and Theological Implications.* Sheffield: Sheffield Academic Press, 1996. http://public. eblib.com/EBLPublic/PublicView.do?ptiID=742500.

Barclay, John M. G. "'Jews' and 'Christians' in the Eyes of Roman Authors c.100 CE." In *Jews and Christians in the First and Second Centuries: How to Write Their History*, edited by Peter J. Tomson and Joshua Schwartz, 313–26. Leiden: Brill, 2014.

Barrett, C. K. *The Gospel According to St. John: An Introduction with Commentary and Notes on the Greek Text.* London: SPCK, 1965.

Barton, Carlin A. and Daniel Boyarin. *Imagine No Religion: How Modern Abstractions Hide Ancient Realities.* New York: Fordham University Press, 2016.

Bassler, Jouette M. "Mixed Signals: Nicodemus in the Fourth Gospel." *Journal of Biblical Literature* 108, no. 4 (1989): 635–46.

Batnitzky, Leora Faye. *How Judaism Became a Religion: An Introduction to Modern Jewish Thought.* Princeton: Princeton University Press, 2013.

Bauckham, Richard. *The Gospels for All Christians: Rethinking the Gospel Audiences.* Grand Rapids: W.B. Eerdmans, 1998.

Baum, Gregory. "Introduction." In *Faith and Fratricide: The Theological Roots of Anti-Semitism.*, edited by Rosemary Radford Ruether, 1–22. New York: Seabury Press, 1974.

Beck, David R. *The Discipleship Paradigm: Readers and Anonymous Characters in the Fourth Gospel.* Leiden: Brill, 1997.

Beck, Norman A. *Mature Christianity: The Recognition and Repudiation of the Anti-Jewish Polemic of the New Testament.* Selinsgrove: Susquehanna University Press, 1985.

Becker, Adam H., and Annette Yoshiko Reed. *The Ways That Never Parted: Jews and Christians in Late Antiquity and the Early Middle Ages.* Fortress Press, 2007.

———, eds. "What 'Parting of the Ways'? Jews, Gentiles, and the Ancient Mediterranean City." In *The Ways That Never Parted: Jews and Christians in Late Antiquity and the Early Middle Ages*, 35–63. Fortress Press, 2007.

Benay, Erin E. *Faith, Gender and the Senses in Italian Renaissance and Baroque Art: Interpreting the Noli Me Tangere and Doubting Thomas.* Visual Culture in Early Modernity. London: Routledge, 2016. https://login.proxy.bib.uottawa.ca/login?url=http://www.taylorfrancis.com/books/9781315094168.

Bennema, Cornelis. *Encountering Jesus: Character Studies in the Gospel of John.* Milton Keynes: Paternoster, 2009.

○ Aune, DE. ~~Prophecy in Early Christianity and the~~ Ancient Medit. World (1983)

———. "The Identity and Composition of Οι Ιουδαιοι in the Gospel of John." *Tyndale Bulletin* 60, no. 2 (2009): 239–63.

Berger, Michael S. *Rabbinic Authority*. New York: Oxford University Press, 1998.

Bernier, Jonathan. *Aposynagōgos and the Historical Jesus in John: Rethinking the Historicity of the Johannine Expulsion Passages*. Leiden: Brill, 2013.

Beutler, Johannes. *Judaism and the Jews in the Gospel of John*. Roma: Pontificio Istituto Biblico, 2006.

Bieringer, R., Didier Pollefeyt, and F. Vandecasteele-Vanneuville, eds. *Anti-Judaism and the Fourth Gospel: Papers of the Leuven Colloquium, 2000*. Assen: Royal Van Gorcum, 2001.

Bieringer, Reimund, Barbara Baert, and Karlijn Demasure, eds. *"Noli me tangere" in Interdisciplinary Perspective: Textual, Iconographic and Contemporary Interpretations*. Leuven: Peeters, 2016.

Bieringer, Reimund, and Didier Pollefeyt. "Wrestling with Johannine Anti-Judaism: A Hermeneutical Framework for the Analysis of the Current Debate." In *Anti-Judaism and the Fourth Gospel: Papers of the Leuven Colloquium, 2000*, edited by R. Bieringer, Didier Pollefeyt, and F. Vandecasteele-Vanneuville, 1–40. Assen: Royal Van Gorcum, 2001.

Black, C. Clifton. *The Rhetoric of the Gospel: Theological Artistry in the Gospels and Acts*. St. Louis: Chalice Press, 2001.

Black, C., and Duane Frederick Watson. *Words Well Spoken: George Kennedy's Rhetoric of the New Testament*. Vol. 8. Studies in Rhetoric and Religion 8. Waco: Baylor University Press, 2008.

Booth, Wayne C. *The Rhetoric of Fiction*. 2nd ed. Chicago: University of Chicago Press, 1983.

Borgen, Peder. *Bread from Heaven; an Exegetical Study of the Concept of Manna in the Gospel of John and the Writings of Philo*. Leiden: E.J. Brill, 1965.

———. "The Gospel of John and Hellenism: Some Observations." In *Exploring the Gospel of John: In Honor of D. Moody Smith*, edited by R. Alan Culpepper, C. Clifton Black, and D. Moody Smith, 98–123. Louisville: Westminster John Knox, 1996.

———. *The Gospel of John: More Light from Philo, Paul and Archaeology: The Scriptures, Tradition, Exposition, Settings, Meaning*. Leiden: Brill, 2014.

Bornhäuser, Karl. *Das Johannesevangelium, eine Missionsschrift für Israel*. Gütersloh: C. Bertelsmann, 1928.

Bowman, John. "The Fourth Gospel and the Samaritans." *Bulletin of the John Rylands Library* 40 (1958): 298–327.

Boyarin, Daniel. "A Tale of Two Synods: Nicaea, Yavneh, and Rabbinic Ecclesiology." *Exemplaria* 12, no. 1 (2000): 21–62.

———. *Border Lines: The Partition of Judaeo-Christianity*. Philadelphia: University of Pennsylvania Press, 2004.

———. "Justin Martyr Invents Judaism." *Church History* 70, no. 3 (2001): 427–461.

———. "The Ioudaioi of John and the Prehistory of Judaism." In *Pauline Conversations in Context: Essays in Honor of Calvin J. Roetzel*, edited by Janice Capel Anderson, Philip Sellew, Claudia Setzer, and C. J. Roetzel, 216–39. London: Sheffield Academic Press, 2002.

Brant, Jo-Ann A. *Dialogue and Drama: Elements of Greek Tragedy in the Fourth Gospel*. Peabody: Hendrickson Publishers, 2004.

———. *John*. Grand Rapids: Baker Academic, 2011.

Brass, Paul R. "Introduction." In *Riots and Pogroms*, edited by Paul R. Brass, 1–55. Houndmills: Macmillan, 1996.

Breed, Brennan. "Biblical Reception History: A Dangerous Supplement," October 2014. http://www.bibleinterp.com/articles/2014/10/bre388022.shtml.

Brown, Raymond E. *The Birth of the Messiah: A Commentary on the Infancy Narratives in the Gospels of Matthew and Luke*. New York: Doubleday, 2008.

———. *The Death of the Messiah: From Gethsemane to the Grave: A Commentary on the Passion Narratives in the Four Gospels*. New York: Doubleday, 1994.

Brown, Raymond Edward. *The Community of the Beloved Disciple*. New York: Paulist Press, 1979.

O ———. *The Gospel According to John*. Garden City: Doubleday, 1966.

O Brubaker, Rogers. *Ethnicity without Groups*. Cambridge, MA: Harvard University Press, 2004.

Brubaker, Rogers, and Frederick Cooper. "Beyond 'Identity.'" *Theory and Society* 29, no. 1 (2000): 1–47. https://doi.org/10.1023/A:1007068714468.

Brunson, Andrew C. *Psalm 118 in the Gospel of John: An Intertextual Study on the New Exodus Pattern in the Theology of John*. Tübingen: J.C.B. Mohr Siebeck, 2003.

Buchanan, George Wesley. "Samaritan Origin of the Gospel of John." In *Religions in Antiquity; Essays in Memory of Erwin Ramsdell Goodenough*, 149–75. Leiden: Brill, 1968.

Buell, Denise Kimber. *Why This New Race: Ethnic Reasoning in Early Christianity*. New York: Columbia University Press, 2005.

O Bultmann, Rudolf. *The Gospel of John: A Commentary*. Philadelphia: Westminster Press, 1971.

Burke, Kenneth. *A Rhetoric of Motives*. Berkeley: University of California Press, 1969.

———. *Counter-Statement*. Los Altos: Hermes Publications, 1953.

Cameron, Averil. *Christianity and the Rhetoric of Empire: The Development of Christian Discourse*. Berkeley: University of California Press, 1991.

Carnazzo, Sebastian A. *Seeing Blood and Water: A Narrative-Critical Study of John 19:34*. Eugene, Oregon: Pickwick Publications, 2012.

Carr, David McLain. *The Erotic Word: Sexuality, Spirituality, and the Bible*. New York: Oxford University Press, 2003. http://www.dawsonera.com/depp/reader/protected/external/AbstractView/S9780195343557.

Carroll, Noël. *The Philosophy of Motion Pictures*. Foundations of the Philosophy of the Arts; Oxford: Blackwell Pub., 2008.

O Carson, D. A. "Syntactical and Text-Critical Observations on John 20:30–31: One More Round on the Purpose of the Fourth Gospel." *Journal of Biblical Literature* 124, no. 4 (2005): 693–714. https://doi.org/10.2307/30041065.

———. "The Purpose of the Fourth Gospel: John 20:31 Reconsidered." *Journal of Biblical Literature* 106, no. 4 (1987): 639–651. https://doi.org/10.2307/3260824.

✓O Brown, R. *An Introduction to NT Christology*: Paulist, 1994.

✓ NB: Burridge, R. What Are the Gospels? & bios approach are

Carter, Warren. *John: Storyteller, Interpreter, Evangelist*. Peabody: Hendrickson, 2007.

Chae, Young S. *Jesus as the Eschatological Davidic Shepherd: Studies in the Old Testament, Second Temple Judaism, and in the Gospel of Matthew*. Tübingen: Mohr Siebeck, 2006.

Chancey, Mark A. *The Myth of a Gentile Galilee*. Cambridge: Cambridge University Press, 2002.

Chatman, Seymour Benjamin. *Story and Discourse: Narrative Structure in Fiction and Film*. Ithaca: Cornell University Press, 1978.

Chazon, Esther G. "Prayers from Qumran and Their Historical Implications." *Dead Sea Discoveries* 1, no. 3 (1994): 265–84.

Chilton, Bruce. "The Godfearers: From the Gospels to Aphrodisias." In *Partings: How Judaism and Christianity Became Two*, edited by Hershel Shanks, 55–71. Washington, D.C.: Biblical Archaeology Society, 2013.

"Chrysostom. Adversus Iudaeos," n.d. http://www.tertullian.org/fathers/chrysostom_adversus_judaeos_01_homily1.htm.

Cicero, Marcus Tullius. *De Oratore*. Edited by H. Rackham. Translated by E. W. Sutton, LCL. Cambridge, MA: Harvard University Press, 1976.

 Clark, Donald Lemen. *Rhetoric in Greco-Roman education*. Westport: Greenwood Pr., 1977.

Clark-Soles, Jaime. *Scripture Cannot Be Broken: The Social Function of the Use of Scripture in the Fourth Gospel*. Boston: Brill Academic Publishers, 2003. http://site.ebrary.com/id/10090611.

Cohen, Jeremy. *Living Letters of the Law: Ideas of the Jew in Medieval Christianity*. Berkeley: University of California Press, 1999. http://hdl.handle.net/2027/spo.baj9928.0110.013.

Cohen, S. J. D. *The Beginnings of Jewishness: Boundaries, Varieties, Uncertainties*. Berkeley: University of California Press, 1999.

Cohen, Shaye J. D. "Crossing the Boundary and Becoming a Jew." *Harvard Theological Review* 82, no. 1 (January 1989): 13–33.

Cohen, Shaye J. D. *From the Maccabees to the Mishnah*. Louisville: Westminster John Knox Press, 2014.

Cohen, Shaye J. D. "Respect for Judaism by Gentiles According to Josephus." *Harvard Theological Review* 80, no. 4 (October 1987): 409–30.

———. "The Significance of Yavneh: Pharisees, Rabbis, and the End of Jewish Sectarianism." *Hebrew Union College Annual* 55 (1984): 27–53.

Cohen, Shaye J. D. "Were Pharisees and Rabbis the Leaders of Communal Prayer and Torah Study in Antiquity? The Evidence of the New Testament, Josephus, and the Church Fathers." *The Echoes of Many Texts: Reflections on Jewish and Christian Traditions: Essays in Honor of Lou H. Silberman*, edited by William G. Denver and J. Edward Wright, 89–105. Atlanta: Scholars Press, 1997.

Collingwood, R. G. *The Idea of History,*. Oxford: Clarendon Press, 1946.

Coloe, Mary L. "Gentiles in the Gospel of John: Narrative Possibilities—John 12:12–43." In *Attitudes to Gentiles in Ancient Judaism and Early Christianity*, edited by David C. Sim and James S. McLaren, 209–23. London: Bloomsbury T & T Clark, 2013.

missing

Coloe, Mary L. *God Dwells with Us: Temple Symbolism in the Fourth Gospel*. Collegeville: Liturgical Press, 2001.

Conley, Thomas M. "Topics of Vituperation: Some Commonplaces of 4th-Century Oratory." In *Influences on Peripatetic Rhetoric: Essays in Honor of William W. Fortenbaugh*, edited by David C. Mirhady, 231–38. Leiden: Brill, 2007.

Cook, John Granger. *The Interpretation of the New Testament in Greco-Roman Paganism*. Peabody: Hendrickson Publishers, 2003. ✻

Cook, John Granger. *The Interpretation of the Old Testament in Greco-Roman Paganism*. Tübingen: Mohr Siebeck, 2004.

Cribiore, Raffaella. *Libanius the Sophist: Rhetoric, Reality, and Religion in the Fourth Century*. Ithaca: Cornell University Press, 2013.

Crossley, James G. *Jesus in an Age of Neoliberalism: Quests, Scholarship and Ideology*. Cambridge: Cambridge University Press, 2014. http://universitypublishingonline.org/acumen/ebook.jsf?bid=CBO9781844657384.

Culpepper, R. Alan. *Anatomy of the Fourth Gospel: A Study in Literary Design*. Foundations and Facets: New Testament. Philadelphia: Fortress Press, 1983.

——. "Anti-Judaism in the Fourth Gospel as a Theological Problem for Christian Interpreters." In *Anti-Judaism and the Fourth Gospel: Papers of the Leuven Colloquium, 2000*, edited by R. Bieringer, Didier Pollefeyt, and F. Vandecasteele-Vanneuville, 61–82. Assen: Royal Van Gorcum, 2001.

——. *John, the Son of Zebedee: The Life of a Legend (Studies on Personalities of the New Testament)*. Columbia: University of South Carolina Press, 1994.

——. *The Gospel and Letters of John*. Nashville: Abingdon Press, 1998.

Culpepper, R. Alan. "The Gospel of John and the Jews." *Review & Expositor* 84, no. 2 (1987): 273–88.

——. "The Relationship between John and 1 John." In *Communities in Dispute: Current Scholarship on the Johannine Epistles*, edited by R. Alan Culpepper and Paul N. Anderson, 95–120. Society of Biblical Literature, 2014. http://www.jstor.org.proxy.bc.edu/stable/j.ctt9qh1w6.

Daise, Michael A. *Feasts in John: Jewish Festivals and Jesus's "Hour" in the Fourth Gospel*. Tübingen: Mohr Siebeck, 2007.

D'Angelo, Mary Rose. "Abba and 'Father': Imperial Theology and the Jesus Traditions." *Journal of Biblical Literature* 111, no. 4 (1992): 611–30. https://doi.org/10.2307/3267435.

——. "Theology in Mark and Q: Abba and 'Father' in Context." *The Harvard Theological Review* 85, no. 2 (1992): 149–74.

Das, A. Andrew. *Paul and the Jews*. Peabody: Hendrickson, 2003.

Davies, Margaret. *Rhetoric and Reference in the Fourth Gospel*. Sheffield: Sheffield Academic Press, 1992.

DeConick, April. "Who Is Hiding in the Gospel of John? Reconceptualizing Johannine Theology and the Roots of Gnosticism." In *Histories of the Hidden God: Concealment and Revelation in Western Gnostic, Esoteric, and Mystical Traditions*, edited by April DeConick and Grant Adamson, 13–29. Gnostica. Durham: Acumen, 2013.

Dennis, John A. "Jesus's Death and the Gathering of True Israel: The Johannine Appropriation of Restoration Theology in the Light of John 11.47–52." Tübingen: Mohr Siebeck, 2006.

✻ e.g. on divine sonship, enthousiasmos, political "non-controversy" (apologetics)

DeVore, David J. "Eusebius' Un-Josephan History: Two Portraits of Philo of Alexandria and the Sources of Ecclesiastical History." In *Studia Patristica*, 161–79. Leuven: Peeters, 2013.

Dixon, Suzanne. *The Roman Family*. New York: ACLS History E-Book Project, 2005.

Donaldson, Terence L. *Jews and Anti-Judaism in the New Testament: Decision Points and Divergent Interpretations*. Waco: Baylor University Press, 2010.

Donaldson, Terence L. *Judaism and the Gentiles: Jewish Patterns of Universalism (to 135 C.E.)*. Waco: Baylor University Press, 2007.

———. "Nicodemus: A Figure of Ambiguity in a Gospel of Certainty." *Consensus* 24, no. 1 (1998): 121–24.

Drake, H. A, ed. *Violence in Late Antiquity: Perceptions and Practices*. London: Routledge, 2016. http://search.ebscohost.com/login.aspx?direct=true&scope=site&db=nlebk&db=nlabk&AN=1432040.

Dray, William H. *History as Re-Enactment: R.G. Collingwood's Idea of History*. Oxford: Clarendon Press, 1995.

Dunn, James D. G. *Jews and Christians: The Parting of the Ways AD 70 to 135*. Wissenschaftliche Untersuchungen Zum Neuen Testament. Tübingen: Mohr, 1992.

Edwards, Ruth B. "Aposynagōgos and the Historical Jesus in John: Rethinking the Historicity of the Johannine Expulsion Passages." *Journal for the Study of the New Testament* 37, no. 5 (August 2015): 53–53.

Efroymson, David P. "Jews and Judaism in Chrysostom on John." In *Proceedings of the Fifth Biennial Conference on Christianity and the Holocaust: "Christianity and Judaism: History, the Holocuast [Sic] and Reconciliation in the Third Millennium": Held at Princeton Marriott Forrestal Village, Princeton, New Jersey, October 18–19, 1998*, 177–90. Lawrenceville: Rider University, 1998.

Ehrman, Bart D. *The New Testament: A Historical Introduction to the Early Christian Writings*. New York: Oxford University Press, 2004.

Epp, Eldon Jay. "Anti-Semitism and the Popularity of the Fourth Gospel in Christianity." *CCAR Journal* 22, no. 4 (1975): 35–57.

Esler, Philip F. "From *Ioudaioi* to Children of God: The Development of a Non-Ethnic Group Identity in the Gospel of John." In *In Other Words: Essays on Social Science Methods and the New Testament in Honor of Jerome H. Neyrey*, edited by Jerome H. Neyrey, Hagedorn, Anselm C., Zeba A. Crook, and Eric Clark Stewart, 106–36. Sheffield: Sheffield Phoenix Press, 2007.

———. "Judaean and Christ-Follower Identities: Grounds for a Distinction." *New Testament Studies* 63, no. 4 (2017): 493–515.

Eslinger, Lyle. "The Wooing of the Woman at the Well: Jesus, the Reader and Reader-Response Criticism." *Literature and Theology* 1, no. 2 (1987): 167–83.

Estes, Douglas. *The Questions of Jesus in John: Logic, Rhetoric and Persuasive Discourse*. Leiden: Brill, 2013.

Eva Mroczek. *The Literary Imagination in Jewish Antiquity*. New York: Oxford University Press, 2016.

Fee, Gordon D. "On the Text and Meaning of John 20, 30–31." In *The Four Gospels: Festschrift Frans Neirynck. Vol. 3*, edited by Frans van Segbroeck, 2193–2205. Leuven: Leuven University Press, 1992.

o Ehrman, Bart. *The NT and Other Early Christian Writings* (2003) - All the apostolic fathers

o Ehrman, Bart. *How Jesus Became God*. (2014) (on evolving christology)

o Edwards, M. *Apologetics in the Roman Empire* ..... (1999)

Fehribach, Adeline. *The Women in the Life of the Bridegroom: A Feminist Historical-Literary Analysis of the Female Characters in the Fourth Gospel*. Collegeville: Liturgical Press, 1998.

Ferreira, Johan. *Johannine Ecclesiology*. Sheffield: Sheffield Academic Press, 1998. http://search.ebscohost.com/login.aspx?direct=true&scope=site&db=e000x na&AN=378316.

Fortna, Robert Tomson. *The Gospel of Signs: A Reconstruction of the Narrative Source Underlying the Fourth Gospel*. London: Cambridge University Press, 1970.

Fowden, Garth. "Late Polytheism." In *The Cambridge Ancient History Volume 12.*, edited by Alan Bowman, Averil Cameron, and Peter Garnsey, 521–37. Cambridge: Cambridge University Press, 2005. http://dx.doi.org/10.1017/CHOL9780521301992.

Fredriksen, Paula. *Augustine and the Jews: A Christian Defense of Jews and Judaism*. New York: Doubleday, 2008.

———. "How Later Contexts Affect Pauline Content, or: Retrospect Is the Mother of Anachronism." In *Jews and Christians in the First and Second Centuries: How to Write Their History*, edited by Peter J. Tomson and Joshua Schwartz, 17–51. Leiden: Brill, 2014.

———. "Mandatory Retirement: Ideas in the Study of Christian Origins Whose Time Has Come to Go." *Studies in Religion* 35, no. 2 (2006): 231–46.

———. *Paul, The Pagan's Apostle*. New Haven: Yale University Press, 2017.

Freed, Edwin D. "Did John Write His Gospel Partly to Win Samaritan Converts." *Novum Testamentum* 12, no. 3 (July 1, 1970): 241–56.

Freed, Edwin D. "Samaritan Influence in the Gospel of John." *The Catholic Biblical Quarterly* 30, no. 4 (October 1968): 580–87.

Frey, Jörg. "Heiden—Griechen—Gotteskinder: zu Gestalt und Funktion der Rede von den Heiden in vierten Evangelium." In *Die Herrlichkeit des Gekreuzigten: Studien zu den Johanneischen Schriften I*, 297–338. Tübingen: Mohr Siebeck, 2013. http://www.zora.uzh.ch/85152.

———. "Temple and Identity in Early Christianity and in the Johannine Community: Reflections on the 'Parting of the Ways.'" In *Was 70 CE a Watershed in Jewish History?: On Jews and Judaism before and after the Destruction of the Second Temple*, edited by Daniel R. Schwartz and Zeev Weiss, 447–507. Leiden: Brill, 2012.

Frey, Jörg, Zimmermann Ruben, J. G. van der Watt, and Gabriele Kern, eds. *Imagery in the Gospel of John: Terms, Forms, Themes, and Theology of Johannine Figurative Language*. Tübingen: Mohr Siebeck, 2006.

Freyne, Seán. "Vilifying the Other and Defining the Self: Matthew's and John's Anti-Jewish Polemic in Focus." In *"To See Ourselves as Others See Us": Christians, Jews, "Others" in Late Antiquity*, edited by Jacob Neusner, Ernest S. Frerichs, and Caroline McCracken-Flesher, 117–43. Chico: Scholars Press, 1985.

Fuglseth, Kåre. *Johannine Sectarianism in Perspective: A Sociological, Historical, and Comparative Analysis of Temple and Social Relationships in the Gospel of John, Philo, and Qumran*. Leiden: Brill, 2005.

○ Friesen, SJ. Twice Neokoros: Ephesus, Asia, . - - - - (1993)

○ Gregerman, . Building on the Ruins of the Temple... (2014) (on early Christian apologetics)

Gager, John G. *The Origins of Anti-Semitism: Attitudes toward Judaism in Pagan and Christian Antiquity*. New York: Oxford University Press, 1983.

Gamble, Harry Y. *Books and Readers in the Early Church: A History of Early Christian Texts*. New Haven: Yale University Press, 1995.

Gaston, Lloyd. *Paul and the Torah*. Vancouver: University of British Columbia Press, 1987.

Geertz, Clifford. *The Interpretation of Cultures: Selected Essays*. New York: Basic Books, 1973.

Gerdmar, Anders. *Roots of Theological Anti-Semitism: German Biblical Interpretation and the Jews, from Herder and Semler to Kittel and Bultmann*. Leiden: Brill, 2010.

Gerrig, Richard J. *Experiencing Narrative Worlds: On the Psychological Activities of Reading*. New Haven: Yale University Press, 1993.

Gibbons, Debbie M. "Nicodemus: Character Development, Irony and Repetition in the Fourth Gospel." *Proceedings (Grand Rapids, Mich.)* 11 (1991): 116–28.

Gowler, David B. "Socio-Rhetorical Interpretation: Textures of a Text and Its Reception." *Journal for the Study of the New Testament* 33, no. 2 (2010): 191–206.

Grafton, Anthony, Glenn W. Most, Salvatore Settis, and Eileen Adair Reeves. *The Classical Tradition*. Cambridge, MA: The Belknap press of Harvard University Press, 2010.

Green, Melanie C., and Timothy C. Brock. "The Role of Transportation in the Persuasiveness of Public Narratives." *Journal of Personality and Social Psychology* 79, no. 5 (2000): 701–721. https://doi.org/10.1037/0022–3514.79.5.701.

Griffith-Jones, Robin. "Apocalyptic Mystagogy: Rebirth-from-Above in the Reception of John's Gospel." In *John's Gospel and Intimations of Apocalyptic*, edited by Catrin H. Williams and Christopher Rowland, 274–99. London: Bloomsbury T & T Clark, 2013.

Guilding, Aileen. *The Fourth Gospel and Jewish Worship: A Study of the Relation of St. John's Gospel to the Ancient Jewish Lectionary System*. Oxford: Clarendon Press, 1960.

Hakola, Raimo. *Identity Matters: John, the Jews, and Jewishness*. Leiden: Brill, 2005. http://public.eblib.com/choice/publicfullrecord.aspx?p=280605.

———. *Identity Matters: John, the Jews, and Jewishness*. Leiden: Brill, 2005.

———. *Reconsidering Johannine Christianity: A Social Identity Approach*. New York: Routledge, 2015.

———. *Reconsidering Johannine Christianity: A Social Identity Approach*. New York: Routledge, 2015.

———. "The Burden of Ambiguity: Nicodemus and the Social Identity of the Johannine Christians." *New Testament Studies* 55, no. 4 (October 2009): 438–55. https://doi.org/10.1017/S0028688509990014.

Hardman, Melissa. "Wine & Viniculture in Roman and Medieval History." *The Vine Daily* (blog), July 20, 2015. https://www.winebags.com/Wine-Viniculture-in-Roman-and-Medieval-History-s/2041.htm#sthash.qYeI1LdP.dpuf.

Harrington, Daniel J. "Pseudo-Philo." In *The Old Testament Pseudepigrapha*, edited by James H. Charlesworth, 2:297–377. New York: Doubleday, 1985.

Harris, Wm. *Ancient Literacy* (1989)

Harland, P. "Honours and Worship..... Ephesus," SR 25 (1996) 319–34.

Harland P. *Associations, Synagogues & Congregations* [Studies in Religion]

Harrison, Carol. *The Art of Listening in the Early Church*. Oxford: Oxford University Press, 2013.   (on reading aloud, even to oneself, p. 5)

Harvey, Graham. *The True Israel: Uses of the Names Jew, Hebrew, and Israel in Ancient Jewish and Early Christian Literature*. Boston: Brill Academic, 2001.

Heemstra, Marius. *The Fiscus Judaicus and the Parting of the Ways*. Tübingen: Mohr Siebeck, 2010.

Hengel, Martin. *The Johannine Question*. London: SCM Press, 1989.

Heschel, Susannah. "Historiography of Anti-Semitism versus Anti-Judaism: A Response to Robert Morgan." *Journal for the Study of the New Testament* 33 (2011): 257–279.

———. "Nazifying Christian Theology: Walter Grundmann and the Institute for the Study and Eradication of Jewish Influence on German Church Life." *Church History: Studies in Christianity and Culture* 63, no. 4 (1994): 587–605. https://doi .org/10.2307/3167632.

———. *The Aryan Jesus: Christian Theologians and the Bible in Nazi Germany*. Princeton: Princeton University Press, 2008.

Hill, Charles E. *The Johannine Corpus in the Early Church*. Oxford: Oxford University Press, 2004.

Horbury, William. "The Benediction of the 'Minim' and Early Jewish-Christian Controversy." *The Journal of Theological Studies* 33, no. 1 (1982): 19–61.

Horowitz, Mary. "Aristotle and Woman." *Journal of the History of Biology* 9, no. 2 (1976): 183–213. https://doi.org/10.1007/BF00209881.

Horrell, David G. "Ethnicisation, Marriage and Early Christian Identity: Critical Reflections on 1 Corinthians 7, 1 Peter 3 and Modern New Testament Scholarship." *New Testament Studies* 62, no. 3 (2016): 439–460. https://doi.org/10.1017/ S0028688516000084.

———. "'Race,' 'Nation,' 'People': Ethnic Identity-Construction in 1 Peter 2.9." *New Testament Studies* 58, no. 01 (2012): 123–43. https://doi.org/10.1017/S00286885 11000245.

Hurtado, Larry W. "Oral Fixation and New Testament Studies? 'Orality', 'Performance' and Reading Texts in Early Christianity." *New Testament Studies* 60, no. 3 (July 2014): 321–40. https://doi.org/10.1017/S0028688514000058.

Hylen, Susan. *Imperfect Believers: Ambiguous Characters in the Gospel of John*. Louisville: Westminster John Knox Press, 2009.

Iverson, Kelly R. "Oral Fixation or Oral Corrective? A Response to Larry Hurtado." *New Testament Studies* 62, no. 2 (April 2016): 183–200. https://doi.org/10.1017/ S0028688515000430.

Jack, Sarah J., and Kevin R. Ronan. "Bibliotherapy: Practice and Research." *School Psychology International* 29, no. 2 (2008): 161–182. https://doi. org/10.1177/0143034308090058.

Jenkins, Richard. *Social Identity*. London: Routledge, 2008.

Johnson Hodge, Caroline. *If Sons, Then Heirs: A Study of Kinship and Ethnicity in the Letters of Paul*. New York: Oxford University Press, 2007. http://www.myilibrary .com?id=116252.

Johnson, Luke Timothy. "The New Testament's Anti-Jewish Slander and the Conventions of Ancient Polemic." *Journal of Biblical Literature* 108, no. 3 (1989): 419–41.

Jones, Christopher P. *Between Pagan and Christian.* Cambridge (Massachusetts): Harvard University Press, 2014.

Jonge, Marinus de. "Signs and Works in the Fourth Gospel." In *Miscellanea Neotestamentica 2*, edited by T. Baarda, A. F. J. Klijn, and W. C. van Unnik, 107–25. NovTSup 48. Leiden: Brill, 1978.

Juel, Donald H. "The Future of the Religious Past: Qumran and the Palestinian Jesus Movement." In *The Bible and the Dead Sea Scrolls: The Second Princeton Symposium on Judaism and Christian Origins. 1, 1,* edited by James H. Charlesworth, 61–74. Waco: Baylor Univ. Press, 2006.

"Juvenal, Satires," n.d. http://www.tertullian.org/fathers/juvenal_satires_14.htm#6.

Katz, Steven T. "Issues in the Separation of Judaism and Christianity after 70 CE: A Reconsideration." *Journal of Biblical Literature* 103, no. 1 (1984): 43–76.

Keen, Suzanne. "A Theory of Narrative Empathy." *Narrative* 14, no. 3 (2006): 207–236. https://doi.org/10.1353/nar.2006.0015.

Keener, Craig S. *The Gospel of John: A Commentary.* Peabody: Hendrickson, 2003.
———. *The Gospel of John: A Commentary.* Peabody: Hendrickson Publishers, 2003.

Kelber, Werner H. *The Oral and the Written Gospel: The Hermeneutics of Speaking and Writing in the Synoptic Tradition, Mark, Paul, and Q.* Bloomington: Indiana University Press, 1997.

Kennedy, George A. *Classical Rhetoric and Its Christian and Secular Tradition from Ancient to Modern Times.* Chapel Hill: University of North Carolina Press, 1980.

———. *New Testament Interpretation through Rhetorical Criticism.* Chapel Hill: University of North Carolina Press, 1984.

Kerr, Alan Richard. *The Temple of Jesus's Body: The Temple Theme in the Gospel of John.* Sheffield: Sheffield Academic Press, 2002.

Kierspel, Lars. *The Jews and the World in the Fourth Gospel: Parallelism, Function, and Context.* Tübingen: Mohr Siebeck, 2006.

———. *The Jews and the World in the Fourth Gospel: Parallelism, Function, and Context.* Wissenschaftliche Untersuchungen Zum Neuen Testament. 2. Reihe; 220. Tübingen: Mohr Siebeck, 2006.

Kile, Chad. "Feeling Persuaded: Christianization and Social Formation." In *Rhetoric and Reality in Early Christianities*, edited by Willi Braun, 219–48. Waterloo: Published for the Canadian Corporation for Studies in Religion/Corporation canadienne des sciences religieuses by Wilfrid Laurier University Press, 2005.

Kimelman, Reuven. "Birkat Ha-Minim and the Lack of Evidence for an Anti-Christian Jewish Prayer in Late Antiquity." In *Jewish and Christian Self-Definition, 2*, 226–44. Philadelphia: Fortress, 1981.

King, Karen L. *The Gospel of Mary of Magdala: Jesus and the First Woman Apostle.* Santa Rosa: Polebridge Press, 2003.

Klink, Edward W. *John.* Grand Rapids: Zondervan, 2016.

esp. on Ephesus as provenance

Klink, Edward W III. "Expulsion from the Synagogue? Rethinking a Johannine Anachronism." *Tyndale Bulletin* 59, no. 1 (2008): 99–118.

Kloppenborg, John S. "Disaffiliation in Associations and the Ἀποσυναγωγός of John." *HTS Teologiese Studies/Theological Studies* 67 (2011). https://doi.org/10.4102/hts.v67i1.962.

Knust, Jennifer Wright. "Early Christian Re-Writing and the History of the Pericope Adulterae." *Journal of Early Christian Studies* 14, no. 4 (2006): 485–536.

———. "Too Hot to Handle? A Story of an Adulteress and the Gospel of John." In *Women of the New Testament and Their Afterlives*, edited by Christine E. Joynes, 143–63. Sheffield: Sheffield Phoenix Press, 2009.

Kobel, Esther. *Dining with John: Communal Meals and Identity Formation in the Fourth Gospel and Its Historical and Cultural Context*. Leiden: Brill, 2011. http://search.ebscohost.com/login.aspx?direct=true&scope=site&db=nlebk&db=nlabk&AN=408440.

Koester, Craig R. *Symbolism in the Fourth Gospel: Meaning, Mystery, Community*. 2nd ed.. Minneapolis: Fortress Press, 2003.

Kümmel, Werner Georg. *Introduction to the New Testament*. Translated by Paul Feine. Nashville: Abingdon Press, 1975.

Kuypers, Jim A. ed. *Rhetorical Criticism: Perspectives in Action*. Lanham: Lexington Books, 2009.

Kuypers, Jim A. and Andrew King. "What Is Rhetoric?" In *Rhetorical Criticism: Perspectives in Action*, edited by Jim A. Kuypers, 1–12. Lanham: Lexington Books, 2009.

Kysar, Robert. "The Expulsion from the Synagogue: The Tale of a Theory." In *Voyages with John: Charting the Fourth Gospel.*, 237–45. Waco: Baylor University Press, 2006. http://search.ebscohost.com/login.aspx?direct=true&scope=site&db=nlebk&db=nlabk&AN=147100.

———. *Voyages with John: Charting the Fourth Gospel*. Waco: Baylor University Press, 2006.

Kysar, Robert Dean. "The Promises and Perils of Preaching on the Gospel of John." *Dialog* 19, no. 3 (1980): 214–20.

Lamb, David A. *Text, Context and the Johannine Community: A Sociolinguistic Analysis of the Johannine Writings*. London: Bloomsbury T & T Clark, 2014.

Langer, Ruth. *Cursing the Christians? A History of the Birkat Haminim*. New York: Oxford University Press, 2011.

Leibig, Janis E. "John and 'the Jews': Theological Anti-Semitism in the Fourth Gospel." *Journal of Ecumenical Studies* 20, no. 2 (1983): 209–34.

Levine, Amy-Jill. *The Misunderstood Jew: The Church and the Scandal of the Jewish Jesus*. San Francisco: HarperSanFrancisco, 2006.

Levine, Lee I. *The Ancient Synagogue: The First Thousand Years*. New Haven: Yale University Press, 2000. (mourners?)

Levine, Lee I. "The Nature and Origin of the Palestinian Synagogue Reconsidered." *Journal of Biblical Literature* 115, no. 3 (1996): 425–48. https://doi.org/10.2307/3266895.

Lieu, Judith. *Christian Identity in the Jewish and Graeco-Roman World*. Oxford: Oxford University Press, 2004.

——— and M. de Boer. *Oxford Handbook of Johannine Studies*. Oxford: Oxford University Press, 2018 (pp. 121-37)

———. *Neither Jew nor Greek? Constructing Early Christianity*. Edinburgh: T & T Clark, 2002.

Limor, Ora, and Guy G. Stroumsa, eds. *Contra Iudaeos: Ancient and Medieval Polemics between Christians and Jews*. Tübingen: J.C.B. Mohr, 1996.

Lincoln, Andrew T. "The Beloved Disciple as Eyewitness and the Fourth Gospel as Witness." *Journal for the Study of the New Testament* 85 (2002): 3–26.

Lincoln, Andrew T. *Truth on Trial: The Lawsuit Motif in the Fourth Gospel*. Peabody: Hendrickson Publishers, 2000.

Lincoln, Bruce. *Discourse and the Construction of Society: Comparative Studies of Myth, Ritual, and Classification*. Oxford: Oxford University Press, 2014.

Lindars, Barnabas. "The Persecution of Christians in John 15:18–16:4." In *Suffering and Martyrdom in the New Testament: Studies Presented to G.M. Styler by the Cambridge New Testament Seminar*, edited by G. M. Styler, William Horbury, and Brian McNeil, 48–69. Cambridge: Cambridge University Press, 1981.

Longenecker, Bruce W. "The Empress, the Goddess, and the Earthquake: Atmospheric Conditions Pertaining to Jesus-Devotion in Pompeii." In *Early Christianity in Pompeiian Light: People, Texts, Situations*, edited by Bruce W. Longenecker, 59–89. Minneapolis: Fortress Press, 2016.

Lowe, Malcolm F. "Who Were the 'ΙΟΥΔΑΙΟΙ?" *Novum Testamentum* 18, no. 2 (1976): 101–30.

Malina, Bruce J. "Was Jesus a Jew? Was Aristotle a Greek-American? Translating *Ioudaios*." Accessed February 19, 2017. http://assemblyoftrueisrael.com/Documents/Yahshuawasnojew%5B1%5D.htm.

Marcus, Joel. "Birkat Ha-Minim Revisited." *New Testament Studies* 55, no. 4 (2009): 523–51.

Marjanen, Antti. "Mary Magdalene, a Beloved Disciple." In *Mariam, the Magdalene, and the Mother*, edited by Deirdre Joy Good, 49–61. Bloomington: Indiana University Press, 2005.

Marjanen, Antti. "Mary Magdalene, a Beloved Disciple." In *Mariam, the Magdalen, and the Mother*, 49–61. Bloomington: Indiana University Press, 2005.

Martyn, J. Louis. "A Gentile Mission That Replaced an Earlier Jewish Mission?" In *Exploring the Gospel of John: In Honor of D. Moody Smith*, edited by R. Alan Culpepper and C. Clifton Black, 124–44. Louisville: Westminster John Knox Press, 1996.

———. *History and Theology in the Fourth Gospel*. Louisville: Westminster John Knox Press, 2003.

———. "The Johannine Community among Jewish and Other Early Christian Communities." In *What We Have Heard from the Beginning: The Past, Present, and Future of Johannine Studies*, edited by Tom Thatcher, 183–90. Waco: Baylor University Press, 2007.

Mason, Steve. *A History of the Jewish War, AD 66–74*. New York: Cambridge University Press, 2016.

———. "Jews, Judaeans, Judaizing, Judaism: Problems of Categorization in Ancient History." *Journal for the Study of Judaism in the Persian, Hellenistic and Roman Period* 38 (2007): 457–512.

MacMullen, R. *Enemies of the Roman Order* (1966)
(prophets; urban unrest)

Kloppenborg, J. & S. Wilson (eds), *Voluntary Associations in the Graeco-Roman World* (1996) (mourners?)

Mason, Steve, and Philip F. Esler. "Judaean and Christ-Follower Identities: Grounds for a Distinction." *New Testament Studies* 63, no. 4 (2017): 493–515. https://doi.org/10.1017/S0028688517000145.

Masuzawa, Tomoko. *The Invention of World Religions or, How European Universalism Was Preserved in the Language of Pluralism.* Chicago: University of Chicago Press, 2007.

Matthews, Shelly. *First Converts: Rich Pagan Women and the Rhetoric of Mission in Early Judaism and Christianity.* Contraversions. Stanford: Stanford University Press, 2001. https://login.proxy.bib.uottawa.ca/login?url=http://hdl.handle.net/2027/heb.04314.

McCaffrey, James. *The House with Many Rooms: The Temple Theme of Jn. 14, 2–3.* Roma: Editrice Pontificio Istituto Biblico, 1989.

McCready, Wayne O., and Adele Reinhartz. *Common Judaism: Explorations in Second-Temple Judaism.* Minneapolis: Fortress Press, 2008.

McCutcheon, Russell T. *Critics Not Caretakers: Redescribing the Public Study of Religion.* Albany: State University of New York Press, 2001.

———. *Studying Religion: An Introduction.* New York: Routledge, 2014.

McWhirter, Jocelyn. *The Bridegroom Messiah and the People of God: Marriage in the Fourth Gospel.* Cambridge: Cambridge University Press, 2006.

Meeks, Wayne A. "'Am I a Jew?'—Johannine Christianity and Judaism." In *Christianity, Judaism and Other Greco-Roman Cults: Studies for Morton Smith at Sixty,* edited by Jacob Neusner, 163–86. Leiden: Brill, 1975.

———. "Breaking Away: Three New Testament Pictures of Christianity's Separation from the Jewish Communities." In *"To See Ourselves as Others See Us": Christians, Jews, "Others" in Late Antiquity,* edited by Jacob Neusner, Ernest S. Frerichs, and Caroline McCracken-Flesher, 93–115. Chico: Scholars Press, 1985.

———. "Man from Heaven in Johannine Sectarianism." *Journal of Biblical Literature* 91, no. 1 (1972): 44–72.

Meier, John P. *A Marginal Jew: Rethinking the Historical Jesus. Volume 4, Law and Love.* New Haven: Doubleday, 2009.

Miller, David. "The Meaning of *Ioudaios* and Its Relationship to Other Group Labels in Ancient 'Judaism.'" *Currents in Biblical Research* 9, no. 1 (2010): 98–126.

Miller, David M. "Ethnicity Comes of Age: An Overview of Twentieth-Century Terms for *Ioudaios.*" *Currents in Biblical Research* 10, no. 2 (2012): 293–311.

———. "Ethnicity, Religion and the Meaning of *Ioudaios* in Ancient 'Judaism.'" *Currents in Biblical Research* 12, no. 2 (2014): 216–65.

Minear, Paul S. *John, the Martyr's Gospel.* New York: Pilgrim Press, 1984.

Moloney, Francis J. "John 21 and the Johannine Story." In *Anatomies of Narrative Criticism,* edited by Tom Thatcher, 237–52. Atlanta: Society of Biblical Literature, 2008.

Moloney, Francis J. *Love in the Gospel of John: An Exegetical, Theological, and Literary Study.* Grand Rapids: Baker, 2013.

———. "Narrative and Discourse at the Feast of Tabernacles: John 7:1–8:59." In *Word, Theology and Community in John,* 155–72. St Louis: Chalice Press, 2002.

(handwritten annotations:)

(2010) 9

10², mo. 2 (2012) 2

☆ Currents in Biblical Research

☆ Currents in Biblical Research 12, no. 2 (2014) 2

○ Metzger, Bruce. *The Canon of the NT* ..... c (1987)

Morgan, Robert. "Susannah Heschel's Aryan Grundmann." *Journal for the Study of the New Testament* 32, no. 4 (June 2010): 431–94. https://doi.org/10.1177/014206410366334.

Motyer, Stephen. "Bridging the Gap: How Might the Fourth Gospel Help Us Cope with the Legacy of Christianity's Exclusive Claim over against Judaism?" In *The Gospel of John and Christian Theology*, edited by Richard Bauckham and Carl Mosser, 143–67. Grand Rapids: William B. Eerdmans Pub., 2008.

———. *Your Father the Devil: A New Approach to John and the Jews*. Carlisle: Paternoster Pr, 1997.

Mournet, Terence C. *Oral Tradition and Literary Dependency: Variability and Stability in the Synoptic Tradition and Q*. Tübingen: Mohr Siebeck, 2005.

Mroczek, Eva. *The Literary Imagination in Jewish Antiquity*. New York: Oxford University Press, 2016.

Murdock, James. *The Syriac New Testament Translated into English from the Syriac Peshitto Version*. Piscataway: Gorgias Press, 2001.

Murray, Michele. *Playing a Jewish Game: Gentile Christian Judaizing in the First and Second Centuries CE*. Waterloo: Published for the Canadian Corp. for Studies in Religion = Corp. canadienne des Sciences religeuses by Wilfrid Laurier University Press, 2004.

Myers, Alicia D. "'Jesus Said to Them . . .': The Adaptation of Juridical Rhetoric in John 5:19–47." *Journal of Biblical Literature* 132, no. 2 (2013): 415–430.

Myers, Alicia D. "Prosopopoetics and Conflict: Speech and Expectations in John 8." *Biblica* 92, no. 4 (2011): 580–96.

Myles, Robert J., and James G. Crossley. "Biblical Scholarship, Jews and Israel: On Bruce Malina, Conspiracy Theories and Ideological Contradictions." The Bible and Interpretation, December 2012. http://www.bibleinterp.com/opeds/myl368013.shtml.

Nagel, Joane. "Constructing Ethnicity: Creating and Recreating Ethnic Identity and Culture." *Social Problems* 41, no. 1 (1994): 152–76.

Needham, Joseph, and Arthur F. W Hughes. *A History of Embryology*. New York: Abelard-Schuman, 1959.

Neyrey, Jerome H. *An Ideology of Revolt: John's Christology in Social-Science Perspective*. Eugene: Wipf & Stock Publishers, 2007.

Neyrey, Jerome H. "Encomium versus Vituperation: Contrasting Portraits of Jesus in the Fourth Gospel." *Journal of Biblical Literature* 126, no. 3 (2007): 529–52.

Neyrey, Jerome H. *The Gospel of John in Cultural and Rhetorical Perspective*. Grand Rapids: William B. Eerdmans Pub. Co., 2009.

Nussbaum, Martha C. "Aristotle on Human Nature and the Foundations of Ethics." In *World, Mind, and Ethics: Essays on the Ethical Philosophy of Bernard Williams*, edited by J. E. J. Altham and Ross Harrison, 86–131. Cambridge: Cambridge University Press, 1995. https://www.cambridge.org/core/books/world-mind-and-ethics/aristotle-on-human-nature-and-the-foundations-of-ethics/28C561667CF0A244E2FDBFE20265ED89.

Nussbaum, Martha Craven. *The Therapy of Desire: Theory and Practice in Hellenistic Ethics*. Princeton: Princeton University Press, 1994.

*O Morgan, . Literate Education in the Hellenistic and Roman World (1998) "Con Homer", "G-R cultures"

*O Neusner, J. Christianity, Judaism and other Greco-Roman Cults ( ) vol 12 "Kinship of Acts & John" pt 1

Oatley, Keith. "A Taxonomy of the Emotions of Literary Response and a Theory of Identification in Fictional Narrative." *Poetics* 23, no. 1 (1995): 53–74. https://doi .org/10.1016/0304–422X(94)P4296-S.

O'Collins, Gerald. "Mary Magdalene as Major Witness to Jesus's Resurrection." *Theological Studies* 48, no. 4 (December 1987): 631–46.

Odeberg, Hugo. *The Fourth Gospel. Interpreted in Its Relation to Contemporaneous Religious Currents in Palestine and the Hellenistic-Oriental World.* Amsterdam: B.R. Grüner, 1968.

Ong, Walter J. *Orality and Literacy: The Technologizing of the Word.* London: Methuen, 1982.

Ovide. *Metamorphoses.* Translated by Stanley Lombardo. Indianapolis: Hackett, 2010.

Painter, John. "John 9 and the Interpretation of the Fourth Gospel." *Journal for the Study of the New Testament* 28 (October 1986): 31–61.

———. "Rereading Genesis in the Prologue of John?" In *Neotestamentica et Philonica: Studies in Honor of Peder Borgen*, edited by David E. Aune, Torrey Seland, and Jarl Henning Ulrichsen, 180–201. Leiden: Brill, 2003.

Pamment, Margaret. "Is There Convincing Evidence of Samaritan Influence on the Fourth Gospel." *Zeitschrift Für Die Neutestamentliche Wissenschaft und die Kunde Der Älteren Kirche* 73, no. 3–4 (1982): 221–30.

———. "John 3:5: 'Unless One Is Born of Water and the Spirit, He Cannot Enter the Kingdom of God.'" *Novum Testamentum* 25, no. 2 (1983): 189–190. https://doi .org/10.1163/156853683X00249.

Pancaro, Severino. *The Law in the Fourth Gospel: The Torah and the Gospel, Moses and Jesus, Judaism and Christianity According to John.* Leiden: Brill, 1975.

Parsenios, George L. *Rhetoric and Drama in the Johannine Lawsuit Motif.* Tübingen: Mohr Siebeck, 2010.

Pecknold, C. C. "Theo-Semiotics and Augustine's Hermeneutical Jew, Or, 'What's a Little Supersessionism between Friends?'" In *Augustine and World Religions*, edited by Brian Brown, John A. Doody, and Kim Paffenroth, 97–112. Lanham: Lexington Books, 2008. http://public.eblib.com/choice/publicfullrecord.aspx?p=1380481.

Petersen, Anders Klostergaard. "At the End of the Road: Reflections on a Popular Scholarly Metaphor." In *The Formation of the Church: Papers from the Seventh Nordic New Testament Conference in Stavanger 2003*, edited by Jostein Ådna, 45–72. Tübingen: Mohr Siebeck, 2005.

Phelan, James. *Narrative as Rhetoric: Technique, Audiences, Ethics, Ideology.* Columbus: Ohio State University Press, 1996.

———. "Rhetorical Literary Ethics and Lyric Narrative: Robert Frost's 'Home Burial.'" *Poetics Today* 25, no. 4 (2004): 627–651.

Pinker, Steven. *How the Mind Works.* New York: Norton, 1997.

Pippin, Tina. "'For Fear of the Jews': Lying and Truth-Tellling in Translating the Gospel of John." *Semeia* 76 (1996): 81–97.

Porter, Stanley E. *John, His Gospel, and Jesus: In Pursuit of the Johannine Voice.* Grand Rapids: William B. Eerdmans Publishing Company, 2015.

———. *John, His Gospel, and Jesus: In Pursuit of the Johannine Voice.* Grand Rapids: William B. Eerdmans Publishing Company, 2015.

————, ed. *The Messiah in the Old and New Testaments*. Grand Rapids: William B. Eerdmans, 2007.

Preus, A. "Science and Philosophy in Aristotle's Generation of Animals." *Journal of the History of Biology* 3 (1970): 1–52.

Pryor, Dwight A. "The Most Jewish Gospel?" Accessed January 1, 2017. http://jc studies.com/the-most-jewish-Gospel/.

Reinhartz, Adele. "A Fork in the Road or a Multi-Lane Highway? New Perspectives on the 'Parting of the Ways' between Judaism and Christianity." In *Changing Face of Judaism, Christianity, and Other Greco-Roman Religions in Antiquity*, 280–95. Gütersloh: Gütersloher, 2006.

————. "'And the Word Was Begotten': Divine Epigenesis in the Gospel of John." *Semeia*, no. 85 (January 1, 1999): 83–103.

————. *Befriending the Beloved Disciple: A Jewish Reading of the Gospel of John*. New York: Continuum, 2001.

————. *Caiaphas the High Priest*. Columbia: University of South Carolina Press, 2011.

————. "Gospel Audiences: Variations on a Theme." In *The Audience of the Gospels: The Origin and Function of the Gospels in Early Christianity*, edited by Edward W. Klink, 134–52. London: T & T Clark, 2009.

————. "Great Expectations: A Reader-Oriented Approach to Johannine Christology and Eschatology." *Literature Theology Literature and Theology* 3, no. 1 (1989): 61–76.

————. "Jesus as Prophet: Predictive Prolepses in the Fourth Gospel." *Journal for the Study of the New Testament* 36, no. 1 (1989): 3–16.

————. "'Jews' and Jews in the Fourth Gospel." In *Anti-Judaism and the Fourth Gospel: Papers of the Leuven Colloquium, 2000*, edited by R. Bieringer, Didier Pollefeyt, and F. Vandecasteele-Vanneuville, 341–56. Assen: Royal Van Gorcum, 2001.

————. "John 8:31–59 from a Jewish Perspective." In *Remembering for the Future 2000: The Holocaust in an Age of Genocides*, edited by John K. Roth and Elisabeth Maxwell-Meynard, 2:787–97. London: Palgrave, 2001.

————. "John 20:30–31 and the Purpose of the Fourth Gospel." PhD, McMaster University, 1983.

————. "On Travel, Translation, and Ethnography: The Gospel of John at the Turn of the Century." In *What Is John? Literary and Social Readings of the Fourth Gospel*, edited by Fernando F. Segovia, 2:249–56. Atlanta: Scholars Press, 1998.

————. "Reproach and Revelation: Ethics in John 11:1–44." In *Torah Ethics and Early Christian Identity*, edited by Susan J. Wendel and David M. Miller, 92–106. Grand Rapids: Eerdmans, 2016.

————. "The Johannine Community and Its Jewish Neighbors: A Reappraisal." In *"What Is John?"* edited by Fernando F. Segovia, 2:111–38. Atlanta: Scholars Press, 1998.

————. *The Word in the World: The Cosmological Tale in the Fourth Gospel*. Atlanta: Scholars Press, 1992.

————. "To Love the Lord: An Intertextual Reading of John 20." In *The Labour of Reading: Essays in Honour of Robert C. Culley*, edited by Fiona Bladk, Roland

Boer, Christian Kelm, and Erin Runions, 56–69. Semeia Studies. Atlanta: Scholars Press, 1999.

———. "Torah Reading in the Johannine Community." *Journal of Early Christian History* 5, no. 2 (2016): 111–16.

✱ O Reinhartz, Adele, Steve Mason, Daniel R. Schwartz, Annette Yoshiko Reed, Joan Taylor, Malcolm F. Lowe, Jonathan Klawans, Ruth Sheridan, and James G. Crossley. "Jew and Judean: A Forum on Politics and Historiography in the Translation of Ancient Texts." Marginalia: A Los Angeles Review of Books Channel, August 26, 2014. http://marginalia.lareviewofbooks.org/jew-judean-forum/.

✱ O Reinhartz, Adele, et al. "Jew and Judean: A Forum on Politics and Historiography in the Translation of Ancient Texts." The Marginalia Review of Books. Accessed August 26, 2014. http://marginalia.lareviewofbooks.org/jew-judean-forum/.

Rensberger, David. "Anti-Judaism and the Gospel of John." In *Anti-Judaism and the Gospels*, edited by Farmer, 120–57. Harrisburg: Trinity Press International, 1999.

———. "The Politics of John: The Trial of Jesus in the Fourth Gospel." *Journal of Biblical Literature* 103 (1984): 395–411.

Rensberger, David K. *Johannine Faith and Liberating Community*. Philadelphia: Westminster Press, 1988.

Reynolds, Joyce Marie, and Robert Tannenbaum. *Jews and God-Fearers at Aphrodisias: Greek Inscriptions with Commentary: Texts from the Excavations at Aphrodisias Conducted by Kenan T. Erim*. Cambridge: Cambridge Philological Society, 1987.

Riesenfeld, Harald. "Zu den Johanneischen Hina-Sätzen." *Studia Theologica* 19, no. 1–2 (1965): 213–20.

Rivera, Mayra. "God at the Crossroads: A Postcolonial Reading of Sophia." In *Postcolonial Theologies Divinity and Empire*, edited by Catherine Keller, Michael Nausner, and Mayra Rivera, 183–203. St. Louis, Missouri: Chalice Press, 2004.

Robbins, Vernon K. *Exploring the Texture of Texts: A Guide to Socio-Rhetorical Interpretation*. Valley Forge: Trinity Press International, 1996.

———. *Jesus the Teacher: A Socio-Rhetorical Interpretation of Mark*. Minneapolis: Fortress Press, 2009.

Robbins, Vernon K., Robert H. von Thaden, and Bart B. Bruehler. *Foundations for Sociorhetorical Exploration: A Rhetoric of Religious Antiquity Reader*, 2016. http://lib.myilibrary.com?id=951528.

Robertson, David. *Word and Meaning in Ancient Alexandria: Theories of Language from Philo to Plotinus*. Farnham: Ashgate Pub., 2008. https://nls.ldls.org.uk/welcome.html?ark:/81055/vdc_100029263789.0x000001.

Robinson, John A. T. "The Destination and Purpose of St John's Gospel." In *New Testament Issues*, 191–209. New York: Harper and Row; S.C.M, 1970.

Rom-Shiloni, Dalit. *Exclusive Inclusivity: Identity Conflicts between the Exiles and the People Who Remained (6th-5th Centuries BCE)*. London: Bloomsbury Publishing, 2015.

Root, Bradley W. *First Century Galilee: A Fresh Examination of the Sources*. Tübingen: Mohr Siebeck, 2014.

Rothschild, Clare. "Embryology, Plant Biology, and Divine Generation in the Fourth Gospel." In *Women and Gender in Ancient Religions: Interdisciplinary Approaches*,

✱O Rodgers, Z etal. *A Wandering Galilean* (2009) (Esler essay on Judeans as ethnic gro[up]

✱O Richardson, Peter, ed. *Building Jewish in the Roman East* " Pre-70 synagogues as collegia in Rome, the diaspora 2004. and Judea." (on ethnic associations)

edited by Stephen P. Ahearne-Kroll, Paul A. Holloway, and James A. Kelhoffer, 125–51. Tübingen: Mohr Siebeck, 2010.

Ruether, Rosemary Radford. *Faith and Fratricide: The Theological Roots of Anti-Semitism.* New York: Seabury Press, 1974.

Runesson, Anders. "Inventing Christian Identity: Paul, Ignatius, and Theodosius I." In *Exploring Early Christian Identity*, 59–92. Tübingen: Mohr Siebeck, 2008.

Runesson, Anders, Donald D. Binder, and Birger Olsson. *The Ancient Synagogue from Its Origins to 200 C.E.: A Source Book.* Leiden: Brill, 2008.

Rutgers, Leonard Victor. *Making Myths: Jews in Early Christian Identity Formation.* Leuven: Peeters, 2009.

Sanders, E. P. *Judaism: Practice and Belief, 63 BCE-66 CE.* London: SCM Press, 2016.

Sanders, E. P. *Paul and Palestinian Judaism: A Comparison of Patterns of Religion.* Philadelphia: Fortress Press, 1977.

Sandmel, Samuel. *Anti-Semitism in the New Testament?* Philadelphia: Fortress press, 1978.

———. *Anti-Semitism in the New Testament?* Philadelphia: Fortress press, 1978.

Schaberg, Jane. *The Resurrection of Mary Magdalene: Legends, Apocrypha, and the Christian Testament.* New York: Continuum, 2002.

Schnackenburg, Rudolf. *The Gospel According to St. John.* New York: Seabury Press, 1980.

———. *The Gospel According to St. John.* London: Burn & Oates, 1980.

Schoeps, Hans-Joachim. *Jewish Christianity: Factional Disputes in the Early Church.* Philadelphia: Fortress Press, 1969.

Schuchard, Bruce G. *Scripture within Scripture: The Interrelationship of Form and Function in the Explicit Old Testament Citations in the Gospel of John.* Atlanta: Scholars Press, 1992.

Schwartz, Daniel R. "'Judean' or 'Jew'? How Should We Translate *Ioudaios* in Josephus?" In *Jewish Identity in the Greco-Roman World = Jüdische Identität in der Griechisch-Römischen Welt*, 3–27. Ancient Judaism and Early Christianity. Leiden: Brill, 2007.

———. *Judeans and Jews: Four Faces of Dichotomy in Ancient Jewish History.* Toronto: University of Toronto Press, 2014.

Schwartz, Seth. "How Many Judaisms Were There?" *Journal of Ancient Judaism* 2, no. 2 (2011): 208–38.

Scott, Martin. *Sophia and the Johannine Jesus.* Sheffield: JSOT Press, 2016.

Segal, Alan F. *Two Powers in Heaven: Early Rabbinic Reports about Christianity and Gnosticism.* Leiden: Brill, 1977.

Seim, Turid Karlsen. "Descent and Divine Paternity in the Gospel of John: Does the Mother Matter?" *New Testament Studies* 51, no. 3 (July 2005): 361–75.

———. "Motherhood and the Making of Fathers in Antiquity. Contextualizing Genetics in the Gospel of John." In *Women and Gender in Ancient Religions: Interdisciplinary Approaches*, edited by Stephen P. Ahearne-Kroll, Paul A. Holloway, and James A. Kelhoffer, 99–123. Tübingen: Mohr Siebeck, 2010.

Setzer, Claudia. *Jewish Responses to Early Christians: History and Polemics, 30–150 C.E.* Minneapolis: Fortress Press, 1994.

° On high christology from a Judean perspective.

+ On Judean acceptance and/or rejection of Christianity (Acts is a major 1st century text)

Sheridan, Ruth. "Issues in the Translation of Οι Ἰουδαῖοι in the Fourth Gospel." *Journal of Biblical Literature* 132, no. 3 (2013): 671–95.

———. *Retelling Scripture "the Jews" and the Scriptural Citations in John 1:19–12:50.* Leiden: Brill, 2012.

Sideris, Athanasios, Archonti Korka, Nikolaos Koutras, and Klio Panourgia, eds. *Ephesus: History, Archaeology, Architecture.* Harvard University Center for Hellenic Studies, 2012.

Siker, Jeffrey S. *Disinheriting the Jews: Abraham in Early Christian Controversy.* Louisville: Westminster/John Knox Press, 1991.

Singh, Yii-Jan. "Semen, Philosophy, and Paul." *Journal of Philosophy & Scripture* 4, no. 2 (2007): 32–42.

Skinner, Christopher W. *Characters and Characterization in the Gospel of John.* London: Bloomsbury T & T Clark, 2013.

Smith, D. Moody. *Johannine Christianity: Essays on Its Setting, Sources, and Theology.* London: T & T Clark, 2006.

———. "Judaism and the Gospel of John." In *Jews and Christians: Exploring the Past, Present, and Future,* edited by James H. Charlesworth, 76–96. New York: Crossroad, 1990.

———. "The Life Setting of the Gospel of John." *Review and Expositor* 85 (1988): 433–44.

Spaulding, Mary B. *Commemorative Identities: Jewish Social Memory and the Johannine Feast of Booths.* London: T & T Clark, 2009.

Stampfer, Shaul. "Did the Khazars Convert to Judaism?" *Jewish Social Studies* 19, no. 3 (2013): 1–72. https://doi.org/10.2979/jewisocistud.19.3.1.

Stegemann, Ekkehard, and Wolfgang Stegemann. *The Jesus Movement: A Social History of Its First Century.* Minneapolis: Fortress Press, 1999.

Stendahl, Krister. *Paul among Jews and Gentiles, and Other Essays.* Philadelphia: Fortress Press, 1976.

Stock, Brian. *Listening for the Text: On the Uses of the Past.* Baltimore: Johns Hopkins University Press, 1990.

Stovell, Beth M. *Mapping Metaphorical Discourse in the Fourth Gospel: John's Eternal King.* Leiden: Brill, 2012. http://dx.doi.org/10.1163/9789004230460.

Stowers, Stanley K. "The Concept of 'Community' and the History of Early Christianity." *Method & Theory in the Study of Religion* 23, no. 3–4 (2011): 238–56.

Stube, John Carlson. *A Graeco-Roman Rhetorical Reading of the Farewell Discourse.* London: T & T Clark International, 2006.

Talmon, Shemaryahu. "Oral Tradition and Written Transmission." In *Jesus and the Oral Gospel Tradition,* edited by Henry Wansbrough, 121–58. Sheffield: JSOT Press, 1991.

Tanzer, Sarah J. "Salvation Is for the Jews: Secret Christians in the Gospel of John." In *The Future of Early Christianity: Essays in Honour of Helmut Koester,* edited by Birger A. Pearson, George W. E Nickelsburg, Norman R. Petersen, and A. Thomas Kraabel, 285–300. Minneapolis: Fortress Press, 1991.

Tellbe, Mikael. *Christ-believers in Ephesus: A Textual Analysis of Early Christian Identity Formation in a Local Perspective.* Tübingen: Mohr Siebeck, 2009.

※ ※ ○ Smith, D. Moody. *John among the Gospels: The Relationship in Twentieth-Century Research.* 2001. (John & Luke)

Theobald, Michael. *Das Evangelium nach Johannes.* Regensburg: Friedrich Pustet, 2009.

Thettayil, Benny. *In Spirit and Truth: An Exegetical Study of John 4:19–26 and a Theological Investigation of the Replacement Theme in the Fourth Gospel.* Leuven: Peeters, 2007.

Thiessen, Matthew. *Paul and the Gentile Problem.* New York: Oxford University Press, 2016.

Townsend, John T. "The Gospel of John and the Jews: The Story of a Religious Divorce." In *Anti-Semitism and the Foundations of Christianity,* 72–97. New York: Paulist Press, 1979.

Toye, Richard. *Rhetoric: A Very Short Introduction.* Oxford: Oxford University Press, 2013. http://dx.doi.org/10.1093/actrade/9780199651368.001.0001.

Trebilco, Paul R. *Self-Designations and Group Identity in the New Testament.* Cambridge: Cambridge University Press, 2011.

Trebilco, Paul R. *The Early Christians in Ephesus from Paul to Ignatius.* Tübingen: Mohr Siebeck, 2004.

Tress, Daryl McGowan. "The Metaphysical Science of Aristotle's Generation of Animals and Its Feminist Critics." In *Feminism and Ancient Philosophy,* edited by Julie K. Ward, 30–50, 227–32. New York: Routledge, 1996.

Ullucci, Daniel C. *The Christian Rejection of Animal Sacrifice.* New York: Oxford University Press, 2012.

Um, Stephen T. *The Theme of Temple Christology in John's Gospel.* London: T & T Clark, 2016.

Unnik, W. C. van. "The Purpose of St. John's Gospel." *Studia Evangelica,* 1959, 382–411.

Upson-Saia, Kristi, Carly Daniel-Hughes, and Alicia J. Batten. *Dressing Judeans and Christians in Antiquity.* Farnham: Ashgate Publishing Group, 2014.

Van Belle, Gilbert. "'Salvation Is from the Jews': The Parenthesis in John 4:22b." In *Anti-Judaism and the Fourth Gospel: Papers of the Leuven Colloquium, 2000,* edited by R. Bieringer, Didier Pollefeyt, and F. Vandecasteele-Vanneuville, 370–400. Assen: Royal Van Gorcum, 2001.

Van der Watt, J. G. *Family of the King: Dynamics of Metaphor in the Gospel According to John.* Leiden: Brill, 2000.

Van der Watt, J. G., and Ruben Zimmermann, eds. *Rethinking the Ethics of John: "Implicit Ethics" in the Johannine Writings.* Wissenschaftliche Untersuchungen Zum Neuen Testament 291. Tübingen: Mohr Siebeck, 2012.

Van der Watt, Jan Gabriel. *Family of the King: Dynamics of Metaphor in the Gospel According to John.* Leiden: Brill, 2000.

von Wahlde, Urban C. *The Earliest Version of John's Gospel: Recovering the Gospel of Signs.* Wilmington: Michael Glazier, 1989.

———. *The Gospel and Letters of John.* 3 vols. Grand Rapids: Eerdmans, 2010.

von Wahlde, Urban C. "The Gospel of John and the Presentation of Jews and Judaism." In *Within Context: Essays on Jews and Judaism in the New Testament,* edited by Mary C. Boys, David P. Efroymson, Eugene J. Fisher, and Leon Klenicki, 67–84. Collegeville: Liturgical Press, 1993.

[handwritten note] Could there have been churches of lower & higher christology in a large city such as Ephesus? (Ephesus receives much attention specif. in Acts.)

von Wahlde, Urban C. "'The Jews' in the Gospel of John." *Ephemerides Theologicae Lovanienses* 76, no. 1 (2000): 30–55.

von Wahlde, Urban C. "The Johannine 'Jews': A Critical Survey." *New Testament Studies* 28 (1982): 33–60.

von Wahlde, Urban C. "The Terms for Religious Authorities in the Fourth Gospel: A Key to Literary-Strata?" *Journal of Biblical Literature* 98, no. 2 (1979): 231–53.

Wander, Bernd. *Gottesfürchtige und Sympathisanten: Studien Zum Heidnischen Umfeld von Diasporasynagogen*. Tübingen: Mohr Siebeck, 1998.

Warren, Meredith J. C. *My Flesh Is Meat Indeed: A Nonsacramental Reading of John 6:51–58*. Minneapolis: Fortress, 2015.

Werblowsky, R. J. Zwi. "Messianism in Jewish History." *Cahiers d'histoire mondiale. Journal of World History. Cuadernos de Historia Mundial* 11, no. 1 (1968): 30–46.

Wheaton, Gerry. *The Role of Jewish Feasts in John's Gospel*. New York: Cambridge University Press, 2015. http://ebooks.cambridge.org/ref/id/CBO9781139942034.

White, E. B. *Charlotte's Web*. New York: Harper & Brothers, 1952.

Wilken, Robert Louis. *John Chrysostom and the Jews: Rhetoric and Reality in the Late 4th Century*. Berkeley: University of California Press, 1983.

Wilson, S. G. *Related Strangers: Jews and Christians, 70–170 C.E.* Minneapolis: Fortress Press, 1995.

Winsor, Ann Roberts. *A King Is Bound in the Tresses: Allusions to the Song of Songs in the Fourth Gospel*. New York: P. Lang, 1999.

Winston, David. *Logos and Mystical Theology in Philo of Alexandria*. Cincinnati: Hebrew Union College Pr., 1985.

Witherington, Ben. *John's Wisdom: A Commentary on the Fourth Gospel*. Cambridge: Lutterworth Press, 1995.

———. "The Waters of Birth: John 3. 5 and 1 John 5. 6–8." *New Testament Studies* 35, no. 1 (1989): 155–160. https://doi.org/10.1017/S0028688500024565.

Yee, Gale A. *Jewish Feasts and the Gospel of John*. Eugene: Wipf & Stock, 2007.

Yuval, Israel Jacob. *Two Nations in Your Womb: Perceptions of Jews and Christians in Late Antiquity and the Middle Ages*. Berkeley: University of California Press, 2006.

Zimmermann, Ruben. "Imagery in John." In *Imagery in the Gospel of John: Terms, Forms, Themes, and Theology of Johannine Figurative Language*, edited by Jörg Frey, Ruben Zimmermann, J. G. van der Watt, and Gabriele Kern, 1–46. Tübingen: Mohr Siebeck, 2006.

———. "'The Jews': Unreliable Figures or Unreliable Narration?" In *Character Studies in the Fourth Gospel: Narrative Approaches to Seventy Figures in John*, edited by Steven A. Hunt, D. F. Tolmie, and Ruben Zimmermann, 71–109. Grand Rapids: Eerdmans, 2016.

Website:

http://holyjoe.org/poetry/howitt.htm

[handwritten notes:]

※ ○ Wills, Lawrence. "Jews, Judeans, Judaism in the Ancient Period," *Journal of Ancient Judaism* 7 (2, 2016): 169–193.

※※ ○ Witmer, S. "Approaches to Scripture in the Fourth Gospel and the Qumran Pesharim." *NovTest* 48:313–28 (...)

Index of
Ancient Sources

Index of
Modern Authors

Subject Index

Abraham, 29, 53, 54, 60, 78
Akiva, Rabbi, 118
Alexandra (fictional figure): as a child of God, 42, 150–1; encounter with John's gospel, xxxi, 6, 17, 18, 67, 94, 121; experience of expulsion, 124, 131; hope for fulfilment of desires, 30; personality, xxix; persuasion of, 43; transformation of identity, 23
Andrew, Apostle, 13, 24, 139
anti-Judaism, 164, 165n4
anti-Semitism, 101, 163, 164, 165n4
anti-Zionism, 101
aposynagōgos passages, 112, 113, 119, 121, 145
Arachne (mortal weaver), xxi, xxxvn18
Aristotle, 16, 33, 39, 40
arrangement (in classical rhetoric), xxv
artistic evidence (in classical rhetoric). *See* internal evidence
audience of Gospel: as children of God, 38–9; cultural profile of, xxix; ethnic identities of, 5, 133–5; external evidence for construction of, 113–14, 141–3; as Gentile outsiders, 135–45; internal evidence for construction of, 136–41; Jewish Christ-believers, 133–4, 135; pagan origins of, 137; rhetorical persuasion of, xxiii–xxiv;

Samaritans, 134–5; scholarly debate on intended, xxxiii, 115, 131, 133, 145, 151n6, 152n7, 153n23, 153n25, 159; transformation of communal identity, 18, 23; *See also* Johannine community

Bar Kokhba, 118
Beloved Disciple (James), 8, 19–20n14, 23–4, 41
Birkat ha-minim (Heretics), 114, 115, 117, 118, 119
birth: infusion of the Holy Spirit during, 41
Bottschaft Gottes, Die (The Message of God), 72
Bread of Life discourse, 73, 74

Caiaphas, the high priest, 138
casting off the withered branches, metaphor of, 60
children of God: audience of Gospel as, 38–9; *vs.* children of the devil, 77–8; communal identity, 42, 51, 62; reborn through water and spirit, 40, 160; relationship with the divine, 41, 51; Samaritans as, 73; separation from outsiders, 67; *vs.* those who are born of man, 77

201

About the Author

Adele Reinhartz, PhD (McMaster University, 1983), is professor in the Department of Classics and Religious Studies at the University of Ottawa (Canada), and general editor of the Journal of Biblical Literature (2012–2018). Her main areas of research are New Testament, early Jewish-Christian relations, and the Bible and film. She is author of numerous articles and books, including *Befriending the Beloved Disciple: A Jewish Reading of the Gospel of John* (Continuum, 2001), *Scripture on the Silver Screen* (Westminster John Knox, 2003), *Jesus of Hollywood* (Oxford, 2007), *Caiaphas the High Priest* (University of South Carolina Press, 2011; Fortress 2012), *Bible and Cinema: An Introduction* (Routledge, 2013), and *The Gospel of John and Jewish-Christian Relations* (Lexington, 2018). Adele Reinhartz was elected to the Royal Society of Canada in 2005 and to the American Academy of Jewish Research in 2014.

CPSIA information can be obtained
at www.ICGtesting.com
Printed in the USA
BVHW03*0028290618
520115BV00002B/6/P